MW00426828

# STANDING AS
# WITNESSES

## Powerful Missionaries
## Through the Ages

# E. DOUGLAS CLARK

GRANITE PUBLISHING & DISTRIBUTION LLC

*Standing as Witnesses: Powerful Missionaries Through the Ages*
Copyright © 2010 by E. Douglas Clark
*All Rights Reserved*

No part of this book may be reproduced in any form whatsoever, whether by graphic, visual, electronic, filming, microfilming, tape recording, or any other means, without the prior written permission of the author, except in the case of brief passages embodied in critical reviews and articles where the title, author and ISBN accompany such review or article.

This book is not an official publication of The Church of Jesus Christ of Latter-day Saints. All opinions expressed herein are the author's alone and are not necessarily those of the publisher or of The Church of Jesus Christ of Latter-day Saints.

Published & Distributed by:

Granite Publishing and Distribution, LLC
868 North 1430 West • Orem, Utah 84057
(801) 229-9023 • Toll Free (800) 574-5779 • Fax (801) 229-1924
www.granitepublishing.biz

Page Layout & Design by Myrna Varga
Cover Design by Adam Riggs


ISBN: 978-1-59936-063-8
Library of Congress Control Number: 2010928058


Printed in the United States of America
First Printing, August 2010
10 9 8 7 6 5 4 3 2 1

*For Christine, Joseph and John*

# TABLE OF CONTENTS

# INTRODUCTION

The Book of Mormon explains that the gift of the gospel comes on condition that we share it with others by "stand[ing] as witnesses of God at all times and in all things, and in all places that [we] may be in, even until death."[1] The Book of Mormon itself helps us do so in two important ways, as described by President Ezra Taft Benson: not only is it "the greatest single tool God has given to convert the world,"[2] but it also provides missionary models like Ammon and his brothers, whose "example is worthy of our emulation."[3]

Ammon is one of the sixteen powerful missionaries featured herein, beginning with Enoch of old and continuing down through prophets of our day. Despite the vast differences in their times and circumstances, all sixteen have unanimously invited mankind to come unto Christ even as they followed Him themselves. Their lives clearly demonstrate the core principles of missionary success, while they not only testify of Him but even typify Him—each in his own unique way that happens to highlight an important facet of missionary work.

Together their stories provide a panoramic view of the Kingdom of God through the ages, helping us appreciate the unique opportunity that is ours to live and labor in this era foreseen by all prophets and patriarchs of old, a time that "has interested the people of God in every age," explained the Prophet Joseph, as "they have looked forward with joyful anticipation to the day in which we live; . . . but . . . we are the favored people that God has made choice of to bring about the Latter-day glory;

it is left for us to see, participate in and help to roll forward the Latter-day glory."[4]

President Thomas S. Monson declared, "All of us living in the world today need points of reference—even models to follow."[5] With the benefit of these powerful missionary models, including the example of President Monson, we can better help to roll forward the Kingdom as we perform what Joseph Smith called our "our greatest and most important duty," namely, "to preach the Gospel."[6]

# I.
# THE PATRIARCHAL
# AND
# EARLY ISRAELITE ERA

# CHAPTER 1

## ~ Enoch ~
## Open Thy Mouth and
## It Shall Be Filled

When Adam was taught the gospel, he was commanded to teach it freely to his children. As mankind multiplied and the missionary work expanded, Adam called others to assist, including his patriarchal line of firstborn male descendants.[1] They are described in the Book of Moses as "preachers of righteousness" who "spake and prophesied, and called upon all men, everywhere, to repent."[2] For most of those illustrious missionaries we know little more than their names—Seth, Enos, Cainan, and so forth—until we come to Enoch, who is the focus of an entire third of the Book of Moses.

### Surprise Mission for a Stammering Lad

In that early age of the world, those first patriarchs lived so long, most of them over 900 years, that the first six generations were all still alive when the seventh was born. He was called Enoch, a name that means "to dedicate"[3] from a word that can also signify "mouth,"[4] apparently expressing the hope that this boy would carry on the missionary legacy of his fore-fathers by becoming a dedicated mouthpiece of the Lord.

How disappointing, then, to discover that Enoch had a speech impediment so severe as to frustrate nearly all with whom he tried to speak.[5] It seemed clear that no matter how otherwise worthy this young man—he received his patriarchal ordination at a much younger age than any of his predecessors[6]—his handicap would prevent him from ever raising his voice to preach the gospel.

But Enoch's story is full of the unexpected. One day as he was journeying, "the Spirit of God descended out of heaven and abode upon him," while a voice from heaven declared:

> Enoch, my son, prophesy unto this people, and say unto them—Repent, for thus saith the Lord: I am angry with this people, and my fierce anger is kindled against them; for their hearts have waxed hard, and their ears are dull of hearing, and their eyes cannot see afar off;
>
> And for these many generations, ever since the day that I created them, have they gone astray, and have denied me, and have sought their own counsels in the dark; and in their own abominations have they devised murder, and have not kept the commandments, which I gave unto their father, Adam.
>
> Wherefore, they have foresworn themselves, and, by their oaths, they have brought upon themselves death; and a hell I have prepared for them, if they repent not.[7]

This account of a hardened and murderous people matches the description of the wicked "giants" found in ancient texts describing Enoch's time. So great was their evil and violence that "the whole earth was filled with blood and oppression,"[8] and they would be remembered as having "caused the downfall of the world."[9] The giants are also mentioned later in the Book of Moses when they attempt to kill Noah.[10]

Enoch would surely have run the same risk, especially when he threatened them with the hell that awaited if they refused to repent. But if they so refused, their fate was sealed, as God further explained to Enoch:

"And this is a decree, which I have sent forth in the beginning of the world, from my own mouth, from the foundation thereof, and by the mouths of my servants, thy fathers, have I decreed it."[11]

This mention of the mouths of his forefathers may well have reminded Enoch about his own terrible inadequacy in speaking, for at that point he could not help but ask a question—not, to his everlasting credit, about his own safety in preaching to such a ferocious people, but rather about how, with his speech impediment, he would be able to deliver the message. "Why is it that I have found favor in thy sight, and am but a lad, and all the people hate me; for I am slow of speech; wherefore am I thy servant?"[12]

While it is possible that Enoch, standing in the presence of his Creator, may have found himself momentarily free of his speech impediment, yet nothing in the record so indicates, leaving us to surmise that Enoch's brief sentence was a mouthful for the stammering lad. But if his faltering words annoyed most mortals, the Lord listened patiently and then rewarded the effort with amazing promises. "Go forth and do as I have commanded thee, and no man shall pierce thee. Open thy mouth, and it shall be filled" —filled with power such as never had been seen among mortals: "I will give thee utterance. . . . Behold my Spirit is upon you, wherefore all thy words will I justify; and the mountains shall flee before you, and the rivers shall turn from their course; and thou shalt abide in me, and I in you; therefore walk with me."[13]

To further prepare Enoch for his remarkable mission, the Lord instructed him to "anoint thine eyes with clay, and wash them, and thou shalt see." When Enoch did so, "he beheld the spirits that God had created; and he beheld also things which were not visible to the natural eye; and from thenceforth came the saying abroad in the land: A seer hath the Lord raised up unto his people."[14]

### Words of Truth and Power

Obedient to the Lord's call, Enoch went forth and opened his mouth. For the first time in his life, his words rang out with clarity and power. "Standing upon the hills and the high places," he "cried with a loud voice, testifying against their works; and all men were offended because of him," saying, "there is a strange thing in the land; a wild man hath come among us." But "no man laid hands on him; for fear came on all them that heard him; for he walked with God."[15]

Then, as the story continues in the Book of Moses, "there came a man unto him, whose name was Mahijah, and said unto him: Tell us plainly who thou art, and from whence thou comest?"[16] A similar incident—of a man with precisely this same name[17] who questions Enoch—is told in the Dead Sea Scrolls,[18] a striking corroboration of the Book of Moses account given to the world a century earlier by the Prophet Joseph Smith.

But the Dead Sea Scrolls version adds an intriguing detail: Mahijah was one of the giants, a fact that would have struck fear into the heart of anyone—except Enoch. As the Book of Moses tells, Enoch answered boldly and, as his descendant Joseph Smith would later do, testified of his experience: "I beheld a vision; and lo, the heavens I saw, and the Lord spake with me, and gave me commandment; wherefore, for this cause, to keep the commandment, I speak forth these words."[19] Confronting even the most dangerous of men, Enoch was fearless in opening his mouth.

He preached of Creation and the brotherhood of all men as recounted in the sacred records.

> The Lord which spake with me, the same is the God of heaven, and he is my God, and your God, and ye are my brethren, and why counsel ye yourselves, and deny the God of heaven?
> The heavens he made; the earth is his footstool; and the foundation thereof is his. Behold, he laid it, an host of men hath he brought in upon the face thereof.

And death hath come upon our fathers; nevertheless we know them, and cannot deny, and even the first of all we know, even Adam.

For a book of remembrance we have written among us, according to the pattern given by the finger of God; and it is given in our own language.[20]

That Enoch was preaching at all was miraculous, but his words were also attended by undeniable power. As he "spake forth the words of God, the people trembled, and could not stand in his presence."[21] And as they fell to the earth, he spoke to them of the consequences of the Fall and of mankind's subsequent fall into error by their own disobedience.

Because that Adam fell, we are; and by his fall came death; and we are made partakers of misery and woe.

Behold Satan hath come among the children of men, and tempteth them to worship him; and men have become carnal, sensual, and devilish, and are shut out from the presence of God.[22]

The answer to mankind's fallen condition, continued Enoch, was repentance as made possible through the Atonement, even as God had once explained to their forefather Adam.

But God hath made known unto our fathers that all men must repent.

And he called upon our father Adam by his own voice, saying: I am God; I made the world, and men before they were in the flesh.

And he also said unto him: If thou wilt turn unto me, and hearken unto my voice, and believe, and repent of all thy transgressions, and be baptized, even in water, in the name of mine Only Begotten Son, who is full of grace and truth, which is Jesus Christ, the only name which shall be given under heaven, whereby salvation shall come unto the children of men, ye shall receive the gift of the Holy Ghost, asking all things in his name, and whatsoever ye shall ask, it shall be given you.[23]

Nor were these things for the benefit of Adam alone, he was told, but for all his posterity, the entire human race.

Wherefore teach it unto your children, that all men, everywhere, must repent, or they can in nowise inherit the kingdom of God, for no unclean thing can dwell there, or dwell in his presence; for, in the language of Adam, Man of Holiness is his name, and the name of his Only Begotten is the Son of Man, even Jesus Christ, a righteous Judge, who shall come in the meridian of time.[24]

Enoch continued to quote from the record, explaining that the Lord again commanded Adam to "teach these things freely unto your children," and even gave him the very words he should say, words that have been restored to us in the latter days and that remain the most powerful description ever given of baptism and the gift of the Holy Ghost.

By reason of transgression cometh the fall, which fall bringeth death, and inasmuch as ye were born into the world by water, and blood, and the spirit, which I have made, and so became of dust a living soul, even so ye must be born again into the kingdom of heaven, of water, and of the Spirit, and be cleansed by blood, even the blood of mine Only Begotten; that ye might be sanctified from all sin, and enjoy the words of eternal life in this world, and eternal life in the world to come, even immortal glory;

For by the water ye keep the commandment; by the Spirit ye are justified, and by the blood ye are sanctified;

Therefore it is given to abide in you; the record of heaven; the Comforter; the peaceable things of immortal glory; the truth of all things; that which quickeneth all things, which maketh alive all things; that which knoweth all things, and hath all power according to wisdom, mercy, truth, justice, and judgment.[25]

After learning about the ordinances, Adam actually received them, explained Enoch. Adam was baptized, being "caught away by the Spirit of the Lord, and . . . carried down into the water, and . . . laid under the water, and . . . brought forth out of the water." Then "the Spirit of God descended upon him, and thus he was born of the Spirit, and became quickened in the inner man. And he heard a voice out of heaven, saying: Thou art baptized with fire, and with the Holy Ghost. . . . Behold, thou art one in me, a son of God; and thus may all become my sons."[26] The great blessing available to Adam and to all through the ordinances was unity, to become one with God and therefore with each other.

Enoch's teaching about Adam was more than a history lesson; Adam had set the example for his posterity, and Enoch now invited them to repent and be baptized.[27]

Jewish tradition tells that as Enoch went forth among the people, "he gathered them about him, and instructed them in the conduct pleasing to God. He sent messengers all over to announce, 'Ye who desire to know the ways of God and righteous conduct, come ye to Enoch!' Thereupon a vast concourse of people thronged about him, to hear the wisdom he would teach and learn from his mouth what is good and right."[28] President John Taylor explained that Enoch "sent out missionaries among the people," and "many believed on them and they were gathered together."[29]

The purpose for gathering the people of God in any age of the world, said Joseph Smith, is to build a temple.[30] Brigham Young indicated that Enoch's people had a temple,[31] and an ancient text that has emerged since Brigham's day tells that Enoch counseled his sons to go to the temple often.[32]

Meanwhile, among the wicked, so great was the uproar over Enoch's preaching that his enemies finally sent their armies to silence him and his followers once and for all. Again Enoch opened his mouth and it was filled, this time with words that not only penetrated hearts but changed the very face of the earth.

> And so great was the faith of Enoch that he led the people of God, and their enemies came to battle against them; and he spake the word of the Lord, and the earth trembled, and the mountains fled, even according to his command; and the rivers of water were turned out of their course; and the roar of the lions was heard out of the wilderness; and all nations feared greatly, so powerful was the word of Enoch, and so great was the power of the language which God had given him.[33]

In exercising the Savior's power to control the elements, Enoch actually resembled the Savior, who would later declare to Abraham that "I stretch my hand over the sea, and it obeys my voice; I cause the wind and the fire to be my chariot; I say to the mountains—Depart hence—and behold, they are taken away by a whirlwind, in an instant, suddenly."[34] And as Enoch opened his mouth and it was filled with the words of God, so would God the Father, according to Isaiah,[35] tell his anointed Servant—the Savior—that "I have put my words in thy mouth."[36]

### Enoch's Zion and His Vision of the Flood and the Savior

As wars and bloodshed raged throughout the rest of the earth during Enoch's day, "the Lord came and dwelt with his people, and they dwelt in righteousness . . . and did flourish," being "of one heart and one mind," with "no poor among them." Therefore they were called Zion, a City of Holiness.[37]

Still Enoch continued to open his mouth, not only directing the great missionary effort but also "preaching in righteousness unto the people of God."[38] He was preparing them for the singular blessing that they eventually received of being translated, or taken up from the earth to dwell in the safety and splendor of a terrestrial realm[39] described as "the bosom of the Father."[40] It was not the celestial kingdom but a paradisiacal place of supernal beauty where their bodies were changed and sanctified, protected from sin and death until they would finally, with the rest of the righteous at the last day, be resurrected in celestial glory.[41]

After Enoch was "high and lifted up,"[42] he saw what was at stake for mortals choosing to accept or reject the gospel, and "heard a loud voice saying: Wo, wo be unto the inhabitants of the earth. And he beheld Satan; and he had a great chain in his hand, and it veiled the whole face of the earth with darkness; and he looked up and laughed, and his angels rejoiced."[43]

From this painful picture, Enoch's attention was drawn to a surprising scene in heaven. "And it came to pass that the God of heaven looked upon the residue of the people, and he wept; and Enoch bore record of it, saying: How is it that the heavens weep, and shed forth their tears as the rain upon the mountains?"[44]

Part of God's answer was a question. "Should not the heavens weep, seeing these shall suffer?"[45]

Enoch himself then "wept and stretched forth his arms, and his heart swelled wide as eternity; and his bowels yearned; and all eternity shook," for "he had bitterness of soul, and wept over his brethren, and said unto the heavens: I will refuse to be comforted."[46]

Comfort came only when Enoch "saw the day of the coming of the Son of Man, even in the flesh; and his soul rejoiced, saying: The Righteous is lifted up, and the Lamb is slain from the foundation of the world."[47]

### Preaching the Gospel and Building Zion in the Latter Days

Enoch then viewed the wickedness that would continue after the Savior's ministry, and again mourned and implored the Lord, "When shall the earth rest? . . . I ask thee if thou wilt not come again on the earth."[48]

"As I live, even so will I come in the last days," answered the Lord, who then foretold the events leading up to His second coming. Despite wickedness and tribulation, the Lord would restore the gospel by bringing righteousness "down from heaven" and truth "out of the earth," and would cause "righteousness and truth . . . to sweep the earth as with a flood, to gather out mine elect from the four quarters of the earth."[49] As one latter-day leader explained:

> Righteousness descending from the heavens was fulfilled in the revelations received by the prophet Joseph Smith including the appearance of the Father and the Son, Moroni's visits, the Savior's appearance in the Kirtland Temple followed by Old Testament prophets delivering priesthood keys. Truth coming forth out of the earth was fulfilled by the publication of the Book of Mormon. The

spread of missionary work and the establishment of the Church in many nations is in fulfillment of the Lord's statement that "righteousness and truth will I cause to sweep the earth."[50]

To accomplish this great work, the Lord has repeated what He once told Enoch, commanding latter-day missionaries to "open your mouths in proclaiming my gospel,"[51] for "the hour of your mission is come; and your tongue shall be loosed, and you shall declare glad tidings of great joy unto this generation."[52] "You shall ever open your mouth in my cause, not fearing what man can do, for I am with you."[53] "Open your mouths and they shall be filled. . . . Yea, open your mouths and they shall be filled."[54]

Accordingly, as Brigham Young said, "we are following the customs of Enoch"[55] as we build "the Holy Order that God has established for his people in all the ages of the world. . . . We may call it the order of Enoch."[56] It is nothing less than the order of Zion, which was Enoch's work and is ours: "Seek to bring forth and establish the cause of Zion"[57] the Lord commands His Latter-day Saints, in order to prepare for the day when we will greet Enoch's Zion returning to earth in what a modern-day apostle termed that "remarkable reunion with our colleagues in Christ from the City of Enoch."[58]

Referring to that future event, the Lord explained that when He comes in glory, the city of Zion will come with Him, as He told Enoch:

> Then shalt thou and all thy city meet them there, and we will receive them into our bosom, and they shall see us; and we will fall upon their necks, and they shall fall upon our necks, and we will kiss each other;
>
> And there shall be mine abode, and it shall be called Zion.[59]

And as Enoch's Zion was required to become "of one heart and one mind" to qualify for the Lord's presence, so latter-day Zion must also qualify. "The Lord Jehovah will return," explained President Henry B. Eyring, "to live with those who have become His people and will find them united, of one heart, unified with Him and with our Heavenly Father."[60]

It is to achieve that celestial unity that latter-day missionaries, like Enoch of old, have received the commandment and promise to "open your mouths and they shall be filled."

## Legacy of Enoch

Born while Adam was still alive, Enoch was the seventh in the line of the early patriarchs who were powerful missionaries. But with his speech impediment, everyone saw he could never be a missionary—everyone except God, who called Enoch to go forth and open his mouth to preach. Enoch obeyed, and his words rang out with unprecedented power. He gathered the obedient and built the city of Zion, which in time was translated. It will soon return, as Enoch himself prophesied, in preparation for which the Lord's servants are again called to open their mouths and speak words of divine power.

CHAPTER 2

# ~ Noah ~
## Blameless Before God

Not quite everyone in Enoch's Zion was translated. His son Methuselah "was not taken, that the covenants of the Lord might be fulfilled, which he made to Enoch; for he truly covenanted with Enoch that Noah should be of the fruit of his loins."[1] Enoch had been gone just four years[2] when Noah was born. It was a time of such wickedness that the earth itself groaned under the burden of evil.[3] But hope for a better world was expressed in Noah's very name, meaning "rest" or "relief."[4] The name was also prophetic, looking ahead to the time when the earth would be cleansed from sin and mankind would live after the pattern set by the righteous and blameless Noah.

### The Boy Noah

The tenth and last in the patriarchal line to be born before the Flood, Noah was baptized at age eight, and then at age ten received his patriarchal ordination by the laying on of hands—by far the youngest among his predecessors to be so ordained.[5]

This information about Noah's youth is supplied exclusively by the Prophet Joseph Smith, but other ancient sources unknown in his day add corroborating details. Jewish tradition tells of Noah that as "the child grew up and was weaned," he was "perfect and upright with God."[6] Early Christian tradition likewise relates that young Noah "did not transgress against God . . . nor did he willfully depart from what pleased God; neither did he ever anger God."[7] And according to one of the Dead Sea Scrolls, the adult Noah wrote that at his birth, "I burst forth for uprightness, and when I emerged from my mother's womb I was planted for righteousness. All of my days I conducted myself uprightly, continually walking in the paths of everlasting truth."[8] Young Noah's righteous life is an enduring example of missionary preparation by a boy who would serve one of the most pivotal missions in history.

Meanwhile, the rest of mankind was stubbornly heading the opposite direction toward a condition that Genesis calls "corrupt" and "filled with violence."[9] Other ancient sources provide additional details, painting a picture alarmingly similar to our day in terms of pride, violence, deceit, immorality, abortion, secret combinations, and every other kind of vice and crime. The Book of Moses reports that the earth itself groaned under the weight of wickedness: "When shall I rest, and be cleansed. . . ? When will my Creator sanctify me, that I may rest?"[10]

Mercifully, however, the Creator delayed the Deluge to allow mankind to change course. As various sources attest, the inhabitants of the earth "were all evil and continuously provoked the Lord sorely, but because he is longsuffering, the flood was delayed"[11] and "a period given to that generation to repent."[12] The man called to proclaim that urgent message of repentance was Noah.

### Preacher and Practicer of Righteousness

The Old Testament relates that God told Noah that mankind would have 120 years to repent or face the Flood,[13] but no mention is made of any missionary activity by Noah. Other ancient sources, however, including the New Testament, remember Noah as a "preacher of righteousness."[14] According to the Book of Moses, "the Lord ordained Noah after his own order, and commanded him that he should go forth and declare his Gospel unto the children of men, even as it was given unto Enoch. And . . . Noah called upon the children of men that they should repent,"[15] and he "prophesied, and taught the things of God, even as it was in the beginning."[16] Noah was following in the footsteps of his patriarchal forefathers, who themselves were "preachers of righteousness."[17]

And like them, he practiced what he preached, teaching by example. Genesis reports that like Enoch, Noah "walked with God," and adds that he was "just . . . and perfect"[18]—or, as most modern translations read, "righteous and blameless."[19] Other ancient sources likewise describe Noah as "pure and kindhearted,"[20] "most upright and true, a most trustworthy man"[21] of "special holiness"[22] who was "a most worthy example of right-eousness."[23] The Jewish historian Josephus says twice that "God loved Noah for his righteousness."[24]

The righteous and blameless Noah was a teacher of great power by exemplifying Him of whom he testified, Jesus Christ, who was described by Enoch as "the Righteous"[25] and by Peter as "a blameless unblemished lamb."[26]

### Preaching the Gospel and Building the Ark

Noah preached the gospel "even as it was given unto Enoch"[27] and sought to persuade all men to "become the sons of God."[28] He was successful with his own three sons,[29] but otherwise met with widespread resistance as his listeners "hearkened not unto his words."[30] He did not give up.

Noah continued his preaching unto the people, saying: Hearken, and give heed unto my words;

Believe and repent of your sins and be baptized in the name of Jesus Christ, the Son of God, even as our fathers, and ye shall receive the Holy Ghost, that ye may have all things made manifest; and if ye do not this, the floods will come in upon you.[31]

The choice was clear. If they refused to be immersed in the waters of baptism, they would be immersed in the waters of the Flood. Still, however, "they hearkened not."[32] Nor were they impressed by Noah's massive visual aid, the great ark that he was constructing.

But why, asks a Jewish source, did God command Noah to make the ark in the first place? After all, "could not [God] have saved him by His word or have borne him up to heaven?"[33] Indeed, God had literally lifted up Enoch and his city, and could easily have done so for Noah during the Flood. So why put Noah to all the trouble of building the ark?

The same Jewish source answers, "In order that mankind should see him engaged in its construction and repent of their ways."[34] For Noah's part, he apparently made the labor of building the ark as conspicuous as possible, for while he could have accomplished his work in much less time, yet "he felt that if people saw his preparations for the Flood, they would change their ways."[35]

With each additional day of labor that Noah and his sons put into the ark, the people saw the depth of Noah's own belief about the coming Flood. Moreover, such an unusual sight was unprecedented—the construction of a massive ship far inland! It was a stunning and constant reminder of Noah's unrelenting message of repentance.

But not only did the people refuse to repent, they "laughed at him,"[36] "mocked and ridiculed him,"[37] and "sneered at him, each one, calling him demented, a man gone mad,"[38] even as they had once called Enoch a "strange" and "wild man."[39] Taunting Noah, they challenged him to bring on the Flood if he was telling the truth.[40]

Finally, as told in the Book of Moses and other sources, they even "sought Noah to take away his life."[41] But he "called upon" the Lord, and "the Lord was with Noah, and the power of the Lord was upon him."[42]

That Noah did make some converts beyond his own family is indicated by ancient sources like an early Christian text telling that "Noah preached repentance, and as many as listened to him were saved."[43] Saved not only spiritually but also temporally from the coming destruction: the Book of Moses tells that they were literally "caught up" out of harm's way "by the powers of heaven into Zion,"[44] that is, translated to the city of Enoch.

## Powerful Warnings of Destruction

Meanwhile, the Lord was offering every inducement for the rest of mankind to repent, as He confirmed Noah's testimony by that of the very elements. According to Jewish tradition:

> The Lord caused the whole earth to shake, and the sun darkened, and the foundations of the world raged, and the whole earth was moved violently, and the lightning flashed, and the thunder roared, and all the fountains in the earth were broken up, such as was not known to the inhabitants before; and God did this mighty act, in order to terrify the sons of men, that there might be no more evil upon the earth. And still the sons of men would not return from their evil ways.[45]

Similar earth-shaking events will happen in our day, again in support of the testimonies by the Lord's missionaries, as foretold in latter-day revelation.

> For after your testimony cometh the testimony of earthquakes, that shall cause groanings in the midst of her, and men shall fall upon the ground and shall not be able to stand.
>
> And also cometh the testimony of the voice of thunderings, and the voice of lightnings, and the voice of tempests, and the voice of the waves of the sea heaving themselves beyond their bounds.
>
> And all things shall be in commotion.[46]

> Lift up your voices and spare not. Call upon the nations to repent, . . . saying: Prepare yourselves for the great day of the Lord;
>
> For if I, who am a man, do lift up my voice and call upon you to repent, and ye hate me, what will ye say when the day cometh when the thunders shall utter their voices from the ends of the earth, speaking to the ears of all that live, saying—Repent, and prepare for the great day of the Lord?

Yea, and again, when the lightnings shall streak forth from the east unto the west, and shall utter forth their voices unto all that live, and make the ears of all tingle that hear, saying these words—Repent ye, for the great day of the Lord is come?[47]

As the day of reckoning arrived for Noah's generation, the heavy rains that fell just before the Flood mirrored God's own sorrow for His wayward children as "the God of heaven looked upon the residue of the people, and he wept," shedding "tears as the rain upon the mountains."[48]

Then, in the greatest catastrophe in history, mankind was violently swept away by the same rising waters that lifted Noah and his family to safety aboard the ark.

### Noah's Covenant and the Latter Days

A year later when the ship came to rest on dry ground, Noah offered sacrifice on the newly cleansed earth finally at rest from wickedness. God accepted the sacrifice and brought forth a rainbow as a token of His covenant. The Genesis account as it has come down to us reports only part of the covenant, promising that the earth would never again be flooded. But more is reported in the Joseph Smith Translation, in which God tells Noah:

> And the bow shall be in the cloud; and I will look upon it, that I may remember the everlasting covenant, which I made unto thy father Enoch; that, when men should keep all my commandments, Zion should again come on the earth, the city of Enoch which I have caught up unto myself.
>
> And this is mine everlasting covenant, that when thy posterity shall embrace the truth, and look upward, then shall Zion look downward, and all the heavens shall shake with gladness, and the earth shall tremble with joy;
>
> And the general assembly of the church of the first-born shall come down out of heaven, and possess the earth, and shall have place until the end come.[49]

Although Noah had missed living in Enoch's Zion, both in its earthly and its translated state, yet he was now assured that that glorious city would one day descend again to the earth. It will come only after a reenactment of Noah's day, as the Savior foretold: "As it was in the days of Noah, so it shall be also at the coming of the Son of Man."[50]

The similarity will be not only in terms of wickedness—"iniquity shall abound"[51]—but also in terms of catastrophe—"the destruction of the wicked."[52] The Prophet Joseph Smith observed that "in the days of Noah, God destroyed the world by a flood, and He has promised to destroy it by fire in the last days."[53]

As He did in Noah's day, the Lord is calling servants to invite mankind to repent and escape the coming destruction. "I the Lord, knowing the calamity which should come upon the inhabitants of the earth, called upon my servant Joseph Smith . . . that the fulness of my gospel might be proclaimed by the weak and the simple"[54] as they "lift a warning voice unto the inhabitants of the earth" and "declare . . . that desolation shall come upon the wicked,"[55] who shall be "consumed away and utterly destroyed by the brightness of my coming."[56]

And as Noah's day is a type of our own, so he remains a powerful example for latter-day missionaries who are commanded to "serve . . . in righteousness"[57] with "all [their] heart, might, mind and strength, that [they] may stand blameless before God at the last day."[58]

Then shall they stand also with the righteous and blameless Noah on the gloriously renewed earth that is finally at rest.

## Legacy of Noah

In a world of nearly incredible wickedness, one man stood out as righteous and blameless: Noah, who was called to testify of Christ and warn of impending disaster if the world did not repent. His testimony was accompanied by that of the very elements, but still mankind did not mend their ways. As the world was cleansed by flood in his day, so it is about to be cleansed by fire at the Savior's glorious appearance. And once again, the Lord has called His servants to go forth as righteous and blameless messengers to invite all to come to Christ and avoid the coming destruction.

CHAPTER 3

# ~ *Abraham* ~
## *Full of Love*

❧

By the tenth generation after Noah, with mankind multiplying and spreading across the earth, the Genesis story suddenly changes focus as it zooms in from universal history to the personal history of one man. His name is Abram, later changed to Abraham—"father of a multitude"—in memorial of the promise he receives of numerous posterity who will bless all nations through the power of love. What this blessing means in terms of missionary work, and what Abraham himself did to fulfill it, is seen more fully in the Book of Abraham restored through Joseph Smith and in other ancient sources that have since come to light.

### Young Abraham in Ur

As the Book of Abraham describes, his people had forsaken the gospel and set "their hearts . . . to do evil," including idol worship, flagrant immorality, and even child sacrifice.[1] As hardened and evil as the generation that perished in the Flood, Abraham's people had all the same vices but with particular emphasis on hatred and war, and were rapidly heading for destruction. According to an early Christian source, "the world was again overspread with errors, and . . . for the hideousness of its crimes destruction was ready for it, this time not by water, but fire, and . . . already the scourge was hanging over the whole earth."[2] As Jewish tradition says, "it was, indeed, high time" that Abraham, the friend of God, "should make his appearance upon earth."[3]

Remarkably, the apostasy had encompassed even the patriarchal line of priesthood leaders into which Abraham was born. There was no one to whom young Abraham could turn for truth, no one who could teach him about God and the purpose of life, leaving the boy entirely on his own to figure things out. As he began contemplating the creations and cosmos, he came to understand that there must be a Creator, and fervently sought Him.

One very ancient source tells that the boy Abraham "began to pray to the creator of all that he would save him from the errors of mankind and that it might not fall to his share to go astray after impurity and wickedness."[4] This same source even mentions that Abraham was fourteen—the very age at which his descendant Joseph Smith would begin to pray. And as with Joseph Smith, Abraham's prayers were answered as he learned of the Creator's reality and of His grand motive in Creation: loving-kindness. Abraham "too then held fast to this quality,"[5] and it became the motivating power of his life.[6]

It was his love for God that prompted young Abraham to reject the immoral practices of his day. "I will set my mind on what is pure," he determined. Various ancient sources attest that he was "pure from sin" and "pure in heart," and "came before the Lord with a pure heart." Thus Abraham "'loved God' because he loved righteousness; this was [his] love of God."[7] And out of love for his fellow men, Abraham to urged them to forsake their evil.

Unfortunately, as he tells in the Book of Abraham, "they utterly refused to hearken to my voice," and "endeavored to take away my life" by making him the intended victim in an ostentatious ceremony of human sacrifice.[8]

The horrific scene is depicted in the first illustration in the Book of Abraham, showing him strapped on the altar as the priest raises the knife. Abraham's cry to God was immediately answered as an angel appeared, smote the priest, and loosed Abraham. In one of the greatest and most dramatic miracles in history, God saved the man whom He would later designate to be the instrument of blessing all the nations of the earth.

But first Abraham and his wife would leave Ur and settle in Haran, where he was able to pore over the precious records—the scriptures—of his righteous forefathers.[9] Abraham's quest for ever greater knowledge is one of the first things mentioned in the Book of Abraham,[10] and was an important part of his preparation to go forth and bless the nations by preaching the gospel. Abraham's call to do so came in a personal appearance of the Lord, who promised that through Abraham's posterity "shall all the families of the earth be blessed, even with the blessings of the Gospel, which are the blessings of salvation, even of life eternal."[11]

This great promise was not for Abraham alone but also equally for his wife, Sarah, a woman of unsurpassed beauty, wisdom, and greatness of soul who possessed a profound "love and compassion . . . for the needy."[12] Her spiritual attainments equaled and in some cases even exceeded those of Abraham, with whom she walked in perfect harmony. As one ancient biographer expressed, "everywhere and always she was at his side, . . . his true partner in life and life's events, resolved to share alike the good and the ill."[13] Together with great love they obeyed, served, and preached the gospel.[14]

It was the same gospel that had been preached by all the earlier patriarchs: the gospel of Jesus Christ, including faith in Him, repentance, baptism, and the gift of the Holy Ghost. Ancient sources attest to Abraham's own baptism and reception of the Holy Ghost.[15] Its effect on

Abraham—as on every righteous recipient, as the prophet Mormon explained—was to fill him "with hope and perfect love."[16] No wonder ancient Jewish tradition remembers that the spread of love and mercy is "the very purpose of the covenant of Abraham."[17]

### Winning People over with the Love of Christ

The great work of blessing all nations began squarely with Abraham himself, whom the Lord instructed to leave Haran, "for I have purposed . . . to make of thee a minister."[18] The event is recorded in the Book of Abraham, which further mentions that when Abraham and Sarah left, they took with them "the souls that we had won."[19]

How had they won them? Jewish tradition reports that Abraham "won people over" with his love and teaching.[20] And powerful teaching it was, for among his many gifts was "a lofty power to convey the truth unto others."[21] He was "an eloquent speaker,"[22] and called out "in a mighty voice to all the world."[23] "He led them to righteousness by speaking persuasively. . . . Even the guilty he led to righteousness."[24]

But Abraham's greatest tool in bringing people to Christ was love. "Abraham our father used to bring them into his house and give them food and drink and be friendly to them . . . and convert them"[25] in a joint effort with Sarah, who was "an equal partner with her husband"[26] in this "large-scale missionary effort."[27]

The people of Haran "readily yielded to the influence of Abraham's humane spirit and his piety. Many of them obeyed his precepts."[28] He "taught them the instruction of the Lord and his ways,"[29] and they "became God-fearing and good."[30] Thus Abraham organized the Church and "founded his Zion."[31]

Abraham's love continued to be the hallmark of his missionary efforts. Journeying south from Haran, "Abraham summoned mankind to believe in God out of his own great love for Him,"[32] and "served Him out of love"[33] by "showing loving-kindness" to everyone.[34] Led by the Spirit in his journeys, Abraham and his followers "were walking and calling and gathering the people from town to town and from country to country."[35] Every stop along the way offered an opportunity to extend hospitality and preach the gospel, and Abraham "was charitable with all his heart and soul."[36] It is said that charity was asleep in the world and Abraham woke it up.[37] Many accepted the gospel and came to Christ, attracted by the Christ-like love they felt from Abraham and Sarah.

## Abraham in Egypt

Shortly after Abraham settled in the promised land, it was struck by a famine so severe that it forced him to take his family and his community of saints to Egypt. Arriving at the border, as told by one of the Dead Sea Scrolls, Abraham had a divinely-inspired dream in which he was represented by a towering cedar of Lebanon, the region's mighty tree that offered shelter and protection like no other. This apt symbol emphasized that Abraham was offering the world the Savior's shelter and protection.[38]

As the story continues in the same scroll, once Abraham had arrived in Egypt, he read to its inhabitants from the records of Enoch, the scriptures of Abraham's day.[39]

But the most significant missionary opportunity in Egypt came later after Abraham and Sarah underwent a great trial. Pharaoh had sent his soldiers and seized Sarah, forcibly bringing her to the palace to become his favorite wife in the royal harem. He would have let nothing stand in his way, including Abraham. But in answer to the fervent prayers of both Abraham and Sarah, God protected her virtue and Abraham's life, and sent a desolating sickness that brought Pharaoh to death's door. At the point of utter despair, the king had a dream in which he saw Abraham healing him by the laying on of hands.

A messenger was quickly sent to Abraham imploring him to come and attend to the dying monarch. Abraham could easily have refused or delayed, allowing his enemy to perish. But the Savior's command to love your enemies was a principle that Abraham followed. By the power of a priesthood blessing, he healed the ailing king—who was so grateful that he invited Abraham to sit on the throne and teach the royal court, as depicted in the third illustration of the Book of Abraham.[40]

Abraham began with a lesson on astronomy, a subject of intense fascination for the Egyptians who were widely renowned for their expertise. To their astonishment, they discovered that Abraham's knowledge exceeded their own. For this very purpose, as the Book of Abraham relates, had God Himself tutored Abraham in astronomy on the night before he entered Egypt.[41]

The royal court was captivated by the superior wisdom of Abraham, who then used the opportunity as a means of preaching the gospel and "proclaiming the name of Christ."[42] Ancient sources recount that Abraham there "taught the faith and true religion," resulting in the conversion of Pharaoh, who took immediate steps to remove idol worship throughout all of Egypt.[43] The king's conversion would have opened the door for multitudes throughout his realm to accept the gospel, not unlike the massive conversions that followed the conversion of certain Lamanite kings in the Book of Mormon.

The ancients rightly remembered Abraham's encounter with Pharaoh as "a crucial event in the history of mankind."[44] Perhaps the most notable thing about it was that it was made possible by Abraham's willingness to forgive an enemy, Pharaoh. Once again, Abraham's loving-kindness had opened an important door for the preaching of the gospel. "It is Abraham the missionary," wrote Hugh Nibley, "who makes brothers of all the world, who abolishes the differences between the nations and the races."[45]

### Blessing, Serving, and Pleading for Mankind

Escorted out of Egypt with royal honors and lavish gifts, Abraham led his family back to the promised land, whose inhabitants, in the words of an early Christian writer, were "dwelling in darkness. He shone over them like a light."[46] Settling in Hebron, Abraham and Sarah "welcomed everyone—rich and poor, kings and rulers, the crippled and the helpless, friends and strangers, neighbors and passersby."[47] He even went in search of wayfarers needing assistance.[48]

Near Abraham's residence was a spring-fed pool of water, which, as described in Jewish tradition, he used for "those who required immediate immersion," for he sought to make "known the true faith to the whole world."[49] This baptismal font was frequently used.

One day three angels arrived and announced the blessing for which Abraham and Sarah had waited for decades: Sarah would finally bear a son. Although she was past the time when this was biologically possible, the angels blessed her that it would be so.

As the angels were leaving, they mentioned to Abraham that they were on their way to the nearby cities of Sodom and Gomorrah to destroy them for their wickedness. Abraham, who had just been granted the blessing for which he had so long hoped and prayed and labored, suddenly risked it all by fervently pleading with God—and even bargaining with Him— for mercy for the wicked cities,[50] "hoping," says Jewish tradition, "that they would perhaps repent."[51] According to Hugh Nibley,

> The impressive thing is the way in which Abraham is willing to abase himself to get the best possible terms for the wicked cities. . . . It was not an easy thing to do—especially for the most degenerate society on earth. It can be matched only by Mormon's great love for a people whom he describes as utterly and hopelessly corrupt, or by the charity of Enoch, Abraham's great predecessor, . . . who "refused to be comforted" until God promised to have compassion on the earth.[52]

Far from being offended by Abraham's insistent intervention, God, according to Jewish tradition, "praised him"[53] and declared, "I love him."[54] Forever after, God would esteem Abraham as "my beloved friend,"[55] reminiscent of God's esteem for "My Beloved Son"—even as Abraham's compassion for sinners echoes the Savior's infinite and atoning compassion. In the words of one writer,

> The tenderness of Abraham's heart is as remarkable as [his] purity.... Sodom was a sink of iniquity. Abraham could not but know that, and could not but hold the habits of its people in unutterable abhorrence. Yet see how he mourns its doom, regarding its sinners with such pity as filled the eyes of Jesus, and drew from his heart this lamentable cry, "O Jerusalem, Jerusalem, how often would I have gathered thy children as a hen gathereth her chickens under her wings, and ye would not!" ... Sodom awakens all [of Abraham's] pity. Considerations of its enormous guilt are swallowed up in the contemplation of its impending doom. Truest, tenderest type of his own illustrious Son, with the spirit that dropped in the tears and flowed in the blood of Jesus, [Abraham] casts himself between God's anger and the guilty city. He asks, he pleads, he prays for mercy.... Compassion, pity, love for sinners, than these there is no surer mark and test of true religion. May they be found in us as in Jesus Christ! —as in Abraham![56]

If they are not found in us, then we are not of Abraham, says Jewish tradition: "Whoever is merciful to his fellow-men is certainly of the children of our father Abraham, and whosoever is not merciful to his fellow-men is certainly not of the children of our father Abraham."[57] According to the Prophet Joseph Smith, "the nearer we get to our heavenly Father, the more we are disposed to look with compassion on perishing souls; we feel that we want to take them upon our shoulders, and cast their sins behind our backs."[58]

But even Abraham's pleading could not save the wicked cities, whose fate was sealed. When the violent destruction drastically reduced the number of visitors to Abraham's home, he moved his family south to Beersheba. There Sarah, after some thirty-five years of waiting, finally bore a son—the son of promise, the son of hope, the son through whom all nations would be blessed: Isaac. His birth was literally miraculous, made possible only by the priesthood blessing given by the angels. The joyous miracle foreshadowed another unique birth, that of Isaac's descendant Jesus Christ, miraculously born of Mary.[59]

Abraham taught Isaac, and involved him in the work of blessing all mankind. Jewish tradition recounts that Abraham planted a lush garden and an orchard, and built a residence that would graciously accommodate all visitors.

> He made four gates for it, facing the four sides of the earth, east, west, north, and south, and he planted a vineyard therein. If a traveler came that way, he entered by the gate that faced him, and he sat in the grove, and ate, and drank, until he was satisfied, and then he departed. For the house of Abraham was always open for all passers-by, and they came daily to eat and drink there. If one was hungry, and he came to Abraham, he would give him what he needed, so that he might eat and drink and be satisfied; and if one was naked, and he came to Abraham, he would clothe him with the garments of the poor man's choice, and give him silver and gold, and make known to him the Lord, who had created him and set him on earth. After the wayfarers had eaten, they were in the habit of thanking Abraham for his kind entertainment of them, whereto he would reply: "What, ye give thanks unto me! Rather return thanks to your host, He who alone provides food and drink for all creatures." Then the people would ask, "Where is He?" and Abraham would answer them, and say: "He is the Ruler of heaven and earth. . . ." When the people heard such words, they would ask, "How shall we return thanks to God and manifest our gratitude unto Him?" And Abraham would instruct them . . . [in] how to praise and thank God. Abraham's house thus became not only a lodging-place for the hungry and thirsty, but also a place of instruction where the knowledge of God and His law were taught.[60]

Abraham's kindness was noised abroad, and many "flocked to him from all parts of the earth,"[61] including "all the lowly and oppressed, the needy and the miserable, the suffering and the downtrodden, the hungry and the naked,"[62] and "Abraham welcomed them with joy and love."[63] He "fed and clothed them, comforted and consoled them and wiped away their tears. And Sarah, his wife, was sharing in the charitable work of her aged husband. Indefatigably she worked day and night."[64]

And for those visitors interested in receiving spiritual nourishment, Abraham and Sarah taught them the gospel and baptized them, welcoming them into the ever-growing Zion community.

### Abraham's Offering of Isaac

Notwithstanding Abraham's lifetime of loving service, there came a time when he was tested as never before.[65] Suddenly and without warning, God spoke, calling to him by the name He Himself had bestowed on him, the name that meant "father of a multitude": "Abraham."

Responsively, submissively, immediately, Abraham answered, "Behold, here I am"[66]—an expression of Abraham's faith in God, of his "readiness to obey His word" and "readiness to answer His call."[67]

God then spoke to Abraham about "thy son . . . Isaac, whom thou lovest." It is the first occurrence of the word "love" in the Old Testament. Significantly, in the New Testament the first occurrence of the word love is also as a heavenly voice mentions the love of a father for his son—the love of God the Father for His Son Jesus.[68]

Abraham's love for his son was the very thing that was being tested, as God, without any explanation whatsoever, directed Abraham to take his beloved Isaac to the land of Moriah and offer him as a burnt sacrifice. Joseph Smith commented that it was the hardest possible trial that God could have designed for his beloved friend Abraham.[69]

On Abraham's part, there was no argument or question or even hesitation, but only total and prompt obedience. He arose early the next morning, split the wood for the sacrifice, and took Isaac and two servants to begin the journey northward to the land of Moriah.

For over two days they traveled, during which we are told neither of the conversation nor of Abraham's agony. He kept the awful secret for as long as he could, sparing the feelings of his beloved son. Only when they came to the place of sacrifice and had left the servants behind did

Abraham disclose what God had asked of them. Isaac willingly agreed but asked to be bound, lest at the last minute he lose his nerve.

When all was ready, Abraham kissed his son, and weeping, raised the knife. A voice from heaven halted the sacrifice, saying that Abraham had proven himself. Only then did Abraham notice behind him a ram caught in a thicket. Sacrificing the ram in the stead of Isaac, Abraham heard a heavenly voice a second time, this time sealing the promises of posterity and eternal life. It was through this sealing, explained Joseph Smith, that Abraham attained "perfect love."[70]

By their willingness to make the sacrifice, Abraham and Isaac had shown the depth of their love for God, which had pointed to an even greater love. For more than any other event in history, Abraham's offering of Isaac was, as the Book of Mormon prophet Jacob would say, a "similitude of God and his Only Begotten Son"[71]—history's greatest act of love in which the Father "so loved the world, that he gave his only begotten Son."[72] Likewise the Beloved Son—the Seed of Abraham through Mary— "loved the world, even unto the laying down of [His] life for the world."[73]

### Transforming the World Through the Love of Christ

To the very end of his life, Abraham continued his ministry of love and caring, inviting all to come unto Christ and paying special attention to the least of his brethren. In the words of Hugh Nibley, Abraham "was 'the Friend of God' because he was the friend of man."[74]

If the hateful world into which the infant Abraham had been born was ripe for destruction, the world he left behind 175 years later had been transformed by his labors of love. He had preached to kings and commoners, and reached out in kindness to the helpless and hopeless, blessing them temporally and spiritually. His was the first great humanitarian mission, combined with proselyting in this great outreach of love. Multitudes had been blessed and comforted by him and Sarah, while their converts numbered into the tens of thousands.[75] His passing occasioned widespread grief.

> According to Jewish tradition, "when the inhabitants of Canaan heard that Abraham was dead, they all came with their kings and princes and all their men to [help] bury Abraham. . . . And all the inhabitants of the land. . . , and all those who had known Abraham, wept. . . , and men and women mourned over him. And all the little children, and all the inhabitants of the land wept on account of Abraham, for Abraham had been good to them all, and . . . had been upright with God and men."

> How many untold stories of compassion and kindness by Abraham are covered in that brief report alluding to what the poet Wordsworth called "that best portion of a good man's life, his little, nameless, unremembered acts of kindness and of love." In addition, "all the great ones of the nations of the world" came to pay their respects, lamenting, "Woe to the world that has lost its leader and woe to the ship that has lost its pilot." How profoundly mankind missed their righteous priesthood patriarch, their loving friend and exemplar.[76]

But the world would continue to be transformed by his noble posterity. "For the sake of being instruments in the hand of God," said one writer, Abraham "and his sons continued all their lives to labor as faithful missionaries, from one kingdom to another . . . , foregoing the comforts of a fixed and fortified habitation, cheerfully encountering the dangers and hardships. . . . Abraham was not only the Father of the Faithful, but he was the . . . father of Missionaries."[77]

Nor would it stop with his sons. In the words of John Taylor, "Abraham's posterity were to stand as messengers of God, as legates of the skies, commissioned of the great Jehovah to proclaim His word to fallen man . . . and bring them to Zion."[78]

Despite periods of apostasy, the covenant sealed upon Abraham would ensure that three and a half millennia later, in the year 1820, the world would again be favored with an opening of the heavens and the restoration of the gospel to Abraham's latter-day posterity, beginning with Joseph Smith.

As Abraham's posterity, it is our privilege and obligation to extend the blessings of the Savior's love to all nations. "Our very identity," explains Elder David A. Bednar, as "the seed of Abraham is in large measure defined by the responsibility to proclaim the gospel."[79] Our guideline in doing so is, as the Lord has commanded, to "do the works of Abraham,"[80] or, in the words of President Spencer W. Kimball, to "follow Abraham's example."[81]

As love was the defining characteristic of Abraham's life and ministry, so it must be with all his posterity who reach out to offer the Savior's atoning love to the world. "No one," the Savior has declared, "can assist in this work except he shall be humble and full of love."[82]

## Legacy of Abraham

Born some ten generations after the Flood, Abraham came to an apostate world whose wickedness and cruelty rivaled that of Noah's time. As Abraham sought God through purity and prayer, he discovered the reality of the Creator and His most important trait: loving-kindness, or charity. Abraham himself exercised this quality as he obeyed the ordinances, received a restoration of the gospel in his day, and then reached out with love to testify of Christ and bless mankind temporally and spiritually. God's covenant to Abraham promised that through him and his posterity all nations of the earth would be blessed. This blessing is now being extended through the preaching of the gospel by Abraham's seed as they extend the love of the Savior—Abraham's Seed—to all mankind.

# CHAPTER 4

## ~ *Isaiah* ~
### *Here Am I, Send Me*

A thousand years after Abraham, his chosen descendants in Jerusalem were admonished by the Lord to do what the righteous since Abraham's day are always commanded to do: "Hearken to me, ye that follow after righteousness, ye that seek the Lord. . . . Look unto Abraham your father, and unto Sarah that bare you."[1] This divine injunction was written by Isaiah, whose own emulation of Abraham set him on an amazing mission that would forever bless Abraham's posterity.

### Salvation for Abraham's Posterity

The name Isaiah means "the Lord is salvation,"[2] holding out hope for a hardened people who had dishonored their Abrahamic heritage by practicing the very evils that Abraham had spent his life opposing: idolatry, immorality, pride, and oppression. The exhortation to remember Abraham was timely indeed, as was the appearance of Isaiah himself.

Born about 760 B.C., Isaiah was the son of Amoz, whom Jewish tradition describes as a prophet and a brother of one of the kings of Judah.[3] This close kinship to the monarchy would explain Isaiah's remarkable access to the royal court and affairs of state in the kingdom of Judah.

## The Lord's Question in His Atoning Ceremony

Isaiah's even more remarkable ministry and prophecies can be explained only by the divine call he received in a vision, which he himself described. It took place in the year that King Uzziah died, about 740 B.C., in the Holy of Holies of the Jerusalem Temple.[4] Isaiah saw Jehovah[5] majestically sitting on His throne guarded by seraphs, winged creatures that were crying out, "Holy, holy, holy, is the LORD of hosts: the whole earth is full of his glory." At the sound of their voices, the temple shook and was filled with a cloud of sweet-smelling incense.[6]

"Woe is me!" cried Isaiah, "for I am undone; because I am a man of unclean lips, and I dwell in the midst of a people of unclean lips: for mine eyes have seen the King, the LORD of hosts."[7]

At this, one of the seraphs used tongs to grasp a live coal, and flying to Isaiah, placed it on his mouth, saying, "thine iniquity is taken away, and thy sin purged"[8]—or in modern translation, "your guilt is taken away and your sin atoned for."[9]

Atonement is precisely what this scene is all about, for Isaiah's description unmistakably identifies it as occurring during the most important ceremony of the Jerusalem Temple, the Day of Atonement.[10] Known as "the Great Day," it was "the supreme festival and the greatest day of the year, . . . a day of unparalleled joy . . . , the whole purpose of [which] is to atone for those who repent and confess their iniquity."[11]

Only on this day of the year did any mortal enter the Holy of Holies where stood the Ark of the Covenant, God's throne guarded by statues of winged creatures. The ceremony called for all Israel to repent and to fast and pray for forgiveness, while the High Priest, as their representative, reverently entered and appeared before the divine throne to seek mercy.

As he proceeded to place incense on live coals, the room filled with fragrant clouds of smoke symbolizing the clouds of heaven. He later returned to sprinkle sacrificial blood in front of and on top of the Ark,[12] a striking demonstration of the fact that the Heavenly King who sat on the throne would one day come to earth and shed His own blood to atone for Israel and all mankind. It was this Atonement, "the atoning blood of Christ,"[13] which now cleansed Isaiah.

No sooner did this happen than Isaiah heard the Lord pose a question: "Whom shall I send, and who will go for us?"[14] The "us" indicates the presence of others, the divine council,[15] which Isaiah seems to have joined on this occasion.

But the question of sending someone clearly meant sending someone to Isaiah's people, the Lord's people Israel. Who would go and cry repentance to this hardened people so that they too might be cleansed through the blood of Christ? It would be a mission fraught with danger and possibly death.

### Echo of the Premortal Council

At this critical moment, Isaiah emulated his forefather Abraham who had so readily responded to God's call. Said Isaiah, "Here am I; send me."[16] But there was another even more important echo. The question that Jehovah asked happened to be precisely the same question asked long ago in the premortal council when the Father had declared, "Whom shall I send?"[17]

Who was willing, in other words, to go and bear the excruciating weight of sin and suffering for all the rest of Father's children? The colossal burden of what was being asked was apparently too great to direct the question to anyone in particular. Whoever accepted would have to volunteer. But everyone knew that there was only One who could actually carry out such a mission, and all eyes must have turned to Jehovah, the firstborn, the most obedient, the most intelligent, and the meekest of all.

He alone could be totally trusted to carry out the unique and painful role upon which the Father's entire plan depended.

Jehovah spoke up. With no hesitation and no attempt to divert the proposed plan to His own ends, He readily responded with those immortal words of submission and self-sacrifice: "Here am I, send me."[18]

Millennia later, as Isaiah now stood before the divine throne, it was Jehovah who now asked the question of whom to send, and it was Isaiah who selflessly echoed Jehovah's own answer spoken so long ago: "Here am I, send me."

### Isaiah's Mission and Message

The Lord did send Isaiah, who went forth to preach. Like his forefather Noah, Isaiah had the burden of warning the people of destruction unless they repented. "Ah sinful nation, a people laden with iniquity," who "have forsaken the LORD" and "provoked the Holy One of Israel unto anger. . . . Your country is desolate" he said, speaking as if it had already happened; "your cities are burned with fire: your land . . . is desolate, as overthrown by strangers."[19]

All this could be averted if the people would but accept the gospel. They must repent—"put away the evil of your doings from before mine eyes; cease to do evil; learn to do well"—and be baptized—"wash you; make you clean"[20] in the "waters of Judah, or . . . the waters of baptism."[21] Then, "though your sins be as scarlet, they shall be as white as snow; though they be red like crimson, they shall be as wool."[22]

This cleansing would come, as Isaiah taught, through the Atonement of the "Prince of Peace,"[23] He who would be born of a virgin[24] and would be "despised and rejected . . . ; a man of sorrows," being "wounded for our transgressions" and "bruised for our iniquities." "Surely he hath borne our griefs, and carried our sorrows," and "with his stripes we are healed."[25]

These and numerous other passages from the Book of Isaiah did the early Christians, and indeed Jesus himself, recognize as prophecies of His mortal ministry. The New Testament quotes or alludes to Isaiah so much—far more than any other Old Testament prophet[26]—that since early times his book as been known among Christians as the "Fifth Gospel."[27] Nor is Isaiah's Messianic message a marginal part of his work, which, as one scholar describes, "is built around three Messianic portraits: the King (chapters 1–37), the Servant (chapters 38–55) and the Anointed Conqueror (chapters 56–66)," which are "meant as facets of the one Messianic person."[28] From first to last, Isaiah's message was centered in Jesus Christ.

## Isaiah's Vision, Writings, and Continued Efforts

One of Isaiah's most devoted readers was the prophet Nephi, born in Jerusalem some decades after Isaiah. In making his own record, Nephi quoted extensively from Isaiah's writings, and then mentioned something about him not found in our Bible. Said Nephi, "he verily saw my Redeemer, even as I have seen him."[29] Nephi's own vision of the Savior had included His birth, mortal ministry, and atoning death.[30]

Nor does the Bible mention what the Prophet Joseph Smith stated about Isaiah, that he attained such righteousness that Jesus Christ appeared to him, introduced the Father, and taught Isaiah face to face, opening to him visions of the heavens and a perfect knowledge of the mysteries of the kingdom of God.[31]

All this is attested by an ancient text that describes a vision of Isaiah very much like what both Joseph Smith and Nephi described. Known as the *Ascension of Isaiah*, the text was cited by a number of early Christian writers,[32] and tells of Isaiah being taken to heaven where he sees both the Father and his Beloved Son, and sees in vision—even as Nephi would later see—the Son's future mortal birth and miraculous ministry culminating in his suffering, crucifixion, and resurrection.[33]

The text further tells that Isaiah testified to his fellow mortals with perfect plainness about the coming of "the Beloved from . . . heaven. . . , and his descent to earth, . . . and the persecution to which he would be subjected,"[34] and that he would "be crucified on a tree"[35] with "wicked men, and that he would be buried in the tomb, and . . . the angel . . . would on the third day open the tomb."[36] All this and more did Isaiah clearly teach his people about the Son of God.

Why, then, do these things not appear in the biblical book of Isaiah? Because, according to the *Ascension of Isaiah*, the prophet Isaiah wrote "parables . . . in the book which contains my public prophecies."[37] That momentous decision to couch his messianic prophecies in parables would assure that when the scriptures would be edited by wicked scribes deleting plain and precious prophecies of Christ,[38] the book of Isaiah would remain nearly intact,[39] a closed book to the unenlightened but a veritable treasure trove for the righteous of future generations.

Thus did Isaiah become a messenger not only to the people of his day but also to those in the future—as for example when Abinadi would quote Isaiah in the preaching that converted Alma,[40] or when John the Baptist would quote Isaiah to convert the Jews,[41] or when the Apostle Paul in his highly successful missionary labors would repeatedly quote Isaiah.[42]

Among Isaiah's own people, however, his message apparently met with little success. We read that his preaching generally fell on deaf ears,[43] and that he himself wistfully remarked, "Who hath believed our report [or 'message']?"[44]

Even so, Isaiah's love for his errant people was as undying as that of the prophet Mormon for his wicked people; and as Mormon continued to lead them in battle as supreme military commander, so Isaiah, as counselor and confidante to the kings of Judah, continued to use his influence at court to attempt to arrange political and military protection for his wayward people as long as possible.

But seeing no way—as Alma would say of his own people—"that he might reclaim them save it were in bearing down in pure testimony against them,"[45] Isaiah fervently preached to his people, "whom he hoped to bring back to the path of righteousness by his prophecies."[46] His audience included his kinsmen of the northern ten tribes constituting the kingdom of Israel, who likewise ignored his preaching. In 722 B.C. they fell to the mighty Assyrians,[47] just as Isaiah had foretold.[48] "To such an end . . . did the Israelites come," commented the historian Josephus, "because they violated the laws and disregarded the prophets who foretold . . . this misfortune."[49]

The survivors were resettled far away in another part of the vast Assyrian empire. Later when political power changed, they traveled northward and out of biblical history. They may well have carried with them the writings of Isaiah "to instruct, inspire, and comfort them throughout the following generations."[50]

### Isaiah's Martyrdom and Great Words

Some twenty-five years after the fall of the northern kingdom, a new king arose in the southern kingdom of Judah. His name was Manassah, and "he did that which was evil in the sight of the LORD."[51] The *Ascension of Isaiah* tells that as a "servant of Satan,"[52] Manassah sought Isaiah's life, for Satan "was especially furious with Isaiah" because of his vision and his plain prophecies of the coming of Christ[53]—even as this same people of Jerusalem just a century later would likewise seek Lehi's life because he "testified . . . plainly of the coming of the Messiah."[54]

According to one version of what happened to Isaiah, he fled when the king sought his life, and hid himself in a hollowed-out cedar tree. Unfortunately, a piece of his clothing stuck out, and when the king and his men saw it, he ordered the tree to be cut through.[55]

But before the order was carried out, Isaiah was offered a way out. His life would be spared if he would admit that everything he had preached and prophesied was wrong, thereby denying the Christ. Isaiah refused, and was sawed in two.[56] Having prophesied about the Savior's future death by crucifixion on a tree, Isaiah sealed his testimony with his blood as he likewise met his own death in a tree.

But his words remained to ever speak hope and inspiration to the house of Israel. With good reason does the Book of Mormon quote extensively from Isaiah, for as Jewish tradition insists, Isaiah "described and proclaimed, in plainer terms than any other prophet, the brilliant destiny in store for the house of Israel."[57] Or, as the resurrected Savior would say to the Nephites about Isaiah, "surely he spake as touching all things concerning my people which are of the house of Israel."[58]

It was on that occasion that the Savior also gave his unparalleled endorsement of Isaiah's writings: "Ye ought to search these things. Yea, a commandment I give unto you that ye search these things diligently; for great are the words of Isaiah."[59]

Just before saying this, the Savior had quoted from Isaiah's great words foretelling the establishment of latter-day Zion when, said the Savior, "the fulness of my gospel shall be preached"[60] by those who, as Isaiah foretold, will bring good tidings and publish peace.[61]

Not surprisingly, Isaiah's great words have echoed throughout the Restoration from its very beginning. When the Father and the Son appeared to Joseph Smith to respond to his question as to which church to join, the Savior answered in the words of Isaiah, saying that they "draw near to me with their lips, but their hearts are far from me."[62] Later when the Savior announced in the opening verse of the Doctrine and Covenants the preaching of the gospel to the world, He again quoted Isaiah: "Hearken ye people from afar; and ye that are upon the islands of the sea, listen together."[63]

To those who would go forth to preach the restored gospel, the Savior has offered this invitation: "If ye have desires to serve God ye are called to the work."[64] In essence, the Lord has again asked the great question He once posed to Isaiah: "Whom shall I send?"

The answer of those who choose to serve will echo what Isaiah said, for of all his great words, none are greater than these, echoing what the Savior Himself once humbly declared: "Here am I, send me!"

## Legacy of Isaiah

Born a thousand years after Abraham as one of his descendants in the land promised to their forefather, Isaiah received a vision in the Jerusalem Temple in which he saw the Lord, who asked whom He should send to preach to the people grown so proud and wicked. Isaiah volunteered with those immortal words, "Here am I, send me," echoing what the Savior had said in the premortal council. Of Him Isaiah prophesied and testified, eventually at the cost of his life. But his written prophecies remained to guide future generations, testifying of the Savior's first coming and of His glorious latter-day work carried out by those who are likewise willing to respond, "Here am I, send me."

# II.
# THE NEPHITE
## AND
# EARLY CHRISTIAN ERA

# CHAPTER 5

# ~ *Abinadi* ~
## *How Beautiful the Feet*

About a century after Isaiah was martyred, the fate that he had foretold for Jerusalem fell violently upon the city as Babylonian soldiers wreaked destruction on its inhabitants and enslaved the survivors. This happened, explains the Old Testament, because they had "mocked the messengers of God, and despised his words, and misused his prophets, until the wrath of the LORD arose against his people, till there was no remedy."[1] One of those prophets was Lehi, who escaped the destruction and brought his family across the ocean to the New World. There his righteous posterity treasured the writings of Isaiah, as seen in the remarkable ministry of Abinadi.

## Called by God, Rejected by the People

As a member of an isolated Nephite colony in about 150 B.C., Abinadi seems to have enjoyed no special position or rank in society, being introduced in the Book of Mormon narrative as merely "a man among them."[2] But he was a man with a message, an urgent divine message for his people. For notwithstanding their Israelite heritage and their outward allegiance to the Mosaic law, they had grown proud and corrupt due in large measure to the influence of their evil king, who ironically bore the name of the righteous and blameless Noah of old. King Noah, in contrast, would be remembered ever after for "his wickedness and his abominations."[3]

A list of those abominations reads like a page out of the writings of Isaiah when he had confronted his people with the same iniquities: pride, oppression, idolatry, immorality, drunkenness, blindness of mind, and hardness of heart.[4] To the errant Israelites of old, God had sent Isaiah; to these later Israelites, God now sent Abinadi.

If Isaiah had been commissioned of God, so was Abinadi: "Thus saith the Lord, and thus hath he commanded me, saying, Go forth, and say unto this people. . . ." If Isaiah had prophesied, so did Abinadi: "He went forth among them, and began to prophesy. . . ." And if Isaiah had foretold disaster and bondage except on condition of repentance, so did Abinadi:

> Wo be unto this people, for I have seen their abominations, and their wickedness, and their whoredoms; and except they repent I will visit them in mine anger.
>
> And except they repent and turn to the Lord their God, behold, I will deliver them into the hands of their enemies; yea, and they shall be brought into bondage; and they shall be afflicted by the hand of their enemies.[5]

Abinadi's audience was "wroth with him, and sought to take away his life; but the Lord delivered him out of their hands."[6] That appeared to be the end of Abinadi's ministry, he having succeeded only in stirring up resistance and resentment, even from King Noah himself. "Who is Abinadi," the haughty monarch demanded, "that I and my people should be judged of him"—and then added, "or who is the Lord, that shall bring upon my people such great affliction? I command you," he ordered, "to bring Abinadi hither, that I may slay him."[7] But Abinadi was nowhere to be found.

### Questions for Abinadi

Two years later he returned in disguise, apparently the only way he could continue to preach. He had been commanded by God again to deliver a message, this one even sterner than before. Abinadi's very willingness to return was heroic, for he surely knew that he was walking into a den of lions.

But he was as bold as before in declaring the word of the Lord, who now warned that in His "fierce anger" He would "visit them in their iniquities and abominations." They would be enslaved, slapped on the face, and driven as beasts of burden; they would be sorely afflicted with famine, pestilence, and plagues of insects, and would "howl all the day long." And they would be killed and their carcasses devoured by vultures, dogs, and wild beasts.

Nor would the king escape. As Isaiah had once predicted disaster on the heads of powerful monarchs,[8] so Abinadi now predicted that Noah's life would be "as a garment in a hot furnace," or "as a dry stalk of the field, which is run over by the beasts and trodden under foot," or as "the blossoms of a thistle" blown "forth upon the face of the land."[9]

As Abinadi must have anticipated, such threats got him an immediate audience with the king, who summarily cast him into prison and convened the royal council of priests. They had Abinadi brought for questioning "that they might cross him, that thereby they might have wherewith to accuse him; but he answered them boldly, and withstood all their questions, yea, to their astonishment; for he did withstand them in all their questions, and did confound them in all their words."[10]

What those questions and answers were, we are not told, with one notable exception. That question by one of the priests—we are not told which one[11]—concerned the meaning of a certain scriptural passage which had been "taught by our fathers."[12] The passage is from Isaiah 52, which was read out to Abinadi:

How beautiful upon the mountains are the feet of him that bringeth good tidings; that publisheth peace; that bringeth good tidings of good; that publisheth salvation; that saith unto Zion, Thy God reigneth;

Thy watchman shall lift up the voice; with the voice together shall they sing; for they shall see eye to eye when the Lord shall bring again Zion;

Break forth into joy; sing together ye waste places of Jerusalem; for the Lord hath comforted his people, he hath redeemed Jerusalem;

The Lord hath made bare his holy arm in the eyes of all the nations, and all the ends of the earth shall see the salvation of our God.[13]

As explained by a modern scholar, this Isaiah passage portrays with "extraordinary vividness . . . a runner coming over the hills and approaching Jerusalem"—which is located in a mountainous region—"with the news that the King himself is on his way, soon to make his triumphal entrance. . . . The watchmen on the towers of the city are the first to catch sight of the oncoming messenger, and as they do so they raise a simultaneous shout of joy. Even the ruins of the city are to come alive and join in the acclamation. . . . What has been dead is to live again. [Jehovah's] victory is to be 'seen' by 'all the ends of the earth.'"[14]

But no such explanation—indeed, no explanation at all—was forthcoming about this Isaiah passage from Abinadi, who, instead of answering the question posed by the royal priests, proceeded to chastise them for not knowing the answer themselves, and then began asking his own questions.

### Questions by Abinadi

"Are you priests," he cried, "and pretend to teach this people, and to understand the spirit of prophesying, and yet desire to know of me what these things mean? I say unto you, wo be unto you for perverting the ways of the Lord! For if ye understand these things ye have not taught them. . . . Therefore, what teach ye this people?"[15]

When they responded that they taught the law of Moses, Abinadi confronted them with more difficult questions: "If ye teach the law of Moses why do ye not keep it? Why do ye set your heart upon riches? Why do ye commit whoredoms and spend your strength with harlots, yea, and cause this people to commit sin?"

The evidence he offered for these accusations was his own presence. It was because of their sins, he declared, "that the Lord has cause to send me to prophesy against this people," adding that "ye know that I speak the truth; and you ought to tremble before God."[16] Bold words for one who, as Abinadi well knew, was on trial for his life!

But it was the priests who now stood accused as Abinadi continued to take charge and ask questions. What, he continued, did they really know about the law of Moses? Did salvation come by the law of Moses?

Yes, they responded.

Abinadi replied that he knew that if they kept the commandments that God had delivered to Moses on Mount Sinai, they would be saved.

It is at this point in the story that we get some idea of Abinadi's remarkable command of the scriptures as he begins to quote verbatim the ten commandments received by Moses. "Thou shalt have no other God before me. Thou shalt not make unto thee any graven image."

But already these first two commandments condemned his listeners. "Have ye done all this? I say unto you, Nay, ye have not. And have ye taught this people that they should do all these things? I say unto you, Nay, ye have not."[17]

### Preaching about the Messiah

King Noah's patience was at an end. "Away with this fellow, and slay him," for "he is mad."[18] But when Abinadi's hostile audience attempted to lay their hands on him, they could not.

"Touch me not," warned Abinadi, "for God shall smite you if ye lay your hands on me, for I have not delivered the message which the Lord sent me to deliver." Nor had he finished answering their question about the Isaiah passage.

As Abinadi spoke, "the Spirit of the Lord was upon him; and his face shone with exceeding luster, even as Moses' did while in the mount of Sinai, while speaking with the Lord." It was a visible and unmistakable witness to the truth of Abinadi's message as he proceeded to quote the remainder of the commandments that Moses had received as written on the stone tablets, "for," declared Abinadi, "I perceive that they are not written in your hearts."[19]

Even so, continued Abinadi, if this wicked people would repent there was hope for them through the Messiah, of whom not only Moses had plainly spoken, but also "all the prophets who have prophesied ever since the world began."[20] Indeed, their message was Abinadi's message:

> Have they not said that God himself should come down among the children of men, and take upon him the form of man, and go forth in mighty power upon the face of the earth?
>
> Yea, and have they not said also that he should bring to pass the resurrection of the dead, and that he, himself, should be oppressed and afflicted?[21]

Having earlier been questioned by his listeners about a scriptural passage from Isaiah 52, Abinadi now quoted to them the whole of Isaiah 53 as evidence of the Savior who, as "a man of sorrows, and acquainted with grief," will have "borne our griefs, and carried our sorrows," having been "wounded for our transgressions" and "bruised for our iniquities."[22]

In other words, explained Abinadi, "God himself shall come down among the children of men, and shall redeem his people" and "make intercession for the children of men," having "taken upon himself their iniquity and their transgressions."[23]

## Beautiful Feet of the Messengers

With this foundation, the master teacher Abinadi was now ready to answer, or complete the answer, to the question about Isaiah 52. Referring to those who previously had borne witness of the Savior, Abinadi declared:

> These are they who have published peace, who have brought good tidings of good, who have published salvation; and said unto Zion: Thy God reigneth!
> And O how beautiful upon the mountains were their feet![24]

And so would it ever be, continued Abinadi.

> And again, how beautiful upon the mountains are the feet of those that are still publishing peace!
> And again, how beautiful upon the mountains are the feet of those who shall hereafter publish peace, yea, from this time henceforth and forever![25]

And if beautiful are the feet of the messengers, how much more beautiful the feet of Him of whom the messengers testify:

> And behold, I say unto you, this is not all. For O how beautiful upon the mountains are the feet of him that bringeth good tidings, that is the founder of peace, yea, even the Lord, who has redeemed his people; yea, him who has granted salvation unto his people.[26]

For it is the Lord, continued Abinadi, who would break the bands of death and thereby bring to pass the resurrection, and His name shall be called Christ; and joining Him in the first resurrection will be all those who have kept His commandments and whom He has redeemed, who will have eternal life.[27]

## Future Events and Repentance Now

Abinadi assured his audience that the truths that he was teaching would eventually "be declared to every nation, kindred, tongue, and people"—and then would be fulfilled the words from Isaiah 52 prophesying that "the Lord shall bring again Zion," and "thy watchmen shall lift up their voice" together in joyful song, for the Lord "hath comforted his people . . . , hath redeemed Jerusalem," and "hath made bare his holy arm in the eyes of all the nations; and all the ends of the earth shall see the salvation of our God."[28]

Providing a vivid illustration of the Lord stretching forth his arm, Abinadi then stretched forth his own arm as he told them that they must repent. Repeating the last phrase of the Isaiah passage he had just quoted, Abinadi declared that "the time shall come when all shall see the salvation of the Lord . . . and shall confess before God that his judgments are just." Then shall the righteous be raised "to the resurrection of endless life and happiness."

But the wicked shall be "cast out, and shall have cause to howl, and weep, and wail, and gnash their teeth." Therefore, Abinadi continued, "ought ye not to tremble and repent of your sins, and remember that only in and through Christ ye can be saved?" Therefore, if they taught the law of Moses, they should also "teach that it is a shadow of those things which are to come" and "that redemption cometh through Christ the Lord."[29]

### The Beautiful Feet of Abinadi

The messenger had delivered his message, and how beautiful were his feet that day to the eyes of one in the audience, a certain Alma who pled with the king to spare Abinadi's life. The king was enraged, and Alma barely escaped with his own life—allowing us to have the account of Abinadi.[30]

For he, like his hero Isaiah, was about to die as a martyr and seal "the truth of his words by his death."[31] Abinadi's death also has similarities to that of the Savior, as seen in some of the very words that Abinadi had quoted: "he was despised, and we esteemed him not," for "we did esteem him stricken, smitten of God, and afflicted."[32]

Abinadi's final affliction was "death by fire,"[33] his flesh being scorched and seared by the flames. Reflecting on the passages he had quoted from

Isaiah, one might well wonder just how such disfigured and charred feet could qualify as beautiful. Commenting on the Isaiah passage about beautiful feet, one modern scholar has observed:

> Considering the geography and customs of the Near East, we can assume that the messenger's feet, after the long journey over the mountains, were not only dusty but very callused and perhaps bleeding. To those feet the witness exclaims, "How beautiful!" For these are feet that bring words that thrill the heart longing for just this announce-ment, "Your God reigns." It is like the old man peering into the still-sparkling eyes of his ninety-year-old wife, eyes bordered by wrinkles enfolding the wisdom of a thousand revelations, and exclaiming, "How beautiful!" It is like the loving husband stroking the stomach of the mother of his children, gently tracing the stretch marks that memorialize her maternal labors, and exclaiming, "How beautiful!" Yes, indeed, how beautiful these feet bruised on behalf of the blessed mission of proclaim-ing the coming of salvation![34]

### The Most Beautiful Feet of All

Such bruised and bleeding feet call to mind those most beautiful feet of all, described by Abinadi as "the feet of him that bringeth good tidings, that is the founder of peace, yea, even the Lord," who by that very bruising and bleeding "has redeemed his people."[35]

It was those beautiful feet which, nearly two centuries after Abinadi, would stand before the righteous Nephites as they came up, one by one, and felt the nail prints and "did fall down at the feet of Jesus, and did worship him."[36]

He then called forth from the multitude a certain man to serve as the chief of the twelve disciples. Obediently approaching, the man "bowed himself before the Lord and did kiss his feet."[37] Who was this man who had the supreme privilege of first kissing those beautiful resurrected feet? He was Nephi, a descendant of Alma, Abinadi's only convert and he who had recorded Abinadi's powerful words about the Savior's bruised and beautiful feet.

Hence if Abinadi's mission had seemed in vain to those who witnessed his execution, that mission turned out to be pivotal for Nephite history. Every major missionary effort and achievement from that point on as recorded in the Book of Mormon can be traced directly back to the remarkable influence of Abinadi, beginning with his one and only convert, Alma.

After Nephi kissed the Savior's feet, so did the rest of the multitude, or as many as could come, "insomuch that they did bathe his feet with their tears."[38] Later they listened to Jesus prophesy of the latter days when he would send messengers to preach the gospel[39]—the same messengers foreseen by Isaiah, whose words Jesus now quoted, but with important additions: "*And then shall they say:* How beautiful upon the mountains are the feet of him that bringeth good tidings *unto them.*"[40]

That day has arrived, and the messengers are being sent in fulfillment of what Abinadi foretold, that "the salvation of the Lord shall be declared to every nation, kindred, tongue, and people."[41] Those messengers are the ones of whom Isaiah prophesied. "Now," asked the Prophet Joseph Smith, "what do we hear in the gospel which we have received?" He answered:

> A voice of gladness! A voice of mercy from heaven; and a voice of truth out of the earth; glad tidings for the dead; a voice of gladness for the living and the dead; glad tidings of great joy. How beautiful upon the mountains are the feet of those that bring glad tidings of good things, and that say unto Zion: Behold, thy God reigneth![42]

How beautiful indeed are the dusty and weary feet of the Lord's latter-day missionaries as they faithfully traverse the earth's highways and byways, proclaiming the restored gospel of Him whose supremely beautiful feet tell the story of His suffering for all mankind.

## Legacy of Abinadi

To an isolated Nephite colony some hundred and fifty years before Christ, the Lord sent a messenger—"a man among them"—named Abinadi, whose bold message of repentance was rejected by King Noah and his wicked priests, with one exception: Alma repented and recorded Abinadi's powerful preaching about the beautiful feet of the Savior and His messengers. How beautiful also are the feet of them who take the Savior's gospel to all nations, testifying of His atoning wounds and healing love.

## CHAPTER 6

# ~ Alma the Younger ~
# Born of God

The impression that Abinadi's message made on Alma could not have been more powerful. He repented of his sins and sought the Lord in mighty prayer; and after receiving divine forgiveness and authority, he privately taught the words of Abinadi and converted hundreds whom he led back to rejoin the main body of the Nephites. There Alma became the head of the Church and did a great work. But his greatest work was what he accomplished with own son, also named Alma, who gets more coverage than any other missionary in the Book of Mormon.

### A Wicked Son Bent on Destruction

This son shared not only his father's name but also the tragedy of growing up as "a very wicked and an idolatrous man."[1] Unlike his father, however, when the younger Alma heard the word of God, he rejected it, being not merely wayward but also bent on taking as many as possible with him. Using "much flattery" and persuading others "to do after the manner of his iniquities," the younger Alma was cunning and conspiratorial, joining forces with the king's sons in a secret campaign to "destroy the church, and to lead astray the people of the Lord." He was extremely effective, becoming "a great hinderment to . . . the church of God."[2]

Alma the elder, having made every effort to teach and rescue his son, resorted to fervent prayer and asked others to join with him.

## A Thunderous Voice and Indescribable Agony

One day as the younger Alma and his companions were on their way to wreak yet more harm, they were literally stopped in their tracks by an angel descending in a cloud of glory. He spoke in "a voice of thunder, which caused the earth to shake upon which they stood." The astonished travelers collapsed without understanding what the angel had said.[3]

The terror increased for Alma when he heard the angel command him to stand up. Thus singled out and forced to obey, Alma now found himself face to face with this powerful being who again spoke in a voice of thunder.

The angel had come, he said, because the Lord had heard the prayers of His people and particularly the elder Alma.

> For he has prayed with much faith concerning thee that thou mightest be brought to the knowledge of the truth; therefore, for this purpose have I come to convince thee of the power and authority of God. . . .
> And now behold, can ye dispute the power of God? For behold, doth not my voice shake the earth? And can ye not also behold me before you? And I am sent from God.[4]

As dull as Alma's spiritual radar had become, there was absolutely no mistaking the quaking of the earth caused by this powerful being, who commanded Alma to remember his fathers and what the Lord had done for them.[5]

Then came the ultimatum for Alma. He himself would be destroyed, he was told, unless he sought "no more to destroy the church of God."[6] Alma later described this as one would describe a blow from a weapon.

"I was struck," he remembered, "with such great fear and amazement lest perhaps I should be destroyed, that I fell to the earth and I did hear no more."[7]

Lapsing into a state of apparent lifelessness, and oblivious to his mortal surroundings, he felt an excruciating anguish of soul that overwhelmed him. Nothing else in all of scripture quite matches the poignancy of his description.

> I was racked with eternal torment, for my soul was harrowed up to the greatest degree and racked with all my sins.
>
> Yea, I did remember all my sins and iniquities, for which I was tormented with the pains of hell; yea, I saw that I had rebelled against my God, and that I had not kept his holy commandments.
>
> Yea, and I had murdered many of his children, or rather led them away unto destruction; yea, and in fine so great had been my iniquities, that the very thought of coming into the presence of my God did rack my soul with inexpressible horror.
>
> Oh, thought I, that I could be banished and become extinct both soul and body, that I might not be brought to stand in the presence of my God, to be judged of my deeds.
>
> And now, for three days and for three nights was I racked, even with the pains of a damned soul.[8]

It seems that Alma is trying to describe something not fully describable, an agony so intense as to be beyond the understanding of mortals—as the Savior Himself has warned in latter-day revelation: "Repent, lest I smite you by the rod of my mouth, and by my wrath, and by my anger, and your sufferings be sore—how sore you know not, how exquisite you know not, yea, how hard to bear you know not."[9]

The description matches that of the agony prepared for the wicked at the last day when, as prophesied by Alma the elder, they will go into "everlasting fire,"[10] or as Abinadi had foretold, they "shall have cause to howl, and weep, and wail, and gnash their teeth."[11] Such incomprehensible pain is reserved for the wicked beyond the grave; only for Alma was an exception made while his mortal body lay in limbo.

Meanwhile, he was carried to his father who rejoiced to hear of what had happened, and called a great crowd to see what the Lord had done for his son. They began to fast and pray.[12] To all of this, however, the son remained oblivious as his suffering continued, which according to mortal time lasted but three days but seemed to him an eternity.

## Joy and Rebirth Through Jesus

The turning point for Alma the younger came when he finally remembered having "heard my father prophesy unto the people concerning the coming of one Jesus Christ, a Son of God, to atone for the sins of the world."

> Now, as my mind caught hold upon this thought, I cried within my heart: O Jesus, thou Son of God, have mercy on me, who am in the gall of bitterness, and am encircled about by the everlasting chains of death.[13]

According to Elder Jeffrey R. Holland, "Perhaps such a prayer, though brief, is the most significant one that can be uttered in this world. Whatever other prayers we offer, whatever other needs we have, all somehow depends on that plea: 'O Jesus, thou Son of God, have mercy on me.'"[14] For Alma, that desperate cry to Jesus was the turning point.

> And now, behold, when I thought this, I could remember my pains no more; yea, I was harrowed up by the memory of my sins no more.
> And oh, what joy, and what marvelous light I did behold; yea, my soul was filled with joy as exceeding as was my pain!
> Yea, . . . there could be nothing so exquisite and so bitter as were my pains. Yea, . . . on the other hand, there can be nothing so exquisite and sweet as was my joy.
> Yea, methought I saw . . . God sitting upon his throne, surrounded with numberless concourses of angels, in the attitude of singing and praising their God; yea, and my soul did long to be there.[15]

Alma's experience is the most dramatic personal transformation on record: from indescribable torment to indescribable joy; from yearning for banishment from God's presence to longing to be there. The gaping chasm between the two opposites had been bridged only by "Jesus, thou Son of God," as he snatched Alma from the very jaws of hell.

Strength returned to Alma's body, and he stood up to speak—no longer the wayward Alma, but a new person: "I have repented of my sins, and have been redeemed of the Lord; behold I am born of the Spirit,"[16] indeed, "born of God,"[17] who had made known to him that this same transformation was available to all mankind.

> And the Lord said unto me: Marvel not that all mankind, yea, men and women, all nations, kindreds, tongues and people, must be born again; yea, born of God, changed from their carnal and fallen state, to a state of righteousness, being redeemed of God, becoming his sons and daughters;
>
> And thus they become new creatures; and unless they do this, they can in nowise inherit the kingdom of God.[18]

Born of God! The principle was not new, of course, having been preached by the elder Alma,[19] who had heard it from Abinadi,[20] who was but echoing the teaching of his predecessors all the way back to Adam.[21] But it is the experience of Alma, more than anyone else on record, that demonstrates the power of that transformation through Christ, who Himself would be born of the Spirit in the waters of Jordan when "the heavens were opened, and the Holy Ghost descended upon him."[22]

## Choosing to Be a Missionary

No sooner had Alma experienced his spiritual rebirth than he went forth "traveling round about through all the land, publishing to all the people the things which [he] had heard and seen, . . . preaching the word of God,"[23] and "zealously striving to repair all the injuries which [he] had done to the church, confessing all [his] sins, . . . publishing all the things which [he] had seen, and explaining the prophecies and the scriptures to all who desired to hear them."[24]

His objective? As he himself stated some twenty years later near the end of his ministry, looking back to his own spiritual rebirth, "From that time even until now, I have labored without ceasing, that I might bring souls unto repentance; that I might bring them to taste of the exceeding joy of which I did taste; that they might also be born of God, and be filled with the Holy Ghost."[25]

His efforts met with immediate success, "bringing many to the knowledge of the truth, yea, to the knowledge of their Redeemer,"[26] despite the "much tribulation" Alma encountered as he himself became a target of persecution.[27]

Soon burdens of a different sort were added when he was ordained as the ranking high priest (the equivalent of the president of the Church) by his father, and then appointed to be the nation's first chief judge, as the Nephite monarchy peacefully came to a close.[28] But it was a turbulent time in many ways, and Alma had his hands full with domestic problems and as commander-in-chief of a nation fighting a defensive war.[29]

His first love, however, was always missionary work, and he took every opportunity to "establish the church" and baptize the large numbers of those he helped to convert.[30] And when he saw the nation sinking spiritually, he finally stepped down from his high political post "that he himself might go forth among his people" to "preach the word of God unto them, . . . seeing no way that he might reclaim them save it were in bearing down in pure testimony."[31] He chose to be a missionary.

### Redeeming Love and the Redeemer

"Have ye spiritually been born of God?" he asked members of the Church. "Have ye received his image in your countenances? Have ye experienced this mighty change in your hearts?"[32] And if so, and "if ye have felt to sing the song of redeeming love, I would ask, can ye feel so now?"[33]

Redeeming love came only from the Redeemer, of whom Alma constantly bore powerful testimony to members and nonmembers alike, that they might be "purified . . . through the blood of him of whom it has been spoken by our fathers, who should come to redeem his people from their sins."[34] For "I know," Alma declared, "that Jesus Christ shall come, yea, the Son, the Only Begotten of the Father, full of grace, and mercy, and truth."[35]

Indeed, of the "many things to come. . . , there is one thing which is of more importance than they all—for behold, the time is not far distant" (it was in fact less than a century away) "that the Redeemer liveth and cometh among his people." He "shall be born of Mary, at Jerusalem," and "shall go forth, suffering pains and afflictions and temptations of every kind," taking upon himself his people's "infirmities, that his bowels may be filled with mercy, according to the flesh, that he may know according to the flesh how to succor his people according to their infirmities."

For although "the Spirit knoweth all things," yet "the Son of God suffereth according to the flesh that he might take upon him the sins of his people, that he might blot out their transgressions according to the power of his deliverance."[36] Therefore, Alma urged,

> Begin to believe in the Son of God, that he will come to redeem his people, and that he shall suffer and die to atone for their sins; and that he shall rise again from the dead, which shall bring to pass the resurrection, that all men shall stand before him, to be judged at the last and judgment day, according to their works.[37]

### First Principles and Pressing Forward

To strengthen his listeners' faith in Christ, Alma helped them understand the nature of faith as not "a perfect knowledge of things," but rather a "hope for things which are not seen, which are true,"[38] even the truth of the coming of the Son of God "to redeem those who will be baptized unto repentance, through faith on his name."[39] Therefore, the Lord "sendeth an invitation unto all men, for the arms of mercy are extended towards them, and he saith: Repent, and I will receive you."[40]

To the Lord's invitation, Alma added his own: "I wish from the inmost part of my heart, yea, with great anxiety even unto pain, that ye would hearken unto my words, and cast off your sins, and not procrastinate the day of your repentance."[41]

Then, "come and be baptized unto repentance, that ye also may be partakers of the fruit of the tree of life."[42] For, as Alma was humble enough to say, "blessed is he that believeth in the word of God, and is baptized without stubbornness of heart"[43] so as to be "led by the Holy Spirit, becoming humble, meek, submissive, patient, full of love and all long-suffering,"[44] and being "sanctified by the Holy Spirit."[45]

But even then all was not done, for they must ever after pray[46] and "nourish the word" with "faith, and . . . diligence, and patience, and long-suffering," thus "looking forward with an eye of faith to the fruit thereof."[47]

It was a theme to which Alma would return again and again: to be completely born of God, a person must first receive the Holy Ghost and then forever after cultivate His continuing presence and increasing influence.

### That All May Be Born of God

In Alma's teachings, he masterfully used the scriptures,[48] questions,[49] and metaphors[50] to help his listeners understand gospel truths. But the single most important component in his teaching was his own qualification for the Spirit, for which he expended tremendous personal effort. Alma "fasted and prayed many days" for revelations of the Holy Spirit,[51] and also "labored much in the spirit, wrestling with God in mighty prayer, that he would pour out his Spirit upon the people" and grant him success in his missionary labors.[52] Alma's own life stands as supreme witness of the fact that no matter how dramatic and joyous the first part of the rebirth process, it will never be complete without continued diligence and obedience to the end.

After years of missionary service, knowing his mortal ministry was drawing to a close, Alma gathered his sons to give them his final instructions, after which he "could not rest, and . . . went forth" yet again to preach the word of God.[53]

Shortly thereafter, Alma exercised the priesthood in bestowing his final blessings on his sons, upon the righteous, and upon the Church. Then he "departed out of the land of Zarahemla, as if to go into the land of Melek. And it came to pass that he was never heard of more; as to his death or burial we know not of."[54] A couple of years earlier, he had expressed the longing of his heart.

> O that I were an angel, and could have the wish of mine heart, that I might go forth and speak with the trump of God, with a voice to shake the earth, and cry repentance unto every people!
>
> Yea, I would declare unto every soul, as with the voice of thunder, repentance and the plan of redemption, that they should repent and come unto our God, that there might not be more sorrow upon all the face of the earth.[55]

In the end, Alma may well have got his wish, or at least the part that would allow him to be an angel and cry repentance.[56] For it was rumored among his people that he had been "taken up by the Spirit," which thing Mormon, who abridged the account, supposed did happen, as had happened earlier with Moses.[57] If Alma was indeed translated, as appears to be the case, he would have become a ministering angel to help proclaim the gospel, even as he had hoped.

But the second part of Alma's wish—that all people everywhere would hear the message of repentance—would have to wait. Not that this wish was not good, arising at it did from a desire to meet the universal need of which God had told him, that men and women everywhere must be born again.[58] But the worldwide missionary program was reserved for the latter days.

Now is the time when what Alma longed for is taking place, when the Lord's latter-day missionaries are going forth to cry repentance "unto all men."[59] And "whosoever believeth on my words," the Lord has promised in our day, "them will I visit with the manifestation of my Spirit; and they shall be born of me."[60]

Finally, just as Alma hoped, all mankind is being offered the opportunity to be born of God through Jesus Christ as He sends forth His missionaries to all nations.

## Legacy of Alma the Younger

For Abinadi's convert Alma, nothing was so painful as to see his own son Alma grow up as a rebellious and wicked young man. The father's mighty prayers, along with those of his fellow saints, brought down mighty intervention when an angel literally stopped the younger Alma in his tracks and commanded him to repent or be destroyed. As Alma's body lay limp for three days, his spirit experienced an agony beyond description. Only when he remembered his father's preaching about Jesus did Alma seize on this thought and cry out for mercy. His intense pain suddenly gave way to profound joy as Alma was born of God and arose to forever after help others be born again, a timeless pattern for the Lord's latter-day missionaries.

# CHAPTER 7

## ~ *Ammon* ~
## *I Will Be Thy Servant*

On that fateful day when an angel appeared to the rebellious young Alma, he was accompanied by his four closest companions in crime, the sons of King Mosiah. They likewise saw the angel and collapsed in astonishment, and began a course correction that would transform them from enemies of the truth to powerful missionaries. The story of those four Nephite princes, and especially that of their leader, Ammon, is one of the most unexpected and intriguing missionary adventures in the Book of Mormon.

### Change of Course for the Royal Princes

But first they "suffered much anguish of soul because of their iniquities, . . . fearing that they should be cast off forever." Even so, "the Spirit of the Lord [did] work upon them,"[1] effecting a profound transformation. They began to prepare themselves to lead souls to Christ, and it would be later said of them:

> They had waxed strong in the knowledge of the truth; for they were men of a sound understanding and they had searched the scriptures diligently, that they might know the word of God.

But this is not all; they had given themselves to much prayer, and fasting; therefore they had the spirit of prophecy, and the spirit of revelation, and when they taught, they taught with power and authority of God.[2]

With Alma, they began to traverse the entire kingdom, seeking to right their wrongs as they testified of their miraculous conversion and preached the gospel of Christ. They thereby became "instruments in the hands of God in bringing many to the knowledge of the truth, yea, to the knowledge of their Redeemer."[3]

### Missionaries Instead of Monarchs

To the aging King Mosiah, all this must have seemed extraordinarily timely. As the latest in a line of Nephite monarchs who were "mighty men in the faith of the Lord" and who "taught the people the ways of the Lord,"[4] Mosiah had undoubtedly grieved over the wickedness of his sons and what this might mean for the kingdom. Now with their miraculous conversion, he could at last ensure that his realm would continue to be ruled by a righteous man, namely Ammon.[5]

To Mosiah's utter surprise, Ammon refused to be king, as did in turn every one of his brothers. History is full of men who spent their lives and fortunes aspiring to and conspiring for kingship, but these four Nephite princes had a different agenda. They requested their father's permission to leave and preach the gospel to the people who had long been their archenemies, the Lamanites.

The proposal seemed preposterous. Not for centuries had any such notion been seriously entertained, and even then every effort to carry it out had been in vain because of the Lamanites' "eternal hatred" against the Nephites.[6] No wonder that Ammon and his brothers were "laughed . . . to scorn"[7] even by their friends, who desperately tried to bring them to reason:

> Do ye suppose that ye can bring the Lamanites to the knowledge
> of the truth? Do ye suppose that ye can convince the Lamanites of the
> incorrectness of the traditions of their fathers, as stiffnecked a people
> as they are; whose hearts delight in the shedding of blood; whose days
> have been spent in the grossest iniquity; whose ways have been the ways
> of a transgressor from the beginning? . . .
>
> Let us take up arms against them, that we destroy them and their
> iniquity out of the land, lest they overrun us and destroy us.[8]

The writer of the account, Mormon, even adds his own comment
on the enormity of the task proposed by Ammon and his brothers.

> And assuredly it was great, for . . . [the Lamanites were] a wild and
> a hardened and a ferocious people; a people who delighted in murdering
> the Nephites, and robbing and plundering them; and their hearts were
> set upon riches, or upon gold and silver, and precious stones; yet they
> sought to obtain these things by murdering and plundering, that they
> might not labor for them with their own hands.
>
> Thus they were a very indolent people, many of whom did worship
> idols, and the curse of God had fallen upon them because of the
> traditions of their fathers.[9]

The hardened condition of the Lamanites would have been known
only too well by Ammon and his brothers, having been raised in the royal
family and acquainted with affairs of state. And yet, it was precisely the
sorry spiritual state of the Lamanites that evoked the compassion of
Ammon and his brothers, "for they could not bear that any human soul
should perish; yea, even the very thoughts that any soul should endure
endless torment did cause them to quake and tremble."[10]

Accordingly, however foolhardy and hazardous their proposed mission
might appear, yet they felt compelled to undertake it on the mere chance
"that perhaps they might bring" the Lamanites "to the knowledge of the
Lord their God, . . . that they might . . . be brought to rejoice in the Lord
their God."[11] After all, if the Lamanites were hardened transgressors, so
once were Ammon and his brothers. Perhaps it was this vantage point
that allowed them to see possibilities that others did not.

### Embarking on a Great Work

With King Mosiah's long experience as the Nephite monarch, and with his practical knowledge of the Lamanites, he was deeply concerned not only for his sons but also for his other subjects, who were lobbying for one of his sons to accept the throne.[12]

Meanwhile, his sons persisted in pleading for permission to go. After many days, the king decided to make it a matter of prayer. The answer apparently surprised him. He was told to let them go, "for many shall believe on their words, and . . . have eternal life," while Mosiah's sons would be protected[13] according to *Mosiah's* faith.[14]

With this divine assurance, King Mosiah finally granted the permission that his sons had so ardently sought. They had "refused the kingdom"[15] in order to preach the gospel. They had chosen to be servants instead of rulers. They had elected to be missionaries instead of monarchs.

Led by Ammon, the small group of missionaries (including Mosiah's sons and a few others[16]) set out for Lamanite territory. Their path led through a long stretch of wilderness, where they engaged in much fasting and prayer "that the Lord would grant unto them a portion of his Spirit to go with them, and abide with them, that they might be an instrument in the hands of God."[17]

The journey was arduous with "many afflictions" and much suffering "both in body and in mind . . . and also much labor in the spirit,"[18] and at one point their "hearts were depressed, and [they] were about to turn back." They could have done so with no dishonor, for they were under no constraint to go. No priesthood leader had sent them on this mission, and all their friends and associates had strongly advised against it. In fact, if they returned now, they would be warmly welcomed back and praised for their good judgment.

Little could they know what a tragic loss it would have been to turn back. Just at this critical moment, "the Lord comforted [them], and said:

Go amongst thy brethren, the Lamanites, and bear with patience thine afflictions, and I will give unto you success."[19]

Arriving at a particular point, they separated and went their ways, boldly preaching anywhere and everywhere they could get an audience—in homes, on the roads, on hills, in synagogues, and in temples. Despite privation and persecution, they achieved astounding success,[20] as best illustrated by the experience of Ammon.

### Ammon the Invincible Servant

No sooner had Ammon entered the land of Ishmael than he was arrested, bound, and brought before the king, whose name was Lamoni. At his royal whim, he might see fit to have the intruder expelled, imprisoned, or killed. Had he known that this particular captive was heir to the Nephite throne, Ammon may well have been doomed.

But it was precisely that royal upbringing that now served Ammon well. Not only did he know enough not to disclose his royal bloodline, he was also familiar with royal protocol and the respect with which a monarch was to be treated.

King Lamoni asked Ammon if he wished to live among Lamoni's people.

Yes, replied Ammon, he did want to live there for a time, possibly the rest of his life.

Something about this Ammon so deeply impressed the king that he offered one of his daughters in marriage—an unexpected second chance for Ammon to again partake of royal power and privilege.

No thank you, Ammon answered, and then humbly declared, "but I will be thy servant."[21] Once again, Ammon's palace upbringing would prove invaluable. He had grown up being served as royalty, and well knew how to serve a king.

Three days later, when Ammon and his fellow servants were watering the king's flocks, robbers appeared and scattered the animals. Ammon's colleagues mourned for their lives, recalling that the last servants to whom this happened had been executed. But Ammon secretly rejoiced, recognizing this as the opportunity he had prayed for. Now, he thought, "I will show forth . . . the power which is in me, in restoring these flocks unto the king, that I may win the hearts of these my fellow-servants, that I may lead them to believe in my words."[22]

Rousing his fellows with words of encouragement, Ammon led them in a swift and successful race to recover the flocks, but then had to face the robbers. "Encircle the flocks," he directed, while "I go and contend with these men."[23]

The odds seemed entirely against Ammon until he began slinging stones with "mighty power" and deadly aim. Six robbers fell in quick succession, but the rest were now angrily closing in with clubs. Switching from sling to sword, Ammon wielded the weapon with such forceful accuracy that he literally severed every arm raised against him, leaving alive his maimed and bleeding enemies except for their leader, whom Ammon killed.

The rest of the robbers scattered like the flocks, which Ammon and his astounded colleagues then finished watering and led back to pasture. His colleagues also brought back the severed arms, and eagerly presented them to King Lamoni, along with the remarkable report of what they had witnessed that day.

### Ammon the Faithful Servant

Learning of "the faithfulness of Ammon in preserving his flocks, and also of his great power," King Lamoni was "astonished exceedingly," and exclaimed, "Surely this is more than a man. Behold, is not this the Great Spirit who doth send such great punishments upon this people, because of their murders?"[24]

Whether it was the Great Spirit or not, the king's servants could not tell. All they knew was that Ammon was a friend to the king, and clearly could not be slain. It seemed he must be something more than a man.

Lamoni was convinced. "Now I know that it is the Great Spirit . . . of whom our fathers have spoken."[25] But the king was also worried, knowing that he had killed many of his servants when they had failed to protect his flocks. "Where is this man that has such great power?" he wanted to know.

When told that Ammon was feeding the horses, the king was still more astonished, for he remembered that when he had given orders to have the flocks watered, he had further ordered that his horses and chariots be prepared. Ammon's singular diligence seemed added proof that he was more than human, whereupon the king exclaimed:

> Surely there has not been any servant among all my servants that has been so faithful as this man; for even he doth remember all my commandments to execute them.
> Now I surely know that this is the Great Spirit, and I would desire him that he come in unto me, but I durst not.[26]

When Ammon finally came of his own accord to report that the horses and chariots were ready, he noticed a change in the king's countenance and prudently began to leave. One of Lamoni's servants spoke up and, addressing Ammon as "Rabbanah" (a word meaning powerful or great king), said, "the king desireth thee to stay."

Turning again to King Lamoni, Ammon respectfully inquired, "What wilt thou that I should do for thee, O king?"

There was silence for a time, and Ammon again asked, "What desirest thou of me?" Again the king remained silent, but this time the Spirit spoke to Ammon, disclosing the king's thoughts.

### *Teaching a Lamanite King About the Heavenly King*

Answering the king's unspoken question, Ammon explained, "Behold, I am a man, and am thy servant."

Seeing that Ammon could read his thoughts, the king asked, "Art thou that Great Spirit, who knows all things?"

"I am not," Ammon responded.

But the king still knew that he was in the presence of a power that exceeded his own, and was willing to make any royal concession.

> How knowest thou the thoughts of my heart? Thou mayest speak boldly, and tell me concerning these things; and also tell me by what power ye slew and smote off the arms of my brethren that scattered my flocks—
>
> And now, if thou wilt tell me concerning these things, whatsoever thou desirest I will give unto thee; and if it were needed, I would guard thee with my armies; but I know that thou art more powerful than all they; nevertheless, whatsoever thou desirest of me I will grant it unto thee.[27]

Ammon—whom the writer Mormon at this point describes as "wise, yet harmless"—replied, "Wilt thou hearken unto my words, if I tell thee by what power I do these things? And this is the thing that I desire of thee."

"Yea," responded Lamoni, "I will believe all thy words."

"Believest thou that there is a God?" Ammon asked.

The king responded that he didn't know what the word "God" meant.

Rephrasing the question, Ammon asked, "Believest thou that there is a Great Spirit?" The question was asked for the king's benefit, of course, since Ammon already knew his thoughts.

"Yea," said Lamoni.

"This is God," explained Ammon. "Believest thou that this Great Spirit, who is God, created all things which are in heaven and in the earth?"

"Yea, I believe that he created all things which are in the earth; but I do not know the heavens."

"The heavens," Ammon explained, "is a place where God dwells and all his holy angels."

"Is it above the earth?" Lamoni questioned.

"Yea," answered Ammon, "and he looketh down upon all the children of men; and he knows all the thoughts and intents of the heart; for by his hand were they all created from the beginning."

"I believe all these things which thou hast spoken," affirmed Lamoni. "Art thou sent from God?"

"I am a man; and man in the beginning was created after the image of God, and I am called by his Holy Spirit to teach these things unto this people, that they may be brought to a knowledge of that which is just and true; and a portion of that Spirit dwelleth in me, which giveth me knowledge, and also power according to my faith and desires which are in God."[28]

Ammon explained the Creation and Fall, and rehearsed scriptural history down through Father Lehi and the rebellions of Laman and Lemuel and the sons of Ishmael—corrective history to the traditions inherited by Lamoni that his forefathers had been deprived of their birthright by Nephi.

Continuing the story, Ammon then "expounded . . . the records and scriptures . . . down to the present time," and taught "the plan of redemption" and "the coming of Christ."[29] Those scriptures included the words of the angel to Ammon's grandfather, King Benjamin,[30] about the "Lord Omnipotent who reigneth" but who would voluntarily leave his divine throne and "come down from heaven" to serve mankind.[31] The words would have had special meaning to King Lamoni as he sat upon his own throne, and would have been rehearsed with special understanding by Ammon, who had relinquished his right to the throne in order to serve.

### Overwhelmed by Redeeming Love

So powerful was Ammon's testimony that the king not only "believed all his words" but began to petition the Heavenly King: "O Lord, have mercy; according to thy abundant mercy which thou hast had upon the people of Nephi, have upon me, and my people."[32] With this, Lamoni collapsed as if dead.

Ammon knew otherwise, and when asked two days later by the queen to take a look at her lifeless husband, Ammon assured her that the king would rise the next day. And so he did, immediately extending his hand to the queen and declaring, "Blessed be the name of God, and blessed art thou. For as sure as thou livest, behold, I have seen my Redeemer; and he shall come forth, and be born of a woman, and he shall redeem all mankind who believe on his name."[33]

Again King Lamoni collapsed, this time overcome with joy, "and the queen also sunk down, being overpowered by the Spirit."[34] Ammon fell to his knees in a prayer of thanksgiving, and was himself overcome with joy, falling to the ground. The king's servants looking on were overcome with the "fear of the Lord," so that they too began to pray, and also fell down lifeless.

Only one remained standing, a woman named Abish who had long been a secret convert due to a vision given to her father. She, hoping her people might believe, ran and gathered as many as she could. As the growing crowd gazed on the spectacle of lifeless figures, there was disagreement as to what all this meant. One of the onlookers, a brother of a robber killed by Ammon, raised his sword to kill Ammon—and immediately fell dead himself.

When the crowd still could not agree on what was happening, Abish tearfully took the hand of the lifeless queen, who immediately arose and said in a loud voice, "O blessed Jesus, who has saved me from an awful hell! O blessed God, have mercy on this people!"[35]

Joyfully clasping her hands together, she spoke other words that were not understood by those around her, and then grasped the hand of her lifeless husband.

He arose and immediately began to teach all who would listen, and they "were converted unto the Lord." Ammon also arose and administered to the people, and all the servants who had fallen now arose and testified that they had seen and conversed with angels.

Many believed and were baptized, the Church was established, and they became a righteous people upon whom the Lord poured out his Spirit.[36]

### The Joy of Service

Thus did Ammon, heir to the Nephite throne, relinquish his right in order to serve a Lamanite king and thereby serve the King of Heaven. It was but the beginning of a fourteen year mission that would reap a nearly incredible harvest of thousands of souls who became renowned for their resolute righteousness.

"If we had not come," Ammon would later tell his brothers, "these our dearly beloved brethren, who have so dearly beloved us, would still have been racked with hatred against us, yea, and they would also have been strangers to God."[37]

Therefore, "how great reason have we to rejoice; for could we have supposed when we started from [our land] . . . that God would have granted unto us such great blessings? . . . For our brethren, the Lamanites, were in darkness, . . . but behold, how many of them are brought to behold the marvelous light of God!"[38]

"Yea, they were encircled about with everlasting darkness and destruction," but now "they are encircled about with the matchless bounty of his love."[39] "Behold, thousands of them do rejoice,"[40] for the which "we will glory in the Lord; yea, we will . . . praise our God forever."[41]

"Now my brethren, we see that God is mindful of every people, whatsoever land they may be in; yea, he numbereth his people, and his bowels of mercy are over all the earth. Now this is my joy, and my great thanksgiving; yea, and I will give thanks unto my God forever. Amen."[42]

Today, some two millennia after Ammon's selfless service, the Heavenly King is offering to "every people, whatsoever land they may be in," His merciful redemption made when He left His heavenly throne to be "among [us] as he that serveth."[43] And representing Him to the nations are His latter-day missionaries—servants of Him[44] and, as He has said, servants also of mankind "for my sake"[45]—who, like Ammon, are willing to humbly say, "I will be thy servant."

## Legacy of Ammon

As a colleague in crime with the younger Alma, Ammon also saw the angel and underwent agony of soul, choosing to repent. Ammon was the heir apparent to the Nephite throne, and his conversion could not have been more timely. Now the Nephites would enjoy another righteous monarch. But Ammon stunned his father and friends by relinquishing his royal claim and serving the King of Heaven as a humble missionary. His faithful and courageous service to a Lamanite king opened miraculous doors that eventually brought thousands to know the joy of Jesus, a timeless pattern for modern missionaries.

# CHAPTER 8

# ~ *Nephi, Son of Helaman* ~
## *With Such Unwearyingness*

A mmon and his brothers would never have been converted, nor would they have converted their many thousands, without the work of Alma the elder, whose own conversion came through Abinadi. Abinadi's ministry proved to be the turning point in Nephite history, creating an unbroken line of righteous leaders for generations, including Alma's son Alma, his son Helaman, then his son Helaman, and his son Nephi. Each made a major contribution, but Nephi's ministry stands out as the mightiest in the Book of Mormon.

### *Critical Decision at a Critical Hour*

Nephi succeeded his father, Helaman, as chief judge and "did fill the judgment-seat with justice and equity; yea, he did keep the commandments of God, and did walk in the ways of his father."[1] In contrast, Nephi's people had grown proud and wicked because of their great prosperity. In their spiritually weakened condition, they were attacked by Lamanite armies who slaughtered many and drove nearly all the rest from their lands.

Only then did the Nephites begin to listen to Nephi and others who "did preach many things unto the people, yea, and did prophesy many things unto them concerning their iniquities, and what should come unto them if they did not repent of their sins."[2]

They did repent in a measure, and were able to win back half of their lost lands. But they remained generally a "stiffnecked people" who "had set at naught the commandments of God" and had "fallen into a state of unbelief and awful wickedness" to the point that "the judgments of God did stare them in the face." For "they who chose evil were more numerous than they who chose good, therefore they were ripening for destruction," and "except they should cleave unto the Lord their God they must unavoidably perish."[3]

At that critical point, having served the people as their chief judge for some nine years, Nephi made a momentous decision. Having grown "weary because of their iniquity," he determined to follow the lead of his great-grandfather Alma the younger in stepping down as chief judge "to preach the word of God all the remainder of his days." Joining him in the ministry was his equally committed and capable brother, Lehi.[4]

### These Are the Words

Mormon, the writer of the account, explains why they chose to be missionaries: "For they remembered the words which their father Helaman spake unto them." So important did Mormon consider those words that he reproduced them verbatim in a lengthy passage on the plates, with a delight that shines through in his introductory sentence: "And these are the words which he spake."[5]

> Behold, my sons, I desire that ye should remember to keep the commandments of God; and I would that ye should declare unto the people these words. Behold, I have given unto you the names of our first parents who came out of the land of Jerusalem; and this I have done that when you remember your names ye may remember them; and when ye remember them ye may remember their works; and when

ye remember their works ye may know how that it is said, and also written, that they were good.

Therefore, my sons, I would that ye should do that which is good, that it may be said of you, and also written, even as it has been said and written of them.[6]

Regarding the ancient Nephi who had come out of Jerusalem, we know some of his good works through his writing on the small plates, which now forms the first part of the Book of Mormon as we have it. But it is only through latter-day revelation that we learn of that first Nephi's valiant missionary work: "Open your mouths and they shall be filled," the Lord has told His Latter-day Saints, "and you shall become even as Nephi of old, who journeyed from Jerusalem in the wilderness."[7] No wonder Helaman's son Nephi would desire to preach the gospel when he remembered the works of his illustrious forefather.

As Helaman continued teaching his sons, he spoke of the glorious rewards of missionary work:

> And now my sons, behold I have somewhat more to desire of you, which desire is, that ye may not do these things that ye may boast, but that ye may do these things to lay up for yourselves a treasure in heaven, yea, which is eternal, and which fadeth not away; yea, that ye may have that precious gift of eternal life, which we have reason to suppose hath been given to our fathers.[8]

Helaman also reminded them of the Atonement of Christ, the central reality for their own personal lives and for the message they would bear as missionaries:

> O remember, remember, my sons, the words which king Benjamin spake unto his people; yea, remember that there is no other way nor means whereby man can be saved, only through the atoning blood of Jesus Christ, who shall come; yea, remember that he cometh to redeem the world.
>
> And remember also . . . that the Lord surely . . . [shall] not come to redeem them in their sins, but to redeem them from their sins.

> And he hath power given unto him from the Father to redeem them from their sins because of repentance; therefore he hath sent his angels to declare the tidings of the conditions of repentance, which bringeth unto the power of the Redeemer, unto the salvation of their souls.[9]

Then Helaman used a metaphor that had been employed anciently by such powerful missionaries as Enoch[10] and Isaiah[11]—the metaphor of the Messiah as the great and sure foundation stone:

> And now, my sons, remember, remember that it is upon the rock of our Redeemer, who is Christ, the Son of God, that ye must build your foundation; that when the devil shall send forth his mighty winds, yea, his shafts in the whirlwind, yea, when all his hail and his mighty storm shall beat upon you, it shall have no power over you to drag you down to the gulf of misery and endless wo, because of the rock upon which ye are built, which is a sure foundation, a foundation whereon if men build they cannot fall.[12]

### With Power and Authority

Nephi and Lehi *did* remember their father's words, "and therefore they went forth, keeping the commandments of God, to teach the word of God."[13] From city to city they went until they had taught throughout all the Nephite lands.

Not stopping there, they boldly proceeded into enemy-occupied territory to teach the Lamanites, and "did preach with great power," for "they had power and authority given unto them that they might speak, and they also had what they should speak given unto them—therefore they did speak unto the great astonishment of the Lamanites, to the convincing them."[14]

As a result, Nephite dissenters among the Lamanites "came forth and did confess their sins and were baptized unto repentance, and immediately returned to the Nephites to endeavor to repair unto them the wrongs which they had done."[15] Meanwhile, some eight thousand of the Lamanites themselves were "baptized unto repentance, and were convinced of the wickedness of the traditions of their fathers."[16]

## *The Prison Miracle*

But not all the Lamanites accepted the presence of these two bold Nephite intruders. Nephi and Lehi were apprehended by a Lamanite army and imprisoned without food for "many days," pending their execution. On the appointed day, when the three hundred or so captors came again to the prison, they "were struck dumb with amazement" to see Nephi and Lehi "encircled about as if by fire" without being burned.[17]

The Lamanites dared not lay hands on these prisoners, whose "hearts did take courage" as they stood up to speak—not words of revenge or retaliation but of consolation and comfort: "Fear not, for behold, it is God that has shown unto you this marvelous thing, in the which is shown unto you that ye cannot lay your hands on us to slay us."[18]

An earthquake suddenly shook the prison as if it would collapse, while the captors now became captive to a dense vapor of darkness that brought upon them an "awful solemn fear." They then heard a voice "of perfect mildness, as if it had been a whisper, and it did pierce even to the very soul," causing the earth to shake mightily. "Repent ye, repent ye," commanded the voice, "and seek no more to destroy my servants whom I have sent unto you to declare good tidings."

Moments later the message was repeated, again shaking the earth and adding a warning that "the kingdom of heaven is at hand."

When the voice came a third time, it shook the earth yet again but also spoke "marvelous words which cannot be uttered by man."[19]

One of the captors was a man named Aminadab, a Nephite dissenter and apostate from the Church. He happened to turn around and see through the darkness the shining faces of Nephi and Lehi, who were gazing upwards and apparently speaking with someone. Aminadab called to his comrades, who upon turning and seeing the same sight, questioned him as to what these things meant and how they could escape the cloud of darkness.

"You must repent," he responded, "and cry unto the voice, even until ye shall have faith in Christ."[20]

They did so, and when the darkness dispersed they discovered that they also were surrounded by fire—an outward sign of what was happening in their souls as they were "filled with that joy which is unspeakable and full of glory," and filled also with the Holy Spirit "as if with fire, and they could speak forth marvelous words."

Then came a pleasant voice, as if a whisper, saying, "Peace, peace be unto you, because of your faith in my Well Beloved, who was from the foundation of the world."

Looking up to see from where the voice came, they saw the heavens open and angels descend and minister to them. Finally, they were instructed to "go forth and marvel not, neither should they doubt."[21]

### Lamanite Righteousness, Nephite Wickedness

The miracle inside the prison reverberated far beyond its walls, as the captors-turned-converts went forth "declaring throughout all the regions round about all the things which they had heard and seen."[22] Over half of the Lamanite population was converted and gave up their weapons of war, their false ancestral traditions, and their hatred of the Nephites, and even surrendered back all territories won in the war.

For the first time in history the two peoples became friendly, opening trade relations and unrestricted travel between the two countries. Two humble missionaries had accomplished more by faith and love than the entire Nephite armies through the centuries had achieved by military force.

And still the influence of the prison miracle crescendoed, as many Lamanites now came to the Nephites preaching "with exceedingly great power and authority, unto the bringing down many of them into the depths of humility, to be the humble followers of God and the Lamb."[23]

Even though their converts were making converts, Nephi and Lehi could not rest, embarking northward on a six-year mission. Their extensive labors are summed up by the short report that they preached and prophesied many things, but were rejected and finally forced to leave.[24]

Returning home they were amazed to find that despite the intense missionary efforts of themselves and of their converts, yet their own people, the Nephites, had become corrupt. For "the Lord had blessed them so long with the riches of the world," comments the historian Mormon, "that they had not been stirred up to anger, to wars, nor to bloodshed," with the tragic result that "they began to set their hearts upon their riches; yea, they began to seek to get gain that they might be lifted up one above another; therefore they began to commit secret murders, and to rob and to plunder, that they might get gain,"[25] and to "commit whoredoms and all manner of wickedness."[26]

In short, the people had not sought that treasure in heaven of which Nephi's and Lehi's father had spoken, but rather the treasures of this earth to "get gain and glory of the world."[27] Money had become the measure of all things, and even the government had grown corrupt, having fallen within the grasp of a powerful, money-crazed secret combination, a criminal cartel led by a man named Gadianton.

### The Prayer on the Tower

A saddened Nephi went home and knelt to pray on his tower, located in his garden next to the thoroughfare leading to the largest market in the city of Zarahemla. His "heart was swollen with sorrow," and "in the agony of his soul" he voiced his frustration at having to live in a day of such wickedness. His prayer happened to be heard by passers-by, and a crowd soon gathered.[28] Rising from his knees, Nephi spoke.

> Behold, why have ye gathered yourselves together? That I may tell you of your iniquities?

Yea, because I have got upon my tower that I might pour out my soul unto my God, because of the exceeding sorrow of my heart, which is because of your iniquities!

And because of my mourning and lamentation ye have gathered yourselves together, and do marvel; yea, and ye have great need to marvel; yea, ye ought to marvel because . . . the devil has got so great hold upon your hearts.

Yea, how could you have given way to the enticing of him who is seeking to hurl away your souls down to everlasting misery and endless wo?

O repent ye, repent ye! Why will ye die? Turn ye, turn ye unto the Lord your God.[29]

Nephi proceeded to decry their iniquities, their excessive ambition "to get gain" and "be praised of men," leading them to all sorts of iniquities. Their pride was their undoing, he declared, and unless they repented they would violently perish from the earth.[30]

In the crowd were several judges who were members of the secret combination. Furious at Nephi's words, they called for his arrest. Others opposed them, acknowledging that Nephi was a good man and had spoken the truth.

Seeing this dissension, Nephi was constrained to speak further. He testified of Christ, He of whom all the prophets had testified and "looked forward, and . . . rejoiced in his day which is to come."[31]

### Foretelling the Future and Uncovering Corruption

As a further witness of Christ, Nephi's listeners had "all things," both "in heaven, and . . . in the earth,"[32] plus something else which Nephi would now provide: a sign. He told them that even as he spoke, their chief judge was lying in his own blood, murdered by his brother, both of whom belonged to the secret combination "whose author is Gadianton and the evil one who seeketh to destroy the souls of men."[33]

Only five members of the crowd were open-minded enough to actually check out Nephi's prediction. They ran to the judgment seat, skeptical but willing to accept his entire message if this part turned out to be true. Finding the chief judge dead and lying in his own blood, they collapsed in astonishment, fearing that the awful judgments predicted by Nephi would surely come to pass. When these five were later discovered lying near the fallen chief judge, they were arrested and imprisoned for his murder.[34]

The next day at the funeral, the wicked judges who had opposed Nephi inquired about the five who had run to the chief judge. No one seemed to know concerning such men, but there were five, it was reported, who were the murderers and were in prison. The judges demanded that the five be brought, who then told their story.

There, exclaimed the judges, this proves that Nephi was complicit in the murder. The five were set free, and despite their protestations of Nephi's innocence, the judges had Nephi arrested and brought to them.

"Thou art confederate," they accused Nephi, but then offered him a plea bargain: money and his life if he would disclose the actual murderer and acknowledge Nephi's complicity in the crime.[35]

"O ye fools," Nephi thundered, "ye uncircumcised of heart, ye blind, and ye stiffnecked people, do ye know how long the Lord your God will suffer you that ye shall go in this your way of sin? O ye ought to begin to howl and mourn, because of the great destruction which at this time doth await you, except ye shall repent."

To induce them to do so, he now offered another sign. They were to go to the house of Seantum, brother of the deceased chief judge, and ask him if Nephi had agreed with him in the murder of his brother. Seantum would answer no.

They were then to ask if Seantum had murdered his brother. He would act astonished and deny it.

They were to examine his clothing, and would find blood, and were then to say, "Do we not know that it is the blood of your brother?"

Seantum would turn pale, whereupon they were to attest they now knew that he was guilty. He would then confess, and would declare that Nephi could know nothing of the matter except by the power of God.

"And then," said Nephi, "shall ye know that I am an honest man, and that I am sent unto you from God."[36]

Everything happened precisely as Nephi had foretold, and he was vindicated. So also were the five who had been wrongly imprisoned—an experience that turned out for the good, for they had been converted while in prison.

Others also believed in what Nephi had said, but a sharp disagreement arose as to who or what this man was: some said a prophet, others a god. The crowd finally dispersed, leaving Nephi free to return home.[37]

### Unwearying Service, Powerful Example

Nephi went his way, "pondering upon the things which the Lord had shown unto him," and feeling "much cast down because of the wickedness of the people." Many and deep were his thoughts; three times the account mentions that he was pondering.[38] In this reflective state, he heard a voice speaking to him.

> Blessed art thou, Nephi, for those things which thou hast done; for I have beheld how thou hast with unwearyingness declared the word, which I have given unto thee, unto this people. And thou hast not feared them, and hast not sought thine own life, but hast sought my will, and to keep my commandments.
>
> And now, because thou hast done this with such unwearyingness, behold, I will bless thee forever.[39]

The Lord further told him that he would be made "mighty in word and in deed, in faith and in works; yea, even that all things shall be done unto thee according to thy word, for thou shalt not ask that which is contrary to my will."

"Behold, thou art Nephi, and I am God. Behold, I declare it unto thee in the presence of mine angels, that ye shall have power over this people" —power, at Nephi's word alone, to bring famine, pestilence, destruction, or the leveling of a mountain, and even power to seal and loose on earth and in heaven.[40]

The Lord's final words to Nephi that day were a commandment: "And now behold, I command you, that ye shall go and declare unto this people, that thus saith the Lord God, who is the Almighty: Except ye repent ye shall be smitten, even unto destruction."[41]

This commandment came as Nephi was well on his way home at the end of a long and exhausting day that had included the funeral of the murdered chief judge, Nephi's arrest and accusation by the judges, his prophecy and its fulfillment when messengers were sent to the guilty Seantum, Nephi's release and the crowd's dispute, and now this revelation in which he had been complimented for his unwearying work, been guaranteed the precious gift of eternal life, and been granted nearly unlimited power in his continuing ministry. Surely the command to tell the people to repent or be destroyed could wait till tomorrow, especially since Nephi had already delivered this same message earlier that day! Certainly this valiant and exhausted servant could finish his walk home to a much-needed and well-deserved rest that evening, and then continue on the morrow.

But the unwearying Nephi turned around. He "did not go unto his own house, but did return unto the multitudes who were scattered about upon the face of the land, and began to declare unto them the word of the Lord which had been spoken unto him, concerning their destruction if they did not repent."[42]

Notwithstanding the miracle he had performed that very day, his listeners hardened their hearts and sought to "lay their hands upon him that they might cast him into prison." Protected by divine power, Nephi was literally conveyed away by the Spirit to preach to another multitude, and from them to yet another, and so on[43]—a vivid illustration that divine intervention comes only after one unwearyingly does everything in one's power. His labors continued day after day, nor did Nephi stop until he had preached or sent word to all the people.

Still this hardened people refused to repent, and again lapsed into war. Nephi prayed that instead of war there might be a famine to humble them into remembering their God. Only when the famine became severe did they finally repent and ask Nephi to ask God to end the famine. Nephi's prayer brought rain, and the people rejoiced, esteeming Nephi a great prophet.

Within a decade, when the people had again forgotten their God and grown arrogant and wicked, God sent other prophets like Samuel the Lamanite. He testified of the Savior and foretold the marvelous signs to transpire among the Nephites at His birth, which was, he said, but five years away. Samuel further foretold the awful destruction that would later be visited upon the Nephites at the Savior's crucifixion.[44]

Finally, after decades of unwearying labor for his Redeemer, Nephi mysteriously "departed out of the land, and whither he went, no man knoweth."[45] Soon thereafter the Redeemer was born. Before Nephi left, he had turned over the scriptural records and sacred artifacts to his son Nephi, who continued the ministry of his father with remarkable results— preaching with convincing power, raising the dead, casting out devils, and conversing with angels. Eventually the prophesied events associated with the Redeemer's death came to pass, including the terrible tempest and destruction followed by darkness, and later the glorious personal appearance of the resurrected Redeemer, who chose this Nephi as His chief disciple. That terrible destruction and glorious appearance of Christ, according to President Ezra Taft Benson,[46] prefigured what will transpire at the Savior's second coming.

To prepare the world for that great event, God has again called messengers, who can learn much from the unwearying labors of Helaman's son Nephi. "Be not weary in well-doing,"[47] the Lord commands his latter-day missionaries, and "labor while it is called today"[48] to serve God "with all your heart, might, mind and strength."[49] In doing so, they follow the example not only of Nephi but of Him of whom Nephi testified: the Redeemer Himself, who for His tireless and selfless mortal ministry has rightly been called "the unwearying Christ."[50]

## Legacy of Nephi, Son of Helaman

Helaman's son Nephi was named for his ancient ancestor and urged by his father to lay up treasures in heaven by building his life on the rock of the Redeemer. Nephi followed the counsel, and after years of serving as the nation's chief judge, stepped down to accomplish far greater good by preaching the gospel. His tireless efforts converted thousands of Lamanites, but his own people were more hardened. Because of his unwearyingness, the Lord gave him mighty power in his ministry, which is an example to latter-day missionaries who are likewise commanded to be not weary in well doing.

CHAPTER 9

# ~ John the Baptist ~
## Prepare Ye the Way of the Lord

When Helaman's son Nephi walked out of human history, he knew that the Savior would soon be born. He knew also that the Savior's foreordained forerunner had just been born or shortly would be, for Nephi's ancient forefather Nephi and his father Lehi had spoken "much . . . concerning this thing," prophesying of "a prophet who should come before the Messiah, to prepare the way of the Lord" and to baptize many, including the Messiah Himself.[1] That prophet's name was John, who for his great work is remembered as John the Baptist.

### Temple Service by a Faithful Jewish Couple

The ancient Nephite prophecies foretelling the ministry of John must have been of intense personal interest to Helaman's sons, Nephi and Lehi, as they followed his counsel to remember their ancestors for whom they were named.[2] Helaman's sons may also have perceived in the prophecy of John's mission a description of their own, since the work given them by their father was intended to prepare the way for "Jesus Christ, who shall come" and provide salvation on "conditions of repentance." Remembering Helaman's words, Nephi and Lehi had gone forth to prepare the way for the Lord, who after His resurrection would appear to Nephi's son Nephi at the temple.

Meanwhile, the magnificent temple after which the Nephite version was patterned stood half a world away in Jerusalem. Originally built by King Solomon, the Jerusalem temple was destroyed shortly after Lehi left Jerusalem, rebuilt decades later, and lavishly expanded by Herod in the first century B.C. Its impressive animal sacrifices and elaborate rituals, all of which symbolized the coming Atonement of Christ,[3] were understood by the Jews to bless not only Israel but the entire world.[4]

Performing that all-important temple service was the exclusive privilege of the descendants of Aaron, whose priests serving in the temple each year numbered probably about 18,000.[5] Among them was a man named Zacharias, meaning "Jehovah has remembered."[6] His wife was Elizabeth, a name indicating trust in God.[7] Scripture describes them as "both righteous before God, walking in all the commandments and ordinances of the Lord blameless,"[8] reminiscent of the righteous and blameless patriarch Noah.

Since both Zacharias and Elizabeth were descendants of Aaron, if they had had a son—as they had long desired—he also would be eligible to serve in the temple.[9] But Zacharias and Elizabeth were childless.

## Miracle at the Incense Offering

Twice a year did Zacharias perform his temple duties, one week at a time. On one of these occasions the lot fell to him to officiate in the incense offering. It was made twice daily in the "holy place," the Temple's second-most sacred room containing the table of showbread, the golden candelabrum, and the golden altar of incense.

Making the incense offering was a high and holy honor that few priests ever received, and never more than once in a lifetime. "This day when he offered incense was of great personal significance for Zacharias,"[10] who on this occasion was "performing the greatest ministry of his priestly career."[11] If the blessing of a son had passed him by, yet the Lord had after all remembered Zacharias by granting him this special privilege.

Entering the holy place, Zacharias sprinkled incense over a vessel of live coals,[12] creating a sweet-smelling cloud symbolizing divine glory.[13] Suddenly the symbol became reality, turning into what Joseph Smith described as "flaming fire and glory"[14] in which appeared an angel of God.

The angel told Zacharias not to fear, and that in answer to his prayer, Elizabeth would bear a son to be called John, a name meaning "Jehovah has shown favor."[15] Zacharias would have "joy and gladness," the angel said, and John would be "great in the sight of the Lord" and be "filled with the Holy Ghost, even from his mother's womb." He would "go before" the Lord in order to "make ready a people prepared for the Lord."[16]

How could Zacharias be sure of this, he asked, since he and his wife were so old?

The angel answered that because Zacharias had not believed the message, he would not be able to speak until John was born. The angel also identified himself: "I am Gabriel, that stand in the presence of God."[17] Gabriel, according to Joseph Smith, was the patriarch Noah.[18] He who once had righteously and blamelessly preached of Christ to a world on the verge of destruction was now sent to announce the birth of Christ's forerunner, John the Baptist, to a righteous and blameless couple.

## Priesthood and Peril for the Infant John

Six months later Gabriel appeared to Elizabeth's relative[19] named Mary, an exquisitely beautiful[20] young woman who lived in Nazareth. Mary was "engaged,"[21] to use our English word that comes closest to describing the first of a two-part Jewish marriage process. First was the formal exchange of promises in the presence of witnesses, along with the payment of the "bride price," whereupon the woman legally belonged to the man and was referred to as his wife, even though she continued to live with her own family. In the second part, usually about a year later, came the actual marriage celebration when the man took his wife home and they began to live together.

Mary was still in the first part of the process when Gabriel appeared to her and announced the event foretold by all the prophets from the beginning: she would give birth to a son, the very Son of God. Gabriel further informed her that even her relative Elizabeth "hath also conceived a son in her old age: and this is the sixth month with her, who was called barren."[22]

"Behold the handmaid of the Lord," Mary replied. "Be it unto me according to thy word."[23]

Shortly thereafter, Mary traveled to visit Elizabeth in the Judean hill country. As soon as Elizabeth heard Mary's voice, she felt the infant within her own womb leap for joy, and marveled at the blessing of being visited by "the mother of my Lord."

Mary responded in the now-famous words: "My soul doth magnify the Lord, and my spirit hath rejoiced in God my Saviour."[24]

Mary remained with Elizabeth for several months to help out with the birth of John.

On the eighth day after John's birth, at his circumcision, Zacharias' mouth was opened as the Spirit gave him utterance. He praised God and pronounced a prophetic blessing upon his infant son: "And thou, child, shalt be called the prophet of the Highest, for thou shalt go before the face of the Lord to prepare his ways, to give knowledge of salvation unto his people, by baptism for the remission of their sins."[25]

On that same day, as told in latter-day revelation, an angel appeared and ordained the infant for a special mission "to overthrow the kingdom of the Jews, and to make straight the way of the Lord before the face of his people, to prepare them for the coming of the Lord."[26]

But the same powers of darkness that would target the infant Christ would also seek the infant John. When Herod (son of the Herod who had remodeled the temple) issued his evil decree to kill the infants in order to destroy the baby Jesus, the baby John also "came under this same edict," noted Joseph Smith.[27] Early Christian sources affirm that Herod specifically sought John to slay him,[28] and that when Zacharias learned this, he took John to the Temple altar and "laid his hand upon him, and bestowed on him the priesthood," and then sent him to safety.[29]

As the Prophet Joseph Smith explained, Zacharias had Elizabeth take their son "into the mountains, where he was raised on locusts and wild honey."[30] When Herod demanded that Zacharias disclose the whereabouts of his son, he refused and "was slain by Herod's order, between the porch and the altar" of the Temple.[31]

## Preparing to Prepare the Way

John would grow up in the Judean wilderness and remain there until called to his ministry. One short scriptural verse summarizes those preparatory years: "And the child grew, and waxed strong in spirit, and was in the deserts until the day of his showing unto Israel."[32] Left fatherless as an infant, John was taught by his faithful mother until her passing left him an orphan while still a child. He was adopted into and raised by a desert community.[33]

But the most important part of John's education was the *divine* instruction he received. Latter-day revelation describes him as one "whom God raised up, being filled with the Holy Ghost from his mother's womb."[34] And since he possessed the keys of the Aaronic Priesthood which—as he himself would explain when he restored them to Joseph Smith—hold "the keys of the ministering of angels,"[35] it seems likely that young John himself would have been tutored by angels to help prepare him for his important mission.[36]

Meanwhile, Jesus was preparing for His mission, and only when "the hour of his ministry drew nigh"[37] did God call John to begin his own preparatory ministry. Preaching in the Judean wilderness near the Jordan River, he attracted immediate attention, due partly to his rough appearance. It "reminded many of the prophet Elijah," for John "wore a garment made of camels' hair and a leather belt, and he ate the food of the poor—locusts and wild honey."[38]

But it was the Spirit that most set John apart and drew crowds, for the Jews of that day recognized that the spirit of prophecy had long since "departed from Israel."[39] Once again, as in times of old, a prophet walked among them. And not just any prophet, but the long-awaited herald of the Messiah. It was in this capacity that John declared repentance:

> Repent ye; for the kingdom of heaven is at hand.
>
> For I am he who was spoken of by the prophet Esaias [Isaiah], saying, The voice of one crying in the wilderness, Prepare ye the way of the Lord and make his paths straight.[40]

The Isaiah prophecy about one who would announce the coming of the Lord, preparing His way and making His path straight, refers to the custom throughout that region of constructing special roads free of obstacles for a visiting king or dignitary, and announcing his visit by heralds sounding trumpets. Likewise the road for Christ, as foretold by Isaiah, "is to be straight, level and free of obstacle, *i.e.*, he will arrive without fail, travel without difficulty and be undelayed by hindrances,"[41] thanks to the work of John.

### Preaching Repentance and Baptizing the Son of God

John's "trumpet-voiced proclamation . . . thrilled the nation to its heart and drew forth the multitude into the wilderness to hear him—men from Jerusalem and men from Galilee, civilians and soldiers, Pharisees and publicans side by side."[42] If the nation was thrilled to the heart, it was also being called upon for a change of heart—"to prepare the way of the Lord . . . by means of repentance."[43]

Convinced of their need to repent, many of John's listeners inquired, "What shall we do?"

"He that hath two coats," John answered, "let him impart to him that hath none; and he that hath meat [or 'food'[44]] let him do likewise."

The repentant tax collectors, notorious for their overcharging, likewise asked, "Master, what shall we do?"

"Exact no more than that which is appointed [or 'authorized'[45]] you," said John.

Even the soldiers sought guidance: "And what shall we do?"

"Do violence to no man, neither accuse any falsely; and be content with your wages."[46]

In short, John was, as his ancient patriarchal forefathers of old, a preacher of righteousness, calling for "the baptism of repentance for the remission of sins"[47] through faith in Christ.

The message was widely received. In the New Testament report of the people's reaction to John, the Joseph Smith Translation adds an important word: "And *many* were baptized of him in Jordan, confessing their sins."[48]

John's converts had followed the same path as that followed by all converts through the ages, but would receive the unique privilege of receiving the Holy Ghost from Christ Himself, as John promised them:

> I indeed baptize you with water, upon your repentance; and when he of whom I bear record cometh, who is mightier than I, whose shoes I am not worthy to bear, (or whose place I am not able to fill,) as I said, I indeed baptize you before he cometh, that when he cometh he may baptize you with the Holy Ghost and fire.[49]

When that momentous day arrived and the Savior of the world came forward, John's witness was brief but powerful: "Behold the Lamb of God."[50]

Then, in fulfillment of the prophecies recorded in the Nephite scriptures, Jesus asked John to baptize him.

John humbly responded, "I have need to be baptized of thee, and comest thou to me?"[51]

"Suffer it to [or 'let it'[52]] be so now," said the Savior, "for thus it becometh us to fulfil all righteousness."[53]

The Gospels describe the sacred event,[54] which is similarly described in latter-day revelation by John the Baptist:

> And I, John, bear record, and lo, the heavens were opened, and the Holy Ghost descended upon him in the form of a dove, and sat upon him, and there came a voice out of heaven saying: This is my beloved Son.
>
> And I, John, bear record that he received a fulness of the glory of the Father;
>
> And he received all power, both in heaven and on earth, and the glory of the Father was with him, for he dwelt in him.[55]

## No Greater Prophet

As John bore witness of Jesus, so Jesus bore witness of John as "a burning and a shining light,"[56] the one foreordained as the forerunner:

> This is he, of whom it is written, Behold, I send my messenger before thy face, which shall prepare thy way before thee.
>
> For I say unto you, Among those that are born of women there is not a greater prophet than John the Baptist.[57]

John's greatness came not by moving mountains, or parting the sea, or healing the lame; the Gospels report that he "did no miracle."[58] But if, as President Harold B. Lee observed, the greatest miracles are the healing of sick souls,[59] then John's ministry was full of miracles. Many of John's converts became Christ's disciples and apostles.[60] So effective was John's ministry that Herod imprisoned him out of fear that he would start a political revolution.[61]

Within the walls of Herod's fortress prison near the Dead Sea, John was visited by a group of his own disciples who came to consult with him and report on the multitudes that flocked to Jesus.

John responded that "Ye yourselves bear me witness, that I said, I am not the Christ, but that I am sent before him," and emphasized that he was not the bridegroom but merely His friend who "rejoiceth greatly because of the bridegroom's voice: this my joy therefore is fulfilled. He must increase, but I must decrease."[62]

John then again bore witness of the Savior, to whom "God giveth . . . not the Spirit by measure," for "the Father loveth the Son, and hath given all things into his hands. And he who believeth on the Son hath everlasting life; and shall receive of his fulness."[63]

It was John's last recorded testimony of Him whose way he had prepared. Soon thereafter, John was beheaded by command of Herod.

### John and the Latter-Day Preparation for the Savior

But no wicked ruler could frustrate the divine plan. John's preparation was not merely for the Savior's first coming but also for His second, as emphasized in the Joseph Smith Translation of Luke's introduction to John the Baptist (additions are in italics):

> And he came into all the country about Jordan, preaching the baptism of repentance for the remission of sins.
>
> As it is written in the book of the prophet Esaias [Isaiah]; and these are the words, saying, The voice of one crying in the wilderness, Prepare ye the way of the Lord, and make his paths straight.
>
> *For behold, and lo, he shall come, as it is written in the book of the prophets, to take away the sins of the world, and to bring salvation unto the heathen nations, to gather together those who are lost, who are of the sheepfold of Israel;*

*Yea, even the dispersed and afflicted; and also to prepare the way, and make possible the preaching of the gospel unto the Gentiles;*

*And to be a light unto all who sit in darkness, unto the uttermost parts of the earth; to bring to pass the resurrection from the dead, and to ascend up on high, to dwell on the right hand of the Father,*

*Until the fulness of time, and the law and the testimony shall be sealed, and the keys of the kingdom shall be delivered up again unto the Father;*

*To administer justice unto all; to come down in judgment upon all, and to convince all the ungodly of their ungodly deeds, which they have committed; and all this in the day that he shall come;*

*For it is a day of power; yea,* every valley shall be filled, and every mountain and hill shall be brought low; the crooked shall be made straight, and the rough ways made smooth;

And all flesh shall see the salvation of God.[64]

Nearly eighteen centuries later, as a glorious resurrected being, John the Baptist returned to earth and restored the Aaronic priesthood and keys to prepare the way for the Lord's second coming, and directed the baptism of the first two converts of this dispensation, Joseph Smith and Oliver Cowdery.[65]

They in turn, and all others who have since entered the latter-day Kingdom, have been instructed that they too must prepare the way for the Lord and herald His coming:

You are called of me to preach my gospel—

To lift up your voice as with the sound of a trump, both long and loud, and cry repentance unto a crooked and perverse generation, preparing the way of the Lord for his second coming.[66]

Go forth baptizing with water, preparing the way before my face for the time of my coming.[67]

Open your mouths and they shall be filled, saying: Repent, repent, and prepare ye the way of the Lord, and make his paths straight; for the kingdom of heaven is at hand;

Yea, repent and be baptized, every one of you, for a remission of your sins; yea, be baptized even by water, and then cometh the baptism of fire and of the Holy Ghost.[68]

Those who accept this divine mandate to prepare the way of the Lord will ultimately find that the Lord has prepared the way for them, even as He promised: "they shall receive a crown in the mansions of my Father, which I have prepared for them."[69]

## Legacy of John the Baptist

To "prepare the way of the Lord" was the high mission entrusted to John the Baptist, a close relative of Jesus and born just six months earlier. John's own years of preparation were spent mostly in an outlying desert community, from where at the appointed time he stepped forth and boldly declared repentance and the coming of Christ. Multitudes accepted and were baptized, and were ready to receive the Savior when a short time later He appeared and was Himself baptized at the hands of John, who was later beheaded by a wicked king. But John's mission was not over. As a glorious resurrected being, he has returned in our day to restore authority so that we may help prepare the way for the Lord at His second coming.

# CHAPTER 10

# ~ Paul the Apostle ~
## I Have Finished My Course

Within a decade after the birth of John the Baptist to Zacharias and Elizabeth, a son was born to another devout Israelite couple. The Hebrew name they gave him—Saul, meaning "asked for"—may indicate that they also had long prayed for a son. The name certainly reflects the family's cherished Hebrew lineage of the tribe of Benjamin, "that martial tribe which, little as it was, had borne itself so gallantly on the battlefields of old."[1] The most famous member of that tribe in all its long history had been Israel's first king, Saul, but his fame was about to be eclipsed by this infant who would be remembered not as Saul the Hebrew but as Paul the Apostle.

### Young Paul

The tribe of Benjamin was further distinguished by the fact that the magnificent Jerusalem temple stood on land originally allocated to this tribe.[2] But Paul's family lived far away in the Jewish Diaspora, or dispersion, referring to the scattered Jewish settlements beyond the borders of Judea. Paul was born in Tarsus, an ancient city located some 350 miles north of Jerusalem at the junction of important trade routes. Capital of the Roman province of Cilicia, Tarsus was a prosperous city widely renowned as a center of culture and learning, providing valuable preparation for this young man who would interact with people throughout the vast Roman Empire.[3]

His travels would be facilitated by his Roman citizenship which he acquired at birth, when he received not only his Hebrew name, Saul, but also his Roman name, Paul, meaning "little one."[4]

But it was Jerusalem, not Rome, that stirred the heart of the young man, for first and foremost he was "a Hebrew of the Hebrews"[5] who, like so many of his fellow Israelites in the Diaspora, prayed facing Jerusalem, went on pilgrimage to Jerusalem, and ever loved her as the holy city of their forefathers and the site of Judaism's most sacred structure, the Temple. "There is no beauty like the beauty of Jerusalem," insisted the rabbis,[6] who kept alive the Psalmist's ideal that "If I forget you, O Jerusalem, let my right hand wither."[7]

To Jerusalem the youthful Paul went, to study under the greatest Jewish rabbi of the day, Gamaliel. Grandson of Hillel, who was considered the wisest sage of the entire Second Temple period,[8] Gamaliel was the president of the Sanhedrin, the ruling Jewish body, and was the supreme authority on the vast body of oral and written Jewish law. He also possessed a "statesmanlike patience and tolerance"[9] after the pattern of Hillel, who had counseled, "What is hateful to yourself do not to another; that is the whole law, all the rest is commentary."[10]

Completing his studies in Jerusalem, Paul returned home to Tarsus, probably as a rabbi, and certainly as an "exceedingly zealous" adherent of Judaism and the traditions of his forefathers.[11] Physically, according to an early Christian source, he was "small of stature" with a balding head and a hooked nose.[12] This overlaps with the more detailed description supplied by Joseph Smith, that Paul was "about five feet high; very dark hair; dark complexion; dark skin; large Roman nose; sharp face; small black eyes, penetrating as eternity; round shoulders; a whining voice, except when elevated, and then it almost resembled the roaring of a lion."[13]

### The Ravenous Wolf of Benjamin

But it was the image of another wild beast that Paul evoked for the first Christians, in apparent fulfillment of the ancient prophecy that Benjamin would be like a ravenous wolf.[14] During Paul's years back in Tarsus, "momentous events had been transpiring in the Holy Land,"[15] events related to the rapidly growing Christian movement that seemed to pose a grave threat to "the law and the customs, the ancestral traditions, and everything that was of value to Judaism."[16]

With the crucifixion of Jesus, the rulers thought the entire movement was dead. They were shocked when just a month later in Jerusalem on the Day of Pentecost, three thousand joined the movement, which soon numbered upwards of five thousand. To the Jewish leaders, the situation seemed like a dangerous wildfire that needed quenching.

It was at this critical time that Paul visited Jerusalem and heard the preaching of a Christian leader named Stephen, "a man full of faith and of the Holy Ghost"[17] and possessed of such power that he "did great wonders and miracles among the people."[18] Stephen spoke with a "wisdom and ... spirit" that could not be withstood,[19] but some of his listeners were angry that he had repeated Jesus' prediction of the downfall of the Temple.

Bringing Stephen before the Sanhedrin, they charged him with the crime of blasphemy against the Temple, punishable by death. As he responded and bore witness of Christ, Stephen's face shone as if "it had been the face of an angel."[20]

Even so, his message so infuriated his listeners that they gnashed their teeth at him.[21] Just at that moment his own view was distracted from "that circle of angry faces and the encircling walls and roof"[22] to a scene visible only to him.

"Behold," he exclaimed, "I see the heavens opened, and the Son of man standing on the right hand of God"[23]—standing, emphasizes one writer, "as though He had started from His Throne to greet" Stephen, who was about to die a martyr's death and thereby gain "that crown of which his name Stephen, 'the Crown,' had been an unwritten prophecy."[24]

As the Sanhedrin proceeded to stone Stephen, Paul watched in support and held the coats of the executioners.[25] It was but the beginning of a severe persecution in which Paul zealously[26] hunted down the Christians in Jerusalem, invading their homes and beating and imprisoning all who refused to deny Christ.[27] The lion was roaring; the ravenous wolf of Benjamin was attacking the sheep. Many Christians fled to the countryside while the apostles stood their ground in Jerusalem.

Not content with purging Benjaminite soil of what he considered to be a threat to "all that made life worth living,"[28] Paul determined to eradicate the movement as far as it had spread. Still "breathing out threatenings and slaughter against the disciples of the Lord,"[29] Paul obtained authority to arrest and bring back for imprisonment and trial all the Christians he could find in the city of Damascus.[30]

### On the Road to Damascus

En route to apprehend the disciples of Christ, Paul was, as he would later say, "apprehended by Christ Jesus."[31] Approaching beautiful Damascus at about midday, Paul and his companions were suddenly confronted by a dazzling light "above the brightness of the sun" which shone around them.[32] Its sudden brilliance overwhelmed them, toppling them all to the ground.

But it was Paul alone who saw in the light a glorious personage[33] and heard His voice,[34] which addressed Paul in his native Hebrew language[35] and by his Hebrew name, repeating it with urgency: "Saul, Saul, why persecutest thou me? it is hard for thee to kick against the pricks [or 'goads']."[36]

That Paul was kicking against the goads, or cattle prods, strangely implied that he was resisting being led where his master was trying to guide him.[37] Stranger still was the question, "Why are you persecuting me?" Such words might be expected from a helpless victim, but they were being asked by this all-powerful personage of blinding splendor. Notwithstanding the question, the stark reality was that suddenly the tables were turned. Paul the prosecutor had become Saul the defendant, arraigned before a supreme authority who somehow knew all about him but was unknown to him.

"Who art thou, Lord?" asked Paul.

"I am Jesus whom thou persecutest," came the reply.[38]

For Paul, the rabid persecutor of the followers of Jesus, this was the most stunning revelation imaginable.

To Paul's everlasting credit, he had the humility to ask the key question that remains a model for all mortals, and particularly for missionaries: "What shall I do, Lord?"[39]

The answer provided yet another surprise.

> Rise, and stand upon thy feet: for I have appeared unto thee for this purpose, to make thee a minister and a witness both of these things which thou hast seen, and of those things in the which I will appear unto thee;
> Delivering thee from the people, and from the Gentiles, unto whom now I send thee,
> To open their eyes, and to turn them from darkness to light, and from the power of Satan unto God, that they may receive forgiveness of sins, and inheritance among them which are sanctified by faith that is in me.[40]

The Lord's command that Paul stand up seemed to underscore the urgency of the mission on which the Lord was sending him. Paul would continue his travels, although with an entirely different agenda. He had sought to destroy the Church; now he would build it. He had sought to protect Judaism; now he would proclaim its culmination in Christ as the fulfillment of the Abrahamic covenant. In fact, the very words with which the Lord now commissioned Paul—"to make thee a minister"—were the same words with which Christ had once commissioned Father Abraham in a face-to-face conversation.[41]

In Paul's case, however, to prepare him to go and "open the eyes" of others, he himself was now left physically blind after seeing Jesus. God "blinded the eyes of his body," observed a seventeenth century writer, "to open and enlighten those of his mind, that he might no longer look upon the vain and transitory things, that he might now see nothing but Jesus."[42]

In his blinded condition, Paul began to discern what he could not see before: Jesus as the light of the world, the fulfillment of all of Jewish law and the Temple sacrifices.

### Brother Saul

The last thing Jesus told Paul was to proceed to Damascus, where he would receive further instructions.[43] In his blinded condition, Paul was literally led by the hand into the city, where after fasting for three days he saw in vision a man named Ananias healing him by the laying on of hands.[44]

Meanwhile, Ananias, a faithful Church member and priesthood holder in Damascus, was told by the Lord to visit Paul and heal him, "for, behold, he prayeth."[45] This instruction took Ananias completely by surprise, who responded that he had heard many reports about this man and the harm he had done to the saints in Jerusalem, as well as the danger he now posed to the Damascus saints.

"Go," the Lord answered, explaining that Paul was a chosen instrument[46] to carry His name before the Gentiles and their kings and before the people of Israel, and would suffer much in doing so.[47]

Arriving at the specified house, Ananias met Paul and placed his hands upon him to pronounce a priesthood blessing. He addressed Paul as if he were already a member of the Church of Christ: "Brother Saul"—the words must have thrilled and comforted Paul—"the Lord, even Jesus, that appeared unto thee in the way as thou camest, hath sent me, that thou mightest receive thy sight, and be filled with the Holy Ghost."[48]

By divine design, Paul's sight had been restored not by Jesus personally, but under the hand of one of His saints whom the spiritually blind Paul had come to arrest.

Paul was then baptized and received the Holy Ghost, giving him greater spiritual vision than ever before. Only then, as a new member of the Church, did Paul resume bodily nourishment and regain his strength, a changed man who would change the course of history.

The wolf of Benjamin had been transformed into one of the sheep of the Good Shepherd. As Christ's servant and even apostle, Paul would go forth to carry the message far and wide, later comparing himself to a kind of Olympic athlete running the race for Christ.

### The Spirit-Led Race and Its Hardships

Both Paul and the course on which he would run had been carefully prepared. The conquests of Alexander the Great centuries earlier had established Greek as the language of culture and learning throughout the region. Encountering diverse peoples throughout the empire with their different native tongues, Paul would use Greek to preach and to write his letters, which would become an important part of the New Testament.

The Roman Empire had made travel much easier, not only by imposing order in the region but also by building those famous roads that linked the capital city of Rome to its far-flung possessions. "The Roman Empire had pacified and united the world in time for the Gospel to be proclaimed everywhere."[49]

The Jewish settlements scattered throughout the empire would further facilitate Paul's preaching, with more Jews living outside the boundaries of Judea than within.[50] The Jewish synagogue was often the first place Paul would preach, proclaiming Christ as the fulfillment of the Jewish law and prophecies. All was ready for the great race Paul would run as a missionary for Christ.

And what a race it was. "From the moment the stewardship was entrusted to him,"[51] Paul pressed unceasingly forward. His labors for the Lord are legendary. New Testament maps meticulously trace the routes of his three lengthy journeys, and there may have been a fourth.[52] Estimates vary of how far he traveled, but it may well have exceeded 10,000 miles— in fair weather and foul, without the benefit of cars, trains, or planes. Throughout those extensive travels, he found the field of souls "white already to harvest," as the mortal Savior had described to His other apostles.[53]

Notwithstanding Paul's mighty efforts and substantial success, he seemed always to be beckoned on by souls yet to be saved, as when one night in the city of Troas he had a vision of a man of Macedonia pleading with him, "Come over into Macedonia, and help us."[54]

Paul did go and help, and kept on going and kept on helping as he preached and converted and established congregation after congregation of saints. He repeatedly counseled them to "walk in the Spirit"[55] and be "led by the Spirit,"[56] following the pattern of his own ministry. "I press towards the finishing line," he wrote to the Philippians, "to win the heavenly prize to which God has called me in Christ Jesus."[57]

No amount of personal affliction could deter him. For years he suffered from what he referred to as "a thorn in the flesh," apparently some sort of painfully chronic ailment that he prayed to have removed. The Lord did not remove it but gave him strength to endure.[58]

Relentless opposition hounded him. His course led through great afflictions, hardships, calamities, beatings, floggings, imprisonments, riots, sleepless nights, and hunger, undergoing numerous difficulties and dangers that brought him often near death.[59] As he himself explained:

> Five times the Jews have given me the thirty-nine strokes; three times I have been beaten with rods; once I was stoned; three times I have been shipwrecked, and for twenty-four hours I was adrift on the open sea. I have been constantly on the road; I have met dangers from rivers, dangers from robbers, dangers from my fellow-countrymen, dangers from foreigners, dangers in the town, dangers in the wilderness, dangers at sea, dangers from false Christians. I have toiled and drudged and often gone without sleep; I have been hungry and thirsty and have often gone without food; I have suffered from cold and exposure.[60]

Through it all, Paul remained undaunted. "We are troubled on every side, yet not distressed; we are perplexed, but not in despair; persecuted, but not forsaken; cast down, but not destroyed."[61] Indeed, through such extremities Paul came to know not only his own weakness, but also the strength of Christ, who gave men weakness precisely so that they would draw on the strength of Christ. So clearly did Paul understand this that, as he said, he actually delighted in weaknesses and difficulties as opportunities to draw upon the Lord's power, "for when I am weak, then am I strong,"[62] and "I can do all things through Christ which strengtheneth me."[63]

Accordingly, "if God be for us, who can be against us? He that spared not his own Son"—the language is a direct echo of what Abraham was told after he showed his willingness to sacrifice Isaac[64] —"but delivered him up for us all, shall he not with him also freely give us all things?"[65]

No wonder that Paul was not afraid of tribulation but actually gloried in it,[66] and recognized that his tribulations had "served to advance the gospel."[67] Hardship in his missionary labors was also an opportunity for fellowship with Christ, even "the fellowship of his sufferings."[68] It was a small price to pay, he knew, for the surpassing value of knowing "Christ Jesus my Lord: for whom I have suffered the loss of all things, and do count them but dung, that I may win Christ, and be found in him."[69]

To do so, Paul knew that he had to help others win Christ and be found in Him. "I determined," Paul wrote to the Corinthians, "not to know any thing among you, save Jesus Christ, and him crucified."[70]

## A Crucified Messiah and His Love

But a crucified Messiah seemed a contradiction in terms for residents of the Roman Empire. "Crucifixion was so abhorred in the Roman world that modern man can hardly feel its full significance. That a crucified person had been selected for worship and was emphasized in Paul's preaching was a startling and vivid matter," making "*Jesus Christ and him crucified* . . . undoubtedly the most scandalous feature of the Christian message."[71] As Paul commented, "the preaching of the cross is to them that perish foolishness."[72]

Only by the "demonstration of the Spirit and of power" that accompanied Paul's preaching[73] could his hearers ever have accepted such a strange message. Through that divine power, Paul and his companion were suddenly released from prison in Philippi by an earthquake.[74] By that power, Paul healed a crippled man in Lystra.[75] And through that same power in Ephesus, "God wrought special [or 'extraordinary'[76]] miracles by the hands of Paul: so that from his body were brought unto the sick handkerchiefs or aprons, and the diseases departed from them, and the evil spirits went out of them."[77]

But the greatest power in Paul's ministry was the power of love, or charity, even the pure love of Christ, which Paul described in detail:

> Charity suffereth long, and is kind; charity envieth not; charity vaunteth not itself, is not puffed up.
>
> Doth not behave itself unseemly, seeketh not her own, is not easily provoked, thinketh no evil;
>
> Rejoiceth not in iniquity, but rejoiceth in the truth;
>
> Beareth all things, believeth all things, hopeth all things, endureth all things.[78]

Christ's love became the core of Paul's ministry, the supreme reality of his life, as reflected in his letter to the Romans:

> Who shall separate us from the love of Christ? shall tribulation, or distress, or persecution, or famine, or nakedness, or peril, or sword? . . .
>
> For I am persuaded, that neither death, nor life, nor angels, nor principalities, nor powers, nor things present, nor things to come,
>
> Nor height, nor depth, nor any other creature, shall be able to separate us from the love of God, which is in Christ Jesus our Lord.[79]

It was this love that Paul sought to nurture in others, as when he exhorted his converts to "love one another"[80] and be "kind one to another, tenderhearted, forgiving one another."[81] Paul himself showed the way.

> Paul cared deeply for his converts. His letters are full of expressions of love for their recipients: . . . he has "abundant love" for the Corinthians; the Philippians, who are his "crown and joy," he regards with "love" and "longing"; because of his "deep care" for the Thessalonians, he longs "with great eagerness" to see them face to face. Paul frequently calls his converts his "beloved." . . . It was his love for his churches which accounted for the intensity of his prayers for them: so he "constantly prays with joy" for all the members of the church at Philippi; similarly he prays "night and day . . . most earnestly" for the church in Thessalonica. Love—as of a parent for a child—was the bedrock of Paul's pastoral care.[82]

His converts reciprocated that love, as when the Galatians welcomed him "as an angel of God."[83] And it appears "certain that the Ephesians at Miletus were not the only converts of his who, at his parting, fell on his neck and kissed him, sorrowing because they were to see his face no more."[84]

An early Christian leader wrote that Paul "was conscious of nothing . . . but what was . . . in harmony with love and godliness," and "clave to these things more and more, and was carried up even to heavenly places, and was borne to Paradise."[85]

Joseph Smith likewise explained that Paul, having attained perfect love, was caught up to heaven where he met, among others, Enoch, and "received instructions from him."[86] An ancient source[87] describes Paul's heavenly meeting with Enoch, who wept at the failure of so many mortals to qualify themselves for the glorious things which "eye hath not seen, nor ear heard, neither have entered into the heart of man."[88]

## Finishing the Course and Winning the Crown

Unlike Enoch, however, Paul's destiny was to return to earth and continue his arduous mortal ministry to preach the precious gospel for the benefit of mankind. For, as he wrote in one of his letters, quoting partially from Isaiah:

> How . . . shall they call on him in whom they have not believed? and how shall they believe in him of whom they have not heard? and how shall they hear without a preacher?
> And how shall they preach, except they be sent? as it is written, How beautiful are the feet of them that preach the gospel of peace, and bring glad tidings of good things![89]

After decades of propelling those feet forward in his missionary marathon for Christ, Paul was prompted to go where he knew prison and persecution awaited. But he went, as he told the saints at Miletus just before departing, "bound in the spirit unto Jerusalem, not knowing the things that shall befall me there: save that the Holy Ghost witnesseth in every city, saying that bonds and afflictions abide [or 'are waiting for'[90]] me."

Paul was unafraid. "But none of these things move me, neither count I my life dear unto myself, so that I might finish my course with joy, and the ministry, which I have received of the Lord Jesus."[91]

In Jerusalem, Paul was arrested and subjected to the first of what would be several trials before powerful rulers. Had not the Lord said that Paul would bear His name before kings, but suffer much in the process?[92] For Paul, the fearless emissary of Christ, these were but opportunities to more effectively proclaim His name, beginning in a trial before the Sanhedrin where years earlier he had supported the conviction of Stephen.

From Jerusalem, Paul was taken to the city of Caesarea where he appeared before Felix, the cruel and corrupt Roman governor of Judea. Felix was unresponsive and let Paul languish in prison.

Meanwhile, Felix was succeeded by Festus, who was visited by King Herod Agrippa (relative of the Herod who had murdered John the Baptist). When King Herod asked to hear Paul's defense, Paul boldly related his experience near Damascus when he saw a light and heard the voice of the resurrected Jesus. Agrippa's reply to Paul is famous: "Almost thou persuadest me to be a Christian."[93] Agrippa found no fault in Paul and would have released him, but could not because Paul had already exercised his right of appeal as a Roman citizen to appear before the Emperor.

Paul was sent to Rome where he was placed under house arrest pending his trial. The only reason he was confined, as he well knew, was because of his voluntary submission to the divine will; one of his letters begins by announcing himself as "Paul, a prisoner of Jesus Christ."[94] But he continued to zealously preach and minister, and, according to one source, "many souls were added to the Lord,"[95] including some close to the Emperor.[96]

Even so, Paul apparently knew that his time was short, for according to early Christian writers, the Lord revealed to him that "the end of his life was near, and that he should crown it with the triumph of martyr-dom."[97]

The Emperor Nero was a man of incredible depravity and brutality. Among his many horrific crimes was secretly starting the fire that burned half of Rome and then blaming it on the Christians, whom he proceeded to arrest and cruelly torture and murder. Paul was among a group of Christians—viewed as "soldiers of Christ" and followers of a king other than the Emperor—whom Nero imprisoned and ordered to appear before him in chains.[98] An early source describes the scene.

> Among the many Paul also was brought bound; to him all his fellow-prisoners gave heed, so that Caesar observed that he was the man in command. And he said to him: "Man of the great king, but now my prisoner, why did it seem good to thee to come secretly into the empire of the Romans and enlist soldiers from my province?"
>
> But Paul, filled with the Holy Spirit, said before them all: "Caesar, not only from thy province do we enlist soldiers, but from the whole world. For this charge has been laid upon us, that no man be excluded who wishes to serve my king. If thou also think it good, do him service! For neither riches nor the splendour of this present life will save thee, but if thou submit and entreat him, then shalt thou be saved. For in one day he will destroy the world with fire."
>
> When Caesar heard this, he commanded all the prisoners to be burned with fire, but Paul to be beheaded according to the law of the Romans [regarding a Roman citizen].[99]

To his missionary companion Timothy, whom he loved like a son, Paul penned these lines shortly before his death:

> I have fought a good fight, I have finished my course, I have kept the faith:
> Henceforth there is laid up for me a crown of righteousness, which the Lord, the righteous judge, shall give me at that day.[100]

Like a victorious Olympic runner who had completed the course, Paul had finished his race, qualifying for the coveted crown. Olympic champions were, in great ceremony, crowned with prized but perishable garlands of olive leaves. In contrast, the crown reserved for Paul was an imperishable, eternal crown of righteousness, prepared by Jesus, who had endured His own crown of thorns until He could finally exclaim, "It is finished."[101]

Paul's life had come full circle, even as a crown. Years earlier he had participated in the execution of the righteous Stephen, whose very name meant "crown." Now, after long and valiant service in the cause for which Stephen had died, Paul was being sent to his own heavenly crown by the

wicked man who wore the Emperor's crown, and who, according to tradition, was present at Paul's execution.[102] The only account of the event is
found in an apocryphal source, which relates that to the very end, Paul
was fearlessly preaching of Christ and assuring his hearers of life after
death.[103]

Thus "having taught righteousness unto the whole world," wrote one
early Christian, "and when he had borne his testimony before the rulers,"
Paul "departed from the world and went unto the holy place," being
remembered as "the greatest example of endurance."[104]

His example is equally powerful for Latter-day Saints who, like Paul,
are commissioned by Christ to preach His gospel. "Continue . . . unto
the end," the Lord has declared, "and you shall have a crown of eternal
life."[105]

No wonder that when the Prophet Joseph exhorted his "brethren in
Christ and companions in tribulation"[106] to continue faithful to the end,
he pointed to the example of Paul:

> In Paul's last letter to Timothy, which was written just previous to his
> death, he says: "I have fought a good fight, I have finished my course,
> I have kept the faith: henceforth there is laid up for me a crown of
> righteousness." . . . Though he once, according to his own word,
> persecuted the Church of God and wasted it, yet after embracing the
> faith, his labors were unceasing to spread the glorious news: and like
> a faithful soldier, when called to give his life in the cause . . . , he laid
> it down, as he says, with an assurance of an eternal crown. . . .
> Reflect . . . whether you would consider yourselves worthy [of] a seat
> at the marriage feast with Paul and others like him, if you had been
> unfaithful? Had you not fought the good fight, and kept the faith, could
> you expect to receive? Have you a promise of receiving a crown of
> righteousness from the hand of the Lord?[107]

## Legacy of Paul the Apostle

Born in the city of Tarsus hundreds of miles north of Jerusalem, Paul,
whose Hebrew name was Saul, was proud of his Israelite heritage and

studied for a time in Jerusalem under the greatest rabbi of the day. Later when he returned to the city shortly after the crucifixion of Jesus, Paul was alarmed at the rapid spread of the Christian movement which seemed to threaten everything he held dear. Like a ravenous wolf he hunted and persecuted the sheep until in a heavenly vision he was confronted by the resurrected Lord, who called him to go forth as his messenger. Paul's travels and labors to preach Christ and Him crucified are legendary, made in the face of tremendous tribulation and trials. As he himself said shortly before his martyrdom, he had fought a good fight, finished his course, and kept the faith—a powerful example, said Joseph Smith, for the Lord's latter-day missionaries.

# III.
# THE LATTER-DAY
# ERA

CHAPTER 11

~ *Joseph Smith* ~
*My Determination to
Ask of God*

early eighteen centuries after Paul's vision of the resurrected Jesus in a light "above the brightness of the sun," that same Jesus appeared—again in a light "above the brightness of the sun"—to another young Israelite. His name was Joseph Smith, and he was, although he didn't know it at the time, of the tribe of Joseph. His vision, the first of many, came in answer to his prayer, also the first of many. Those prayers would continue to open the heavens and open the way for the restoration of the long-lost Church of Jesus Christ and the preaching of the restored gospel to all the world.

### Asking of God who Gives Liberally

As a fourteen-year-old farm boy in upstate New York in 1820, Joseph had been searching for the true Church of Christ. It was nowhere to be found, for the "falling away"[1] (or, as another translation has it, "the Great Apostasy"[2]) that Paul had foretold had long since set in. "I found," Joseph related, "that mankind did not come unto the Lord but that they had apostatized from the true and living faith,"[3] notwithstanding the "war of words and tumult of opinions"[4] among the competing religious factions.

It was a matter of deep concern for the young man, who reflected again and again on how he might learn the truth. Like his forefather Abraham, Joseph was left alone to seek God in a world gone astray. "I pondered many things in my heart concerning the situation of the world . . . and the darkness which pervaded the minds of mankind," and "my mind became exceedingly distressed." And as young Abraham had done, young Joseph began to ponder the beauty of nature and the cosmos, and came to the conclusion that these majestic creations were unmistakable evidence of a Creator.[5]

But it was the Bible that showed him what to do. One day while reading the New Testament, he came upon this verse in James: "If any of you lack wisdom, let him ask of God, that giveth to all men liberally, and upbraideth not; and it shall be given him."[6] The words struck him as lightning.

> Never did any passage of scripture come with more power to the heart of man than this did at this time to mine. It seemed to enter with great force into every feeling of my heart. I reflected on it again and again, knowing that if any person needed wisdom from God, I did; for how to act I did not know, and unless I could get more wisdom than I then had, I would never know. . . .
>
> I came to the conclusion that I must either remain in darkness and confusion, or else I must do as James directs, that is, ask of God. I at length came to the determination to "ask of God."[7]

And "so, in accordance with this, my determination to ask of God, I retired to the woods to make the attempt."[8] Like his forefather Abraham had done at the same age, fourteen-year-old Joseph would seek God in the solitude of prayer.

An ancient Jewish proverb says that "there is no stirring above" in the heavens "till there is a stirring below" on earth.[9] In the case of Joseph

Smith, his decision to pray stirred also the powers of hell. Retiring to a secluded grove of trees one beautiful spring morning, he knelt down and, in his own words, "began to offer up the desires of my heart to God."[10] It was his first spoken prayer. To his great surprise, he was immediately assailed by an unseen hostile force of such astonishing power as to bind his tongue. Thick darkness closed in on the boy, overwhelming him to the point that he felt that his very life was threatened.

At "this moment of great alarm," summoning all his energy to "call upon God to deliver me out of the power of this enemy," Joseph saw overhead a descending pillar of light "above the brightness of the sun."[11] So brilliant was this light that Joseph expected it to consume the trees, but when it reached the earth it enwrapped everything in a luminous splendor[12] and filled the young man "with unspeakable joy."[13] Within the light were two indescribably glorious men, one of whom pointed to the other and said, "Joseph, this is My Beloved Son. Hear Him!"[14]

Later in his life Joseph would comment that a person can learn more by gazing into heaven for five minutes than by reading all the books ever written on the subject.[15] How many minutes Joseph's first vision lasted we are not told, but at its close he knew more about God than did all the world's leading theologians combined. No wonder the boy was told not to join any of the churches. He was also promised that the fulness of the gospel would later be revealed to him. And all of this had come from the power of prayer: "I had found the testimony of James to be true—that a man who lacked wisdom might ask of God, and obtain, and not be upbraided."[16] It would be a guiding principle throughout his life.

And where had James learned about prayer? From his half-brother, Jesus,[17] who as one writer notes, "taught us how to pray not in word only but also in act. Christ showed us how to pray by praying."[18] Joseph Smith's face-to-face encounter with the risen Lord had come only after acting on the same determination that the Lord Himself had constantly acted on during His mortal ministry: to ask of God. Jesus was truly "the praying Christ,"[19] who had now appeared in glory to the praying Joseph Smith.

## The Spirit and Power of All the Prophets

Long after the outward glory of Joseph Smith's first vision had withdrawn, an inner glow remained. "My soul was filled with love," he wrote, "and for many days I could rejoice with great joy and the Lord was with me"—and then added in the same sentence that he "could find none that would believe the heavenly vision."[20] None outside of his family, he meant, for they did believe him. But his statement shows how urgently he sought to share his glorious experience, and what motivated him to do so: love. He had discovered what his ancestor Abraham discovered, that God's most important characteristic is love.

To Joseph's great dismay, his efforts to reach out in love and share news of the heavenly vision met with "the most bitter persecution and reviling,"[21] causing him to identify closely with one of his heroes from the Bible, the Apostle Paul.

> I have thought since, that I felt much like Paul, when he made his defense before King Agrippa, and related the account of the vision he had when he saw a light, and heard a voice; but still there were but few who believed him; some said he was dishonest, others said he was mad; and he was ridiculed and reviled. But all this did not destroy the reality of his vision. He had seen a vision, he knew he had, and all the persecution under heaven could not make it otherwise; and though they should persecute him unto death, yet he knew, and would know to his latest breath, that he had both seen a light and heard a voice speaking unto him, and all the world could not make him think or believe otherwise.
>
> So it was with me.[22]

Joseph's tribulation never ceased, nor did his sense of identification with the Apostle Paul, whose language he would echo years later when penning a letter from Liberty Jail: "Your humble servant, Joseph Smith, Jun., prisoner for the Lord Jesus Christ's sake . . ."[23] Later Joseph would reflect that "deep water is what I am wont to swim in. It has all become a second nature to me; and I feel, like Paul, to glory in tribulation."[24] For Joseph, Paul was not just another prophet from the past, but a "beloved brother."[25] So much did these two powerful prophets have in common that, according to one biographer, "Joseph Smith's case is that of Saint Paul's over again."[26]

Joseph Smith's case is also that of John the Baptist, who prepared the way of the Lord; and of Abinadi, who published peace; and of Isaiah, who spoke the word of the Lord to all the house of Israel; and of Abraham, who prayed for and received divine guidance at the age of fourteen; and of Noah, who called a wicked world to repentance prior to global destruction; and of the youthful Enoch, who opened his mouth and built Zion; and of other prophets of the past. In the words of Joseph Smith's brother and faithful friend, Hyrum, "Joseph has the spirit and power of all the prophets."[27]

While all those former prophets were men of prayer, so pronounced was this aspect of Joseph's life as to lead one of his biographers to emphasize it in the opening line of his book: "A salient characteristic of Joseph Smith's life, both as a youth and as an adult, was his persistent reliance on the power of prayer."[28]

### Prayer and the Book of Mormon

It was the power of prayer, for example, that brought the visit of the angel Moroni in 1823 one night after Joseph had knelt in "prayer and supplication to Almighty God."[29] The next day Joseph went to the appointed place to see the sacred record Moroni had buried many centuries earlier, but each time Joseph reached down to pick it up, he experienced a shock. Only "by prayer and faithfulness," he was told, would he one day be able to obtain the record. It had, after all, been "sealed by the prayer of faith" to eventually come forth in answer to "the prayer of faith" of those who had written it.

Moroni's parting instruction that day to Joseph was: "Forget not to pray, that thy mind may become strong, that ... thou mayest have power to escape the evil, and obtain these precious things."[30]

Four years and countless prayers later, Joseph was entrusted with the sacred record that he would later describe as "the most correct of any book on earth, and the keystone of our religion," such that a person "would get nearer to God by abiding by its precepts, than by any other book."[31]

As its translator, Joseph himself would be the first person of our age to get nearer to God by reading the book that may well be the greatest treatise ever written on prayer. By its own account the book came forth in answer to prayer,[32] and its testimony of the power of prayer appears in the first chapter and the last, and repeatedly in between, urging readers to call on God always and everywhere; to pray over every activity and concern; to ask and you shall receive; to seek and you shall find; to knock and it shall be opened to you. Most impressive of all is the repeated command of the resurrected Christ to "watch and pray always,"[33] along with His promise that "whatsoever ye shall ask the Father in my name, which is right, believing that ye shall receive, behold it shall be given unto you"[34]—a promise repeatedly echoed elsewhere in the book.[35]

### Organizing the Church and Preaching with Power

Joseph did watch and pray always, and did ask and receive, even a flood of revelations as the Lord proceeded to restore the keys and Kingdom until again there was, in the person of Joseph Smith, an authorized mortal minister of salvation to a world in dire need thereof. Upon receiving the necessary priesthood authority from John the Baptist, Joseph performed the first baptism of this last dispensation. Later came additional priesthood authority from Peter, James, and John.

Where Joseph was, there was the Kingdom of God, for as he would later say, "where there is a priest of God—a minister who has power and authority from God to administer in the ordinances of the Gospel and officiate in the priesthood of God—there is the kingdom of God."[36]

But it was God's further design that from the hands of Joseph, "the kingdom of God go forth, that the kingdom of heaven may come." Hence, "the keys of the kingdom of God are committed unto man on the earth" so that the gospel will "roll forth unto the ends of the earth, as the stone which is cut out of the mountain without hands shall roll forth, until it has filled the whole earth."[37]

To that end Joseph was directed to formally organize the Church on April 6, 1830. It was a day of restoration, a day of power, and a day of baptisms, including that of Joseph's father. "Joseph stood on the shore," his mother recounted, "when his father came out of the water, and as he took him by the hand he cried out, . . . 'I have lived to see my father baptized into the true church of Jesus Christ,' and he covered his face in his father's bosom and wept aloud for joy."[38]

Those present, numbering about fifty in all, received an outpouring of the Holy Ghost "to a very remarkable degree"[39] and learned of the pivotal role the prayers of their young prophet had played in the rise of the restored Church: "For thus saith the Lord God: Him have I inspired to move the cause of Zion in mighty power for good, and his diligence I know, and his prayers I have heard."[40]

Joseph the missionary was valiantly rolling forth the stone, but his work had only begun. "Joseph Smith was commanded by the Lord to take the gospel to every nation, kindred, tongue, and people; and he immediately started out to do it. He was a missionary from the beginning."[41] Convinced that the Church's "greatest and most important duty is to preach the Gospel,"[42] he himself was "ever the missionary," and, like Enoch of old, "never passed up the opportunity to 'open his mouth,'"[43] and "never missed an opportunity to preach the gospel."[44]

In fact, his "unceasing efforts to bring people to the Lord resulted in the organization of several little branches in the same year the Church was organized." Even thereafter, shouldering the colossal burden of presiding over the rapidly expanding Church, "he was almost continually a missionary. When he visited Washington, D.C., he told the President of the United States about the gospel. While in prison, he taught the gospel to the guards. He also went on many missions."[45]

Like the Apostle Paul, Joseph preached Christ and Him crucified, for "the fundamental principles of our religion are the testimony of the Apostles and Prophets, concerning Jesus Christ, that He died, was buried, and rose again the third day, and ascended into heaven; and all other things which pertain to our religion are only appendages to it."[46]

As a teacher, Joseph spoke in a natural tone of voice without pride or pretense,[47] and tailored his teaching to the understanding of his audience. "He is a man that you could not help liking," wrote George Washington Taggart; "neither is he puffed up with his greatness. . . . And I assure you, it would make you wonder to hear him talk and see the information which comes out of his mouth and it is not in big words either but that which any one can understand."[48]

Brigham Young similarly reported that Joseph "could reduce heavenly things to the understanding of the finite. . . . He reduced his teachings to the capacity of every man, woman, and child, making them as plain as a well-defined pathway. . . . No other man could teach as he could."[49]

Parley Pratt likewise observed that Joseph's language was "not polished—not studied . . . but flowing forth in its own native simplicity. . . . He interested and edified, while, at the same time, he amused and entertained his audience; and none listened to him that were ever weary with his discourse. I have even known him," continued Parley, "to retain a congregation of willing and anxious listeners for many hours together, in the midst of cold or sunshine, rain or wind, while they were laughing at one moment and weeping the next. Even his most bitter enemies were generally overcome, if he could once get their ears."[50]

But the most memorable part of his teaching was the powerful Spirit that attended him, often manifesting itself visibly. The journals of those who were present make "continual references . . . to the light which his face radiated at the times when he communed with heaven."[51] Brigham Young noted that as Joseph preached on one occasion, "he was clothed upon with the Spirit and power of God. His face was clear as amber. The room was filled as with consuming fire."[52]

On another occasion as related by another witness, "the Holy Spirit lighted up his countenance till it glowed like a halo around him," and "his words penetrated the hearts of all who heard him."[53]

Another time when Joseph recounted his first vision, his "countenance lighted up, and so wonderful a power accompanied his words that everybody who heard them felt his influence and power, and none could doubt the truth of his narration."[54]

The same kind of convincing power was present when he addressed a large group in Philadelphia. According to Parley Pratt, "The entire congregation were astounded; electrified, as it were, and overwhelmed with the sense of the truth and power by which he spoke, and the wonders which he related. A lasting impression was made; many souls were gathered into the fold."[55]

How Joseph qualified for such power is explained in a revelation he himself received: "the Spirit shall be given unto you by the prayer of faith."[56] Prayer was a constant in his life, as reflected, for example, in what he wrote to his wife, Emma, in 1832: "I have visited a grove which is just back of the town almost every day," he explained. "There I can be secluded from the eyes of any mortal and there give vent to all the feelings of my heart in meditation and prayer."[57] In another letter to her a decade later, written when enemies sought his life, he urged: "Tell the children it is well with their father as yet; and that he remains in fervent prayer to Almighty God for the safety of himself, and for you, and for them."[58]

When others heard him pray, they described it as something extra-ordinary. A Church member recalled:

> Never until then had I heard a man address his Maker as though He was present listening as a kind father would listen to the sorrows of a dutiful child. . . . There was no ostentation, no raising of the voice as by enthusiasm, but a plain conversational tone, as a man would address a present friend. It appeared to me as though, in case the veil were taken away, I could see the Lord standing facing His humblest of all servants I had ever seen.[59]

Wilford Woodruff stated that "I have heard the prophet Joseph pray when the power of God rested down upon him, and all who heard him felt it; and I have seen his prayers answered in a marvelous manner almost immediately."[60]

Prayer further proved the key that unlocked solutions to the most difficult of problems, as when faced with a crisis of Church members being deceived by Satan. "We thought best to inquire of the Lord concerning so important a matter,"[61] he noted. The Lord did not let him down; the problem was soon resolved.

To his fellow saints, Joseph advised, "Supplicate at the throne of grace, that the Spirit of the Lord may always rest upon you. Remember that without asking we can receive nothing; therefore, ask in faith, and ye shall receive such blessings as God sees fit to bestow upon you." And "be plain and simple and ask for what you want."[62]

### The Principle of Love

What Joseph himself apparently most wanted, and received in abundance, was what the Apostle Paul calls the Spirit's greatest gift—charity, which the prophet Mormon said comes by praying "with all the energy of heart."[63] Joseph's first prayer had introduced him to the divine love that filled his soul during and after his first vision; and, as with Abraham, love would become Joseph's most prominent character trait, and a key factor in his remarkable missionary success. "Sectarian priests," he observed, "cry out concerning me, and ask, 'Why is it this babbler gains so many followers, and retains them?' I answer, It is because I possess the principle of love. All I can offer the world is a good heart and a good hand."[64]

Love was, he insisted, the very essence of the religion that he was instrumental in restoring. "Let us pour forth love," he urged, and "show forth our kindness unto all mankind."[65] For it was kindness, he explained, that had the greatest potential to persuade others to repent.

> Nothing is so much calculated to lead people to forsake sin as to take them by the hand, and watch over them with tenderness. When persons manifest the least kindness and love to me, O what power it has over my mind, while the opposite course has a tendency to harrow up all the harsh feelings and depress the human mind.[66]

Those privileged to know the Prophet felt his love as a great force. George Laub recounted that when he returned from a journey "longing" to see the Prophet Joseph, "I then had the opportunity of striking glad hands with him and my heart leaped in me for joy, for I had greater affection towards him than for any person on earth."[67]

William Taylor spoke of Joseph's "geniality and personal magnetism," noting that "I was a witness of this—people, old and young, loved him and trusted him instinctively."[68]

Enoch Dodge remarked that "every Saint who knew him loved him, and would have been willing to lay down his life for him if it had been necessary."[69]

And Mary Alice Lambert attested:

> The love the saints had for him was inexpressible. They would willingly have laid down their lives for him. If he was to talk, every task would be laid aside that they might listen to his words. He was not an ordinary

man. Saints and sinners alike felt and recognized a power and influence which he carried with him.[70]

Joseph's heart swelled with compassion for all mankind. "I feel for my fellow men," he exclaimed. "Oh, that I could snatch them from the vortex of misery, into which I behold them plunging themselves, by their sins; that I might be enabled by the warning voice, to be an instrument of bringing them to unfeigned repentance."[71]

And in a statement that reflected his own desire to travel and preach, he declared that "a man filled with the love of God, is not content with blessing his family alone, but ranges through the whole world, anxious to bless the whole human race."[72]

## Converting the World

Ironically, Joseph himself was not permitted to journey very far to preach, for he was needed to build Zion at its headquarters, and from there to organize and empower missionaries to go forth. From the beginning, many who joined the Church "approached the Prophet with a simple, humble, worthy request: 'Joseph, would you please inquire of the Lord and see what he would like me to do; I would like to do the will of the Lord.'. . . The [revealed] answer was always the same to all of these requests: 'I say unto you, that the thing which will be of most worth unto you will be to . . . bring souls unto me.'"[73]

As missionaries were sent forth, the Lord's mandate and promise to them through His Prophet was to preach "my gospel—repentance and baptism by water, and then cometh the baptism of fire and the Holy Ghost, even the Comforter."[74]

To assist them in their labors, the missionaries were armed with the book that Joseph had translated, the Book of Mormon—designed, as Enoch had foreseen, to "sweep the earth as with a flood, to gather out [the] elect from the four quarters of the earth."[75] Not only is the book "the greatest witness for the truth of the Bible that has ever been published,"[76] as Heber J. Grant said, but it is also, in the words of President Ezra Taft Benson, "the greatest single tool God has given to convert the world."[77]

Converting the world was exactly what Joseph set out to do. President Gordon B. Hinckley observed:

> Joseph Smith set in motion a program for carrying the gospel to the nations of the earth. I marvel at the boldness with which he moved. Even in the infant days of the Church, in times of dark adversity, men were called to leave homes and families, to cross the sea, to proclaim the restoration of the gospel of Jesus Christ. His mind, his vision encompassed the entire earth.[78]

One of those times of adversity was in Kirtland in the fall of 1833, when despite the tribulation at home, Joseph responded to the prompting that he himself should go and preach. He "felt that the field of souls was white for the harvest and that it was incumbent upon him to thrust in his sickle and gather the honest in heart." Taking two brethren, he journeyed to Canada, stopping at various locations along the way to preach the gospel.[79] In the town of Mount Pleasant, as he bore testimony of the Book of Mormon, those present saw—as so many others on other occasions had seen—Joseph's "face become white and a shining glow seemed to beam from every feature."[80] Sixteen baptisms resulted from his labors in that town.

In 1837, during another tumultuous time for the Church in Kirtland, Joseph courageously obeyed the revelation directing him to send away a number of his most faithful followers to serve missions abroad.[81] Nor was he worried in the least when he learned that some of these same missionaries, shortly after arriving in Liverpool, England, had been violently accosted by hosts of evil spirits. "When I heard of it," Joseph later remarked, "it gave me great joy, for I then knew that the work of God had taken root in that land."[82]

Knowing that sacrifice is required for salvation,[83] Joseph was not afraid to ask for sacrifice by those who would preach the gospel, as in 1839 when he called the for Quorum of the Twelve Apostles to leave their families for a season and preach in England. The sacrifice increased when, in preparing to leave, nearly all the quorum members and their families fell gravely ill.

But their resolve to fulfill their mission was unswerving, and they obediently departed in dire conditions of sickness and poverty. For his part, according to one biographer, Joseph "secretly yearned to accompany the Twelve on their mission to the British Isles," as is "evident from the avid way in which he watched and recorded in his journal every aspect of their journeys and ministry."[84] Meanwhile, their astounding success was the most remarkable confirmation yet of the revelations promising that "the field is white already to harvest."[85] Thousands joined the Church and emigrated to America. But as Joseph well knew, it was but the beginning. He wrote to the Twelve in England that before leaving, they should send the gospel from there "into as many parts" of the world "as you possibly can."[86]

At home, Joseph continued to call for additional missionaries. So persuasive was one such plea in a discourse he delivered in Nauvoo, that 380 elders immediately stepped forth and volunteered.[87]

At times he had to offer special encouragement, as when he told John Page that the Lord was calling him on a mission to Canada. "Why, brother Joseph," came the reply, "I can't go on a mission to Canada. I don't even have a coat to wear." Joseph removed his own coat and handed it to John, saying, "Wear this, and the Lord will bless you." Page did so and went to Canada, where Joseph's coat must have seemed like the mantle of Elijah. In the next two years he would walk five thousand miles and baptize six hundred souls.[88]

### Prayerfully Rolling Forward the Mighty Stone

If only John Page got the Prophet's coat, all departing missionaries left with the authority that had been restored through him, along with inspired counsel on how to exercise it. "Go in all meekness, in sobriety, and preach Jesus Christ and Him crucified," and do "not . . . contend with others on account of their faith."[89] "Beware of pride,"[90] he advised. "Declare the first principles, and let mysteries alone,"[91] and "seek to help save souls, not to destroy them."[92]

For "souls are as precious in the sight of God as they ever were; and the Elders were never called to drive any down to hell, but to persuade and invite all men everywhere to repent, that they may become the heirs of salvation."[93] Joseph promised that "if you do your duty, it will be just as well with you, as though all men embraced the Gospel."[94]

The Prophet Joseph would continue to counsel the saints on how to succeed in their ministry even *after* he left mortality, as when he taught Brigham Young in a dream:

> Tell the brethren to be humble and faithful and be sure to keep the Spirit of the Lord. . . . Be careful and not turn away the still, small voice; it will teach them what to do and where to go; it will yield the fruits of the kingdom. . . . They can tell the Spirit of the Lord from all other spirits—it will whisper peace and joy to their souls; it will take malice, hatred, strife and all evil from their hearts, and their whole desire will be to do good.[95]

It was counsel that Joseph himself followed during his own lifetime by means of constant prayer, urging missionaries to do likewise. "Call on the Lord day and night,"[96] for "if thou wilt lead a soul unto salvation . . . thou must commune with God."[97] The Lord Himself had declared through Joseph, "Ask, and ye shall receive; knock, and it shall be opened unto you."[98] "Be faithful, praying always,"[99] "ever lifting up your heart unto me in prayer and faith."[100] "All victory and glory is brought to pass unto you through your diligence, faithfulness, and prayers of faith."[101] "Call upon the Lord, that his kingdom may go forth" until "it has filled the whole earth."[102]

Nor was this great work limited to the mortal sphere, but would embrace the world of spirits with its hosts of the dead. Referring to what the Apostle Paul had written about baptisms for the dead in his day, Joseph promised the saints that they would have the privilege of being baptized for their kindred dead who accept the gospel in the spirit world.[103] Hence "the work in which Joseph Smith was engaged was not confined to this life alone," but included "teaching the gospel in the world of spirits and ... performing saving ordinances for literally billions of our Father's children."[104]

The Kingdom that God had brought forth through Joseph was rolling forth, and nothing could stop it, not even his imprisonment with some of his brethren in the oppressive humiliation and squalor of the jail at Liberty, Missouri. In this the most agonizing point of his life, Joseph prayed from the depths of his soul:

> O God, where art thou? ...
>
> How long shall thy hand be stayed, and thine eye, yea thy pure eye, behold from the eternal heavens the wrongs of thy people and of thy servants, and thine ear be penetrated with their cries?
>
> Yea, O Lord, how long shall they suffer these wrongs and unlawful oppressions, before thine heart shall be softened toward them, and thy bowels be moved with compassion toward them?
>
> O Lord God Almighty, maker of heaven, earth, and seas, and of all things that in them are, and who controllest and subjectest the devil, and the dark and benighted dominion of Sheol—stretch forth thine hand; let thine eye pierce; ... let thy hiding place no longer be covered; let thine ear be inclined; let thine heart be softened, and thy bowels moved with compassion toward us.[105]

There was no immediate response. Not long afterwards, letters arrived from Emma and others, letters "breathing a kind and consoling spirit." The effect on the prisoners was profound, as Joseph recorded:

> The floodgates of our hearts were lifted and our eyes were a fountain of tears, but those who have not been enclosed in the walls of prison without cause or provocation, can have but little idea how sweet the

voice of a friend is; one token of friendship from any source whatever awakens and calls into action every sympathetic feeling; it brings up in an instant everything that is passed; it seizes the present with the avidity of lightning; it grasps after the future with the fierceness of a tiger; it moves the mind backward and forward, from one thing to another, until finally all enmity, malice and hatred, and past differences, misunderstandings and mismanagements are slain victorious at the feet of hope; and when the heart is sufficiently contrite, then the voice of inspiration steals along and whispers, "My son, peace be unto thy soul; thine adversity and thine afflictions shall be but a small moment; and then, if thou endure it well, God shall exalt thee on high; thou shalt triumph over all thy foes."[106]

What followed was one of the crown jewels among latter-day revelations, the most sublime on record about the power of the priesthood[107]—a revelation borne of profound suffering and persistence in prayer.

The ultimate triumph God had promised Joseph would be reserved for the next life, for a few years later, in June 1844 in another jail in Carthage, Illinois, Joseph and his brother Hyrum were martyred. As the Apostle Paul had once done before his martyrdom, Joseph and Hyrum preached the gospel in jail to the very end. A visitor who came shortly before their death reported seeing these "two wisest and most virtuous men on the earth . . . preaching tenderly from between the iron bars of their jail the gospel of peace to those who wanted to kill them."[108]

As reported in another account, "Joseph bore a powerful testimony to the guards of the divine authenticity of the Book of Mormon, the restoration of the Gospel, the administration of angels, and that the kingdom of God was again established upon the earth."[109]

As their cell was stormed and Joseph was hit by a rain of bullets, he fell from the upper-story jail room and uttered his last words in mortality: "O Lord my God!"[110] To his final breath, he was faithful to his determination to commune with God.

In martyrdom, Joseph joined such powerful missionaries as Abinadi, Isaiah, John the Baptist, Paul, and others "of whom the world was not worthy."[111] But Joseph's role had been uniquely pivotal, allowing him, in the words of John Taylor, to have accomplished "more, save Jesus only, for the salvation of men in this world, than any other man that ever lived in it."[112]

Nor was death the end of Joseph's missionary labors. Wilford Woodruff explained that "it was required of him, as the head of this dispensation, that he should seal his testimony with his blood, and go hence to the spirit world, holding the keys of this dispensation, to open up the mission that is now being performed by way of preaching the Gospel to the 'spirits in prison.'"[113]

Writing shortly after Joseph's death, Parley Pratt declared of him: "He has restored the fulness of the gospel, we will spread it abroad. . . . He has quarried the stone from the mountain; we will cause it to . . . fill the whole earth."[114]

As that stone was quarried by young Joseph's "determination to ask of God," it can be rolled forward only by that same determination on the part of all who go forth to preach the gospel. In words echoing the very language from the epistle of James that inspired Joseph Smith, the Savior has similarly commanded his latter-day servants to do what He Himself also did in His mortal ministry: "Ask of God, who giveth liberally."[115]

By so doing, they can assist in the great latter-day miracle described by the Prophet Joseph:

> The gloomy cloud is burst, and the Gospel is shining with all the resplendent glory of an apostolic day;... the kingdom of the Messiah is greatly spreading, [and] the Gospel of our Lord is carried to divers nations of the earth.[116]

> The Standard of Truth has been erected; no unhallowed hand can stop the work from progressing; persecutions may rage, mobs may combine, armies may assemble, calumny may defame, but the truth of God will

go forth boldly, nobly, and independent, till it has penetrated every continent, visited every clime, swept every country, and sounded in every ear, till the purposes of God shall be accomplished, and the Great Jehovah shall say the work is done.[117]

## Legacy of Joseph Smith

After the long night of apostasy foretold by the Apostle Paul, a fourteen-year-old farm boy in upstate New York walked into the forest and knelt down. Inspired by a verse in the New Testament, young Joseph Smith proceeded with his determination to ask of God. In the glorious vision that burst upon him, there appeared both the Father and the Son, who called Joseph to restore the Church of Jesus Christ. Joseph was not only its founding prophet but also its first missionary, one of the Lord's most effective and powerful witnesses ever as he gathered souls into the Kingdom and directed the work of sending the restored gospel to the nations of the earth. Meanwhile, he continued to be a mighty conduit of revelation as he held fast to his determination to ask of God—a powerful example for all those who would seek to roll forth the Kingdom restored through the mighty Prophet Joseph.

# CHAPTER 12

## ~ *Wilford Woodruff* ~
## *Led by the Spirit*

About a year after young Joseph Smith arrived at his determination to ask of God, another fourteen-year-old in a neighboring state began his own quest for divine truth. His name was Wilford Woodruff, and he lived in Connecticut. Until then his favorite pastime had been fishing the forestal streams that fed his father's millpond. In fact, Wilford and one of his brothers were considered the best fishermen in the area. Wilford would always be an avid angler, but his quest for God would eventually transform him into one of history's greatest fishers of men and mightiest instruments of the Spirit of the Lord.

### Where Are the Prophets and Apostles?

Already in his young life he had unmistakably felt the influence of two unseen powers, one of which seemed to be "watching my footsteps in search of an opportunity to destroy my life." He had fallen into a pot of scalding water and been badly burned; fallen down a flight of stairs and broken his arm; fallen across some timber and broken the other arm; been charged by an enraged bull; broken his leg in a sawmill; been kicked in the stomach by an ox; tumbled from a haywagon and been buried by a load of hay; fallen fifteen feet out of a tree onto his back; sunk into thirty feet of river water and nearly drowned; fallen asleep in a heavy snowstorm and nearly frozen to death; split open the instep of his foot with an ax; been bitten by a rabid dog; been thrown from a galloping horse; and been nearly crushed in a flour mill.[1]

Equally astonishing, however, was the protection afforded him by another unseen power, even "a merciful Providence, whose hand has been stretched out to rescue me from death when I was in the presence of the most threatening dangers."[2]

But it was for the welfare of his soul that young Wilford was most concerned. "From the age of 14 to 23," he later recalled, "my mind was often exercised upon the subject of my soul's salvation."[3] In what one writer called "a consuming quest for religion and meaning,"[4] Wilford searched the Bible, investigated the churches, and pondered deeply. But the young man could not seem to find what he was looking for.

"Where," he soberly reflected, "are the Prophets and Apostles? . . . Gone, gone, all gone."[5] Based on what he understood from the Bible, he was earnestly looking for the ancient Church of Christ "to rise again."[6]

After years of feeling like "a ship tossed upon the waves of the sea, up and down, unstable and unsettled,"[7] he began to pray more frequently "night and day as I had an opportunity," and came to be deeply impressed by the handiwork of God. "All things to me seemed to praise the Lord— the sun, moon and stars, sky, air, land and water, mountains, hills, rocks and dales, forests, groves, meadows and grain."[8]

Wilford's experience is remarkably like that of young Joseph Smith, who likewise perceived in creation the unmistakable signature of the Creator. And like Joseph Smith, Wilford sought the Creator in a secluded tract of His marvelous creation. Not far from the flour mill where Wilford was working, in the middle of a large, swift stream, there was an island whose banks were "thickly studded with tall waving pines" surrounding "an open level field covered with wild flowers of various kinds."[9] To this pristine paradise Wilford was drawn again and again.

> I chose this island day and night as my place of retirement for prayer, praise and meditation before the Lord. I spent many a midnight hour alone upon that island in prayer before the Lord, and the many happy hours in sweet meditation which I spent in my lonely walks upon that pleasant retreat I shall never forget.
>
> The roaring waters, the waving pines, giving room to the passing winds, the field of flowers crusted with the silver rays of the moon, [were] all open to the eye and ear while the curtain of heaven [was] decked with the stars and moon. . . . These things resting upon my mind as the handy work of God in connection with prayer and meditation accompanied by the Holy Spirit gave unto me a peculiar charm, sensation, joy, and happiness which I had never before enjoyed and experienced in my life.[10]

In such serene beauty, Wilford began to pray. "I . . . pleaded with the Lord many hours . . . for light and truth and for His Spirit to guide me in the way of salvation."[11] There came not only a peace but an assurance that the Lord "was about to set up His church and Kingdom in . . . fulfilment of promises made by ancient prophets and apostles."[12]

### Resolved to Be Led by the Spirit

At the age of twenty-three, Wilford settled on a resolution that would prove as significant for his future as young Joseph Smith's determination was for his. And as had happened with Joseph, Wilford's resolve came by reading the New Testament. It was a passage written by Paul that stirred young Wilford. "I resolved," Wilford wrote and quoted Paul, "by the grace of God assisting me, to be led by the Spirit and word of God into that truth which maketh free thereby."[13]

One of the ways the Spirit had already led young Wilford was through the influence of an elderly gentleman named Robert Mason, affectionately referred to as "Father Mason" or "Old Prophet Mason." He believed the Lord would again raise up His Church with apostles, prophets, and gifts of the Spirit as of old. Father Mason frequently visited young Wilford's house and taught these things to him and his brothers.[14]

His final visit to the Woodruff home was in the spring of 1830, when he described a dream he had had thirty years earlier. He had been walking through an orchard looking for fruit to satisfy his hunger. Finding none, he began to weep. Suddenly the trees all fell, and new trees immediately grew, laden with the finest fruit he had ever seen. He picked as much as he could hold, but woke up before he could taste it.

Praying for the interpretation of the vision, Mason was told that the original trees represented the men of his generation, among whom the Church of Christ was not to be found. "But in the next generation, I the Lord will set up my kingdom and my church upon the earth, and the fruits of the kingdom and church of Christ . . . shall again be found in all their fulness upon the earth. You will live to see the day, and handle the fruit; but will never partake of it in the flesh." Then, according to Wilford,

> When the old prophet had finished relating the vision and interpretation, he said to me, calling me by my . . . name: "I shall never partake of this fruit in the flesh; but you will, and you will become a conspicuous actor in that kingdom." He then turned and left me. These were the last words he ever spoke to me upon the earth.
>
> This was a very striking circumstance, as I had spent many hours and days, during twenty years, with this old Father Mason, and he had never named this vision to me before. But at the beginning of this last conversation he told me he felt impelled by the Spirit of the Lord to relate it to me. . . .
>
> This vision, with his other teachings to me, made a great impression upon my mind, and I prayed a great deal to the Lord to lead me by His Spirit, and prepare me for His church when it did come.[15]

### True Servants of God

In 1832, Wilford left Connecticut for New York, where he and his married brother Azmon bought a farm and sawmill just east of Palmyra. The following year in the dead of winter, on December 29, 1833, two

Mormon elders knocked at the door. Wilford and Azmon were out working, but Azmon's wife took a message about a meeting to be held that evening in the local schoolhouse. Wilford recorded what happened after work that day.

> Upon my arrival home my sister-in-law informed me of the meeting. I immediately turned out my horses and started for the schoolhouse without waiting for supper. On my way I prayed most sincerely that the Lord would give me His Spirit, and that if these men were the servants of God I might know it, and that my heart might be prepared to receive the divine message they had to deliver.
>
> When I reached the place of meeting, I found the house already packed. My brother Azmon was there before I arrived. He was equally eager to hear what these men had to say. I crowded my way through the assembly and seated myself upon one of the writing desks where I could see and hear everything that took place.
>
> Elder Pulsipher opened with prayer. He knelt down and asked the Lord in the name of Jesus Christ for what he wanted. His manner of prayer and the influence which went with it impressed me greatly. The Spirit of the Lord rested upon me and bore witness that he was a servant of God. After singing, he preached to the people for an hour and a half. The Spirit of God rested mightily upon him and he bore a strong testimony of the divine authenticity of the Book of Mormon and of the mission of the Prophet Joseph Smith. I believed all that he said. The Spirit bore witness of its truth. Elder Cheney then arose and added his testimony to the truth of the words of Elder Pulsipher.
>
> Liberty was then given by the elders to any one in the congregation to arise and speak for or against what they had heard as they might choose. Almost instantly I found myself upon my feet. The Spirit of the Lord urged me to bear testimony to the truth of the message delivered by these elders. I exhorted my neighbors and friends not to oppose these men; for they were the true servants of God. They had preached to us that night the pure gospel of Jesus Christ.[16]

Then, as Wilford further describes, not only did he open his "eyes to see" and his "ears to hear" and his "heart to understand," but also his "doors to entertain him who had administered unto us."[17] Wilford and Azmon took the elders home and sat up late conversing about the restored gospel and the Book of Mormon, which Wilford commenced to read. "As

I did so," he explained, "the Spirit bore witness that the record which it contained was true."[18]

Two days after the first meeting with the elders, on the icy winter morning of December 31, 1833, Wilford and his brother were led by the elders—and led by the Spirit!—into baptismal waters that were literally freezing. "The snow was about three feet deep," Wilford later recalled, "the day was cold, the water was mixed with ice and snow, yet I did not feel the cold."[19]

That evening Wilford received the precious privilege he had fervently sought for so long. "The Holy Ghost fell upon us and we had a time of great rejoicing."[20] He now possessed what he would later call "the greatest gift that can be bestowed upon man,"[21] a gift that serves as "a leader to dictate and guide"[22] inasmuch as "it leads into all truth and reveals to man the will of his Maker."[23] Accordingly, he would say, "there is nothing that we ought to labor more to obtain while in the flesh than the Spirit of God, the Holy Ghost, the Comforter, which we are entitled to receive by reason of our having obeyed the requirements of the Gospel."[24]

One of the first people Wilford thought of on the day he was baptized was his old friend Father Mason, to whom he wrote not long afterwards.

> I informed him that I had found the true gospel with all its blessings; that the authority of the Church of Christ had been restored to the earth as he had told me it would be; that I had received the ordinances of baptism and the laying on of hands; that I knew for myself that God had established through Joseph Smith, the Prophet, the Church of Christ upon the earth.
>
> He received my letter with great joy and had it read over to him many times. He handled it as he had handled the fruit in the vision. He was very aged and soon died without having the privilege of receiving the ordinances of the gospel at the hands of an elder of the Church.[25]

## Learning from the Prophet Joseph

Wilford soon traveled to Church headquarters in Kirtland, Ohio, to meet Joseph Smith, whom Wilford later described as "the greatest prophet that ever breathed the breath of life, excepting Jesus Christ."[26] Wilford had already read a copy of Joseph's vision of the degrees of eternal glory (D&C 76), and knew that it was from God. "Before I saw Joseph I said I did not care how old he was, or how young he was; I did not care how he looked—whether his hair was long or short; the man that advanced that revelation was a prophet of God."[27]

Wilford described his first encounter with Joseph:

When I first saw him and his brother they were shooting at a mark with a brace of pistols. When they stopped shooting I was introduced to them. Brother Joseph shook hands heartily with me and invited me to go to his house and make his habitation my home while I stayed in Kirtland. I gladly accepted the invitation and went home. In a few moments he brought into the room a wolf skin and said come Brother Woodruff, I want you to help me tan this wolf skin as I want to put it on my seat while I go [on] my journey to the west. So I pulled off my coat, rolled up my sleeves, and went at it and soon tanned it over a chair post. While employed at this I smiled at the appearance of my first labour with the Prophet.[28]

Several days later, Wilford heard Joseph preach at a meeting where others were also invited to bear their testimonies, including Hyrum Smith, Brigham Young, Heber C. Kimball, and Parley and Orson Pratt. When they finished, Joseph commented:

Brethren, I have been very much edified and instructed in your testimonies here tonight, but I want to say to you before the Lord, that you know no more concerning the destinies of this church and kingdom than a babe upon its mother's lap.[29]

Wilford was "rather surprised" to hear this and what Joseph said next: "It is only a handful of priesthood you see here tonight, but this church will fill North and South America—it will fill the world."[30]

Whether Wilford sensed that evening how instrumental he would be in helping to bring about that destiny, he did not say. He did record that "there was more light made manifest at that meeting respecting the gospel and Kingdom of God than I had ever received from the whole sectarian world."[31]

Wilford continued to learn from the Lord's prophet, particularly on the Zion's Camp march to Missouri during which Joseph often spoke while "clothed upon with much of the Spirit of God."[32] The opportunity was invaluable, as Wilford explained many years later as a Church leader.

> We gained an experience that we never could have gained in any other way. We had the privilege of beholding the face of the prophet, and we had the privilege of traveling a thousand miles with him, and seeing the workings of the Spirit of God with him, and the revelations of Jesus Christ unto him and the fulfilment of those revelations. . . . Had I not gone up with Zion's Camp I should not have been here today.[33]

### Desiring to Serve

Remaining with the saints in Missouri, Wilford recorded his willingness—borrowing language from the Apostle Paul[34]—to surrender himself as "a living sacrifice holy and acceptable unto God," and to "stand as a bold witness for the gospel of Jesus Christ and follow him through evil as well as good report."[35] For Wilford, missionary service would always be of supreme importance, as he would later declare: "What greater calling can any man have on the face of the earth than to hold in his hands power and authority to go forth and administer in the ordinances of salvation? . . . There is nothing given to the children of men that is equal to it."[36]

It was precisely because he esteemed so highly the calling of missionary that young Wilford did not disclose his desire to serve a mission. He wanted to avoid the appearance of aspiring to so great a calling. Only to God did Wilford disclose his secret yearning as he went into the woods and poured out his heart in prayer.

"Before I arose from my knees," he recounted, "the Spirit of the Lord rested upon me and bore witness that my prayer was heard and should be answered upon my head." Walking back to the road, he encountered one of the brethren who said, "Brother Wilford, the Spirit of the Lord tells me that you should be ordained to go and preach the gospel."[37]

Days later Wilford was ordained to the Aaronic Priesthood and assigned to go to the southern states. His journal entry suggests that he sensed this was the beginning of something grand: "This is my first mission or the first commencement of my travels to preach the gospel."[38]

### A Missionary at Last

Thanks to Wilford's prodigious journal keeping—performed in obedience to counsel given by Joseph Smith[39]—we have more information about Wilford's missionary career than about any other missionary in history. It all began rather humbly as Wilford and his companion simply "put some Books of Mormon and some clothing into our valises, strapped these on our backs, and started on foot. . . . We picked and ate raw corn [and] slept on the ground."[40]

One morning after walking twelve miles in the rain, and with no supper the night before, they came to a house where a man and his family were just sitting down to breakfast. Southern hospitality required them to feed their two drenched guests, despite the family's hostility to Mormons: the man had been in the anti-Mormon mob at Jackson County, Missouri. Wilford recalled:

> He knew we were Mormons; and as soon as we began to eat, he began to swear about the Mormons. He had a large platter of bacon and eggs, and plenty of bread on the table, and his swearing did not hinder our eating, for the harder he swore the harder we ate, until we got our stomachs full; then we arose from the table, took our hats, and thanked him for our breakfast. The last we heard of him he was still swearing. I trust the Lord will reward him for our breakfast.[41]

Other groups Wilford encountered were more open. One day as he was about to address a congregation of five hundred, he began by kneeling. "I prayed to the Lord to give me His Spirit," and then "arose and spoke one hour and a half, and it was one of the best sermons of my life."[42]

The experience was typical, for Wilford and his companion proceeded, as one biographer describes, "to preach openly, boldly declaring that the Church of Jesus Christ had been restored with all its gifts, powers, and blessings, and calling upon the people to repent and to come into the fold through the waters of baptism. Their meetings and conversations were marked by an unusual fervency and by demonstrations of spiritual power."[43] Later in life he would repeatedly comment that he never enjoyed more of the Spirit of the Lord than when he labored on his mission as a priest in the Aaronic Priesthood.[44]

The Spirit came to Wilford as the revelation to the Prophet Joseph said it would come to any missionary: by the prayer of faith.[45] Wilford's "pervasive and persistent practice" of prayer, says one biographer, was "the first and most important ingredient" in his remarkable missionary success.[46] At times even his journal became a vehicle for communion with the Almighty. "O God the Eternal Father," Wilford wrote one evening, "I ask thee in the name of Jesus Christ to prepare me for thy use and give me the spirit of my mission."[47]

The Lord did use Wilford, often with manifestations of mighty power which were truly "extraordinary."[48] Wilford prophesied, had visionary dreams, spoke in tongues, and healed.[49] "And the instances in which he received the 'whisperings of the Spirit' are too numerous to mention."[50] With that divine direction, Wilford taught, converted, and baptized, often despite tribulation and opposition. His highest aspiration was to be a worthy instrument, as reflected in journal entries like the following, penned at the end of a busy first year of preaching: "O God, enable my heart and hands to be clean for a year to come."[51]

By the end of his mission he had baptized some seventy people. These "first fruits of my ministry," he wrote, are "bound to me closer than the ties" of family, for they are "the ties of the blood of Christ," and "eternity cannot break [such] ties of celestial love."[52]

Returning home to Kirtland, he married and was in the process of settling down when the Spirit soon manifested that he must again go and preach, this time to the Fox Islands off the coast of Maine. With the approval and blessing of the Twelve Apostles, he began his journey which took him across a stretch of ocean. Wilford the fisherman noted with some excitement in his journal the names of over fifty kinds of the "great fish that inhabit the waters," adding that there were "many others not named."[53]

But it was as a fisher of men that he had come, and his journal repeatedly attests to the powerful influence of the Spirit. "We . . . preached in the school house. . . . The Spirit of God rested upon us."[54] "The Spirit of God is like leaven through the Island."[55] "The Spirit of God rested upon us."[56] "The Spirit of God caused our souls to rejoice."[57] Leading his converts into the waters of baptism, Wilford "truly felt to rejoice," as "the Spirit of God rested upon me."[58] "O may the Lord roll on his work amid the Islands of the sea and give us a rich harvest of souls."[59] The harvest would include his own father and stepmother, as well as other family members, whom he converted on his return trip home.

## Power and Prompting in Manchester

With all he had already accomplished, Wilford might well have felt he had done his part and then some. But like the unwearying Nephi of old, Wilford was untiring in his effort to bring souls to Christ. When a call came to serve a third mission, this time to England as a newly ordained apostle, he accepted without hesitation. Sailing across the Atlantic Ocean, Wilford noticed, and described in his journal, "a large school of porpoises and blackfish. Some of the blackfish were supposed to be as much as twenty feet in length. They would roll on top of the water all around the ship."[60] This vast school of fish was a harbinger of the vast missionary success that Wilford was about to experience.

Arriving at Liverpool, he felt deeply the need for divine help. "We have need of much faith and humility before God," he wrote.[61] He later commented that "if I have any *forte*, it is prayer to God,"[62] adding that "I have more faith in prayer before the Lord than almost any other principle on earth."[63] As he labored in the region of Manchester, his prayers brought rich outpourings of the Spirit, as noted in numerous journal entries. "I had the Spirit of God."[64] "The power of God rested upon me."[65] "The Spirit made manifest."[66] "The power of God rested upon me and I bore testimony."[67]

Wilford and his companion were constantly asked for priesthood blessings. "The saints in England," Wilford recorded, "have great confidence in God and his servants, and there [are] so many [that] apply for the laying on of hands that we need as much faith as St. Paul had, that at the touch of our garments or handkerchiefs . . . they might be healed."[68]

He baptized frequently, adding a steady stream of converts whose gratitude and love for this humble servant of God were immeasurable. He found it difficult to leave meetings "for the press of saints wishing to shake hands" with him.[69] One faithful sister insisted on washing his feet[70]—beautiful feet to those who had accepted the gospel from this messenger of peace.

The work was flourishing, and Wilford had teaching appointments set for weeks in advance.[71] It seemed that he had "a good field open for labor."[72] Then one evening at the beginning of a meeting—it happened to be on his thirty-third birthday—the Spirit whispered to him: "This is the last meeting that you will hold with this people for many days." When he arose to speak, "the Spirit and power of God rested upon me"[73] to the convincing of several to be baptized.[74] But it was a shock for the saints to hear Wilford announce that he would be leaving them. They were "as much astonished as I was."[75]

"They asked me . . . where I was going. I told them I did not know. I went before the Lord in my closet and asked him where he wished me to go, and all the answer I could get was to go to the south,"[76] for "the Lord had a great work for me to perform there, as many souls were waiting for the word of the Lord."[77]

The next day "I got into a stage and rode eighty miles south, as I was led by the Spirit of the Lord."[78] He stopped only when he arrived at Herefordshire, at the mansion-like farmhouse of a wealthy farmer named John Benbow. Wilford introduced himself as "an elder of the Church of Jesus Christ of Latter-day Saints, who had been sent to him by the commandment of God as a messenger of salvation, to preach the gospel of life to him and his household and the inhabitants of the land."

Benbow and his wife received Wilford "with glad hearts and thanksgiving," fed the weary traveler, and then kept him up till two in the morning talking.[79] Wilford learned that the Benbows were members of a group of about six hundred who had broken off from the Wesleyan Methodist Church and "were calling upon the Lord continually to open the way before them and send them light and knowledge, that they might know the true way to be saved. When I heard these things," Wilford added, "I could clearly see why the Lord had commanded me . . . to leave . . . and go to the south."[80]

### Mighty Works in Herefordshire

The next evening as Wilford began to preach at a meeting to which Benbow had invited his neighbors, the Spirit whispered that there were "many present who would be saints."[81] The following day Wilford preached again and baptized the Benbows and four others. He spent the next day "cleaning out a pool of water and preparing it for baptizing, as I saw that many would receive that ordinance."[82]

The pool was finished in time for the Sabbath, when a thousand people came to the Benbow home to hear Wilford preach. All of these would normally have attended the Herefordshire parish church, so that in their absence that day, a mere fifteen souls showed up to hear a very incensed parish rector. He turned to law enforcement, as Wilford described.

> When I arose to speak at Brother Benbow's house, a man entered the door and informed me that he was a constable, and had been sent by the rector of the parish with a warrant to arrest me. I asked him, "For what crime?" He said, "For preaching to the people." I told him that I, as well as the rector, had a license for preaching the gospel to the people, and that if he would take a chair I would wait upon him after [the] meeting. He took my chair and sat beside me. For an hour and a quarter I preached the first principles of the everlasting gospel. The power of God rested upon me, the Spirit filled the house, and the people were convinced. At the close of the meeting I opened the door for baptism, and seven offered themselves. Among the number were four preachers and the constable. The latter arose and said, "Mr. Woodruff, I would like to be baptized." I told him I would like to baptize him. I went down into the pool and baptized the seven. We then came together. I confirmed thirteen, administered the Sacrament, and we all rejoiced together.
>
> The constable went to the rector and told him that if he wanted Mr. Woodruff taken for preaching the gospel, he must go himself and serve the writ; for he had heard him preach the only true gospel sermon he had ever listened to in his life. The rector did not know what to make of it, so he sent two clerks of the Church of England as spies, to attend our meeting, and find out what we did preach. They both were pricked in their hearts, received the word of the Lord gladly, and were baptized and confirmed members of the Church of Jesus Christ of Latter-day Saints. The rector became alarmed, and did not venture to send anybody else.[83]

Several days later Wilford had to endure rotten eggs being thrown at him,[84] harassment by a "desperate mob" that blocked a baptismal service,[85] and a "pelting [of] my body with stones, one of which hit me in the top of my head [and] nearly knocked me down into the water with the man that I was baptizing, but the Lord saved me from falling, and I continued until I had closed my baptizing, and my mind was stayed on God."[86] None of this slowed Wilford down in the least.

> I continued to preach and baptize daily. . . . The first thirty days after my arrival in Herefordshire, I had baptized forty-five preachers and one hundred and sixty members of the United Brethren, who put into my hands one chapel and forty-five houses, which were licensed according to law to preach in. This opened a wide field for labor, and enabled me to bring into the Church, through the blessings of God, over eighteen hundred souls during eight months. . . . In this number there were also some two hundred preachers of various denominations.[87]

It was, says one biographer, a "veritable Pentecost,"[88] accompanied by repeated displays of divine power to bless the faithful. "The power of God rested upon us and upon the mission," wrote Wilford, as "the sick were healed, devils were cast out, and the lame made to walk."[89]

At the end of one particular day, he recorded that "after standing upon my feet eight hours in conference, conversing much of the time, ordaining about thirty, confirming some, healing many that were sick, shaking hands with about 400 saints, walking two miles, and preaching four hours . . . , I then lay down and dreamed of catching fish."[90]

### Led by the Spirit in Rolling forth the Kingdom

His remarkable success—"I have never seen so many," he marveled, "receive the word of God in so short a time"[91]—was, as he keenly realized, part of the larger miracle of the latter-day Restoration. "Roll on, O ye mighty wheel of the Kingdom of God," Wilford wrote, "until ye become a mountain and fill the whole earth."[92]

And with this rolling forth came an outpouring of love, especially manifest when the time came to say goodbye to the many saints to whom he had brought blessing and salvation. "Multitudes . . . crowded around me, and hands were presented on every side, to bid me farewell. Many called for me to bless them before I departed." For over an hour they "crowded around me as children around their father," asking his parting counsel and advice on a wide variety of matters. Then "many of the saints parted from me in tears."[93]

A similar scene unfolded with another group, as "I was almost three hours shaking hands with the saints, healing the sick, and giving counsel to the multitude which surrounded me, many of whom were in tears when we parted."[94]

Reflecting on his miraculous experience, Wilford wrote that "the whole history of this Herefordshire mission shows the importance of listening to the still small voice of the Spirit of God, and the revelations of the Holy Ghost. The people were praying for light and truth, and the Lord sent me to them. I declared the gospel of life and salvation, [and] some eighteen hundred souls received it."[95] Wilford felt "to render unto God the gratitude of my heart for giving me so many souls as seals to my ministry; and I note the remarkable fact that I had been led by the Spirit."[96]

Wilford continued to be led by the Spirit as he completed his missionary service in England, returned home to Church duties, served another mission to England, and again returned home where, at the first possible occasion, he was baptized in the font of the Nauvoo Temple for his departed friend Father Mason.[97]

Wilford helped lead the saints west to the Great Salt Lake, served a mission to the eastern states, served as president of the St. George Temple, and finally served as President of the Church. In that capacity he led the great missionary effort and the temple work to redeem the dead, dedicating the Salt Lake Temple and pressing forward with the construction of other temples. "There is hardly any principle the Lord has revealed that I have rejoiced more in," he once said, "than in the redemption of our dead."[98]

Toward the end of his life, he calculated that he had traveled some 175,000 miles[99] and preached the gospel "to millions of my fellow men."[100] "I have waded swamps and swum rivers," he reminisced, "and have asked my bread from door to door; and have devoted [many] years to this work.

And why? Was there gold enough in California to have me hired to do it? No, verily; . . . what I . . . and . . . my brethren have done, we have done because we were commanded of God."[101] Thus "I will say as Paul did, 'Woe be unto me if I preach not the gospel.'"[102]

Heber J. Grant stated about Wilford Woodruff: "I believe that no other man who ever walked the face of the earth was a greater converter of souls to the gospel of Jesus Christ."[103] Wilford's example is powerful for all missionaries, for as he said, "when they go abroad to the nations of the earth, [they] need the Spirit of God, to tell them to go here, or go there, that they may search out the honest in heart."[104]

In fact, it is "the privilege" of every worthy missionary, continued President Woodruff, "to have . . . the Holy Ghost as a constant companion, that he may be able to thoroughly gather out . . . the meek of the earth and bring them to the fold of Christ."[105]

Besides a privilege, it is the Lord's commandment to his missionaries: "Go forth in the power of my Spirit, preaching my gospel."[106] As they do so they will not only testify of the Savior, but actually follow the example He set in His own mortal ministry of being constantly led by the Spirit.[107]

## Legacy of Wilford Woodruff

When young Joseph Smith began searching for God, another teenager in a neighboring state was on a similar quest. Wilford Woodruff's prayers and searching led him to the conclusion that Christ's ancient Church was no longer on the earth, but would soon be restored, and Wilford resolved to be "led by the Spirit." Years later when two elders showed up one evening to preach the restored gospel, Wilford stood up in the meeting and bore testimony that they were sent of God. Baptized two days later, Wilford received the precious gift of the Holy Ghost, which led him constantly during his decades of dedicated and miraculous missionary service that gathered multitudes into the Kingdom of God. He remains one of the greatest examples for latter-day missionaries as they seek to obey the Lord's command to go forth in the power of the Spirit.

# CHAPTER 13

# ~ *Joseph F. Smith* ~
## *I Am Clean!*

"Joseph F. Smith," wrote Wilford Woodruff in his journal, "was the son of Hyrum Smith. He has the spirit of his father and uncle Joseph . . . who [were] martyred for the gospel's sake."[1] Just five years before that martyrdom in Carthage Jail, Joseph F. had entered the world while his father and uncle languished in another jail at Liberty, Missouri, during "the most strife-torn year in the Church's history."[2] Thus born amid tribulation, Joseph F. would experience much of it throughout his life, but through courage and purity would rise to become a mighty missionary and powerful prophet in the Lord's latter-day Kingdom.

### Paternal Heritage and Heavenly Gift

While yet a boy, Joseph F. felt the witness of the Spirit as he listened to his Uncle Joseph.

> As a child I knew the Prophet Joseph Smith. As a child I have listened to him preach the gospel that God had committed to his charge and care. As a child I was familiar in his home, in his household, as I was familiar under my own father's roof. I have retained the witness of the Spirit that I was imbued with as a child . . . that Joseph Smith was a prophet of God.[3]

Equally etched in his memory was the last time he saw his uncle and his father alive. Decades later in Nauvoo, Joseph F. pointed to "the exact spot where I stood when the brethren came riding up on their way to Carthage. Without getting off his horse father leaned over his saddle and picked me up off the ground. He kissed me goodbye and put me down again and I saw him ride away."[4]

Not long afterwards little Joseph F. saw the two martyrs lying in their coffins. "I remember my mother lifting me up to look upon the faces of my father and the Prophet, for the last time."[5]

So ended what one biographer called the "abbreviated childhood" of Joseph F. Smith, who forever after found strength in the sacrifice made by his father and uncle. "This martyrdom," he would say, "has always been an inspiration to the people of the Lord. It has helped them in their individual trials; has given them courage to pursue a course in righteousness and to know and to live the truth, and must ever be held in sacred memory."[6]

It was a sacrifice of love, he continued, for although they could easily have chosen not to go to Carthage, yet when they felt "they were needed as a sacrifice for the protection of their worthy followers," Joseph and Hyrum "returned and calmly went to their death. . . . Their courage, their faith, their love for the people were without bounds, and they gave all that they had for their people." And "the Lord permitted the sacrifice, that the testimony of those virtuous and righteous men should stand as a witness."[7]

John Taylor wrote of the two brothers: "In life they were not divided, and in death they were not separated!"[8] The Prophet Joseph himself had written: "Brother Hyrum, what a faithful heart you have got! Oh may the eternal Jehovah crown eternal blessings upon your head, as a reward for the care you have had for my soul! O how many are the sorrows we have shared together."[9]

Hyrum was, in the words of a blessing he had received, "as firm as the pillars of heaven,"[10] and if the Lord loved Hyrum for "the integrity of his heart,"[11] so did his brother Joseph: "Hyrum possesses the integrity of a Job, and . . . the meekness and humility of Christ; and I love him with that love that is stronger than death."[12]

Such was the heritage passed down to Joseph F. from his noble father: integrity and loyalty to the Prophet Joseph, whose very name Hyrum had bestowed on his son. It had "special significance" to him, notes a biographer; "throughout his life it would be a reminder to him of his identity and mission."[13]

But the greatest reminder came with the gift of the Holy Ghost which young Joseph F. received at baptism.

> The feeling that came upon me was that of pure peace, of love and of light. I felt in my soul that if I had sinned—and surely I was not without sin—that it had been forgiven me; that I was indeed cleansed from sin. . . . I felt as if I wanted to do good everywhere to everybody and to everything. I felt a newness of life, a newness of desire to do that which was right. There was not one particle of desire for evil left in my soul. I was but a little boy, it is true, when I was baptized; but this was the influence that came upon me, and I know that it was from God, and was and ever has been a living witness to me of my acceptance of the Lord.[14]

## Influence of a Righteous Mother

Also significant for Joseph F. was his maternal heritage as reflected in his middle name, Fielding, from his angel mother. Mary Fielding Smith taught her son unforgettable lessons of faith, as when they were at Winter Quarters heading west with the saints. Taking a side trip to purchase provisions, she and nine-year-old Joseph F., accompanied by Mary's brother, stopped and made camp on an open prairie not far from a herd of cattle. Arising the next morning, they were alarmed to discover that their best team of oxen had disappeared.

They spread out and spent the morning searching the area, all to no avail. When the dejected Joseph F. returned to camp, he was drenched from the heavy dew clinging to the tall grass through which he had tromped. As he later recalled,

> In this pitiable plight I was the first to return to our wagons, and as I approached I saw my mother kneeling down in prayer. I halted for a moment and then drew gently near enough to hear her pleading with the Lord not to suffer us to be left in this helpless condition, but to lead us to recover our lost team, that we might continue our travels in safety. When she arose from her knees I was standing nearby. The first expression I caught upon her precious face was a lovely smile, which, discouraged as I was, gave me renewed hope and assurance that I had not felt before.

A few minutes later Mary's brother returned to camp and reported that the oxen were still missing.

> Mother replied in a voice which fairly rang with cheerfulness, "Never mind, your breakfast has been waiting for hours, and now, while you and Joseph are eating, I will just take a walk out and see if I can find the cattle." My uncle held up his hands in blank astonishment, as if the Missouri river had suddenly turned to run upstream. . . . "Why Mary," he exclaimed, "what do you mean? We have been all over this country, all through the timber and through the herd of cattle and our oxen are gone—they are not to be found. I believe they have been driven off, and it is useless for you to do such a thing as to attempt to hunt for them."

Undeterred, Mary set out. She was immediately approached by a herdsman on horseback who told her that he had seen her oxen in the opposite direction from which she was walking.

> We heard plainly what he said, but mother went right on, paid no attention to his remark and did not even turn her head to look at him. . . . My mother continued straight down the little stream of water, until she stood almost on the bank of the river, and then she beckoned to us. . . . I outran my uncle and came first to the spot where my mother stood. There I saw our oxen fastened to a clump of willows growing in the bottom of a deep gulch which had been washed out of the sandy

banks of the river by the little spring creek, perfectly concealed from view. We were not long in releasing them from bondage and getting back to our camp, where the other cattle had been fastened to the wagon wheels all the morning, and we were soon on our way homeward bound, rejoicing.[15]

The experience "made an indelible impression upon my mind," Joseph F. later recalled, "and has been a source of comfort, assurance and guidance to me throughout my life."[16]

In Utah, young Joseph F. worked hard as the man of his mother's family. From the potatoes they raised, Mary insisted on selecting the best for the tenth that they paid in tithing, bringing much-needed blessings to the struggling family. "She prospered," remembered Joseph F., "because she obeyed the laws of God. She had abundance to sustain her family."[17]

## Orphan and Committed Missionary

Just before Joseph F.'s fourteenth birthday, his mother became ill and died. It "was one of the most painful experiences of Joseph F.'s life,"[18] who was left an orphan to care for his younger sister. Two years later while attending general conference, Joseph F. was shocked to hear his name read by President Brigham Young as one of those called to serve a mission. Notwithstanding his difficult circumstances, Joseph F. would not turn down a call from the Prophet.

We have no record of the counsel President Young gave to Joseph F. and the other newly called missionaries on that particular occasion, but we do know what the President had told missionaries a year and a half earlier at another conference, undoubtedly attended by young Joseph F. Speaking to "those who are going out on missions," President Young urged:

> One thing must be observed and be before them all the time in their meditations and in their practice, and that is, *clean hands* and *pure hearts* before God, angels, and men. . . .

Start from here with clean hands and pure hearts, and be pure from the crown of the head to the soles of your feet; then live so every hour. Go in that manner, and in that manner labor, and return again as clean as a piece of pure white paper. This is the way to go. . . . How can you do it? Is there a way? Yes. . . . You cannot keep your own hands clean and your hearts pure without the help of the Lord; neither will he keep you pure without your own help.[19]

Joseph F. was called to serve in Hawaii, then known as the Sandwich Islands. It was the fastest growing mission in the Church, with over four thousand converts in the previous four years. Joseph F. was one of about twenty new elders called to continue the work.

Arriving in Honolulu after the long ocean journey, he was assigned to begin his labors on the island of Maui, from where he wrote to a relative at home: "I am ready to go through thick and thin for this cause, and truly hope and pray that I may prove faithful to the end, . . . and I am ready to bear my testimony . . . at any time, or at any place."[20] He further requested that those at home pray for him, and then expressed his absolute commitment to serve an honorable mission.

I had rather die on this mission, than to disgrace myself or my calling. These are the sentiments of my heart. My prayer is that we may hold out faithful to the end, and eventually be crowned in the kingdom of God, with those that have gone before us.[21]

Another letter written months later reveals both his desire and his resolve to be worthy and effective.

I well know that I am young and inexperienced at present, therefore I wish to be humble, prayerful before the Lord, that I may be worthy of the blessings and love of God to protect me at all times. . . . I feel anxious to see the cause of truth speed forth to earth's remotest bounds, and I hope that I may become an instrument in the hands of the Lord in doing much good in helping to spread righteousness.[22]

## A Life-Changing Dream and Faithful Mission

Young Joseph F. worked hard. He learned the language quickly and "prized righteousness, obedience, and diligence,"[23] despite the temptations that seemed to abound. As described many years later by his son, "if a missionary was in any manner inclined to be tempted and lose his virtue, surely he had every opportunity among the natives of those islands in that early day."[24]

Tribulation of other sorts challenged him. Illness, persecution, and poverty all took their toll on this young missionary who, after all, was "still an orphan boy in his mid-teens, working in a strange land a long way from home," such that his difficulties "combined for a time to give him a deep sense of degradation and inferiority."[25]

Food was so scarce that, notwithstanding the natives' willingness to share, the missionaries would sometimes go for days with little or nothing to eat. Clothing also was scarce. With no funds being sent from home, Joseph F. had to rely on the generosity of Church members who themselves had little. "The Saints are poor," he commented, "but I am poorer."[26]

Such difficulties could not help but diminish his self-esteem. "I was very much oppressed," he later recalled. "I was almost naked and entirely friendless, except [for] the friendship of a poor, benighted, degraded people. I felt as if I was so debased in my condition of poverty, lack of intelligence and knowledge, just a boy, that I hardly dared look a white man in the face."[27]

In this discouraged state, Joseph F. fell asleep one night "alone on a mat, away up in the mountains of Hawaii," and had a dream.

> I dreamed that I was on a journey, and I was impressed that I ought to hurry—hurry with all my might, for fear I might be too late. I rushed on my way as fast as I possibly could, and I was only conscious of having just a little bundle, a handkerchief with a small bundle wrapped in it. I did not realize just what it was, when I was hurrying as fast as I could;

but finally I came to a wonderful mansion, if it could be called a mansion. It seemed too large, too great to have been made by hand, but I thought I knew that was my destination. As I passed towards it, as fast as I could, I saw a notice, "Bath." I turned aside quickly and went into the bath and washed myself clean. I opened up this little bundle that I had, and there was a pair of white, clean garments, a thing I had not seen for a long time, because the people I was with did not think very much of making things exceedingly clean. But my garments were clean, and I put them on. Then I rushed to what appeared to be a great opening, or door. I knocked and the door opened, and the man who stood there was the Prophet Joseph Smith. He looked at me a little reprovingly, and . . . said: "Joseph, you are late." Yet I took confidence and said: "Yes, but I am clean—I am clean!"

At that point in the dream, the Prophet Joseph grasped his nephew's hand and ushered him into a place where Joseph F. saw "the chosen, . . . the exalted," including his mother and father, Brigham Young, and numerous others. The experiences of that night wrought a powerful transformation in the young missionary.

When I awoke that morning I was a man, although only a boy. There was not anything in the world that I feared. I could meet any man or woman or child and look them in the face, feeling in my soul that I was a man every whit. That vision, that manifestation and witness that I enjoyed at that time has made me what I am, if I am anything that is good, or clean, or upright before the Lord, if there is anything good in me. That has helped me out in every trial and through every difficulty.

Now, I suppose that is only a dream? To me it is a reality. There never could be anything more real to me. . . . When I woke up I felt as if I had been lifted out of a slum, out of despair, out of the wretched condition that I was in; and . . . I was not afraid of any white man nor of anyone else, and I have not been very much afraid of anybody else since that time. I know that that was a reality, to show me my duty, to teach me something, and to impress upon me something that I cannot forget.[28]

With newly found confidence, Joseph F. forged ahead in his missionary labors. He was soon called to leadership, to preside first over three districts and then over the entire island. Although only sixteen years old, he was responsible for two other missionaries and twelve hundred saints. The Lord blessed his labors with spiritual gifts like a facility with the language, the power to heal, and the power to cast out evil spirits.[29] But the most significant gift that came was described by him years later.

>On my first mission I began to learn something for myself; I had hitherto believed the testimonies of the servants of God whom I had heard converse and preach, as well as the instructions I received from a most kind and affectionate mother, as also what I could comprehend through reading the Book of Mormon, the Doctrine and Covenants, and the Bible. But in the ministry, where I labored earnestly, I began to comprehend more fully, through the inspiration of the Holy Spirit, what I had read and been taught, and so they became in my mind established facts, of which I was as absolutely certain as I was of my own existence.[30]

## Man of Courage and Power

On the way home from his nearly four-year mission, Joseph F. and other returning missionaries sailed to San Francisco, and from there began making their way overland toward Salt Lake City. One evening after they made camp, a group of armed and drunken men on horses rode up threatening to kill any Mormon they found. Joseph F.'s companions managed to cautiously slip out of sight, but he boldly went about his business until one of the cursing men confronted him. Pointing his pistol at Joseph F., he demanded, "Are you a Mormon?"

Joseph F. later said that at that moment he fully expected to be shot. But he looked the man in the eye and replied without hesitation, "Yes, siree; dyed in the wool; true blue; through and through."[31]

His courageous response can be explained only in light of what he himself said years later:

>No matter what may come to me, if I am only in the line of my duty, if I am in fellowship with God, if I am worthy of the fellowship of my brethren, if I can stand spotless before the world, without blemish,

without transgression of the laws of God, what does it matter to me what may happen to me?[32]

What *did* happen on that occasion was nothing short of remarkable. The ruffian suddenly put away his pistol and reached out his hand to Joseph F., exclaiming—while still cursing—that he was the "pleasantest man" he had ever met. "Shake, young fellow, I am glad to see a man that stands up for his convictions."[33]

Back in Salt Lake City, Joseph F. soon married. A year later President Young called him on a second mission, this one to the British Isles where he served for three years. He had not been back a year before President Young called him on yet a third mission, back to Hawaii. One of his fellow workers in Hawaii was Lorenzo Snow, who reported after one talk given by Joseph F.: "It seemed impossible for any man to speak with greater power and demonstration of the Spirit."[34]

### The Mantle and Humility of the Prophets

Home again from Hawaii, Joseph F. remained a powerful preacher. His manner was forthright, "simple, plain and unaffected,"[35] but magnified mightily by the Spirit, as attested in an intriguing journal entry by Apostle Wilford Woodruff on August 26, 1865. Summarizing a meeting in which he had participated that day, Wilford, ever the record keeper, tabulated not only the names of those who spoke but exactly how many minutes each had taken. These speakers included some of the mightiest men in the Kingdom, including Brigham Young, John Taylor, Lorenzo Snow, and George Q. Cannon. But Wilford's only substantive comment on any of the talks was reserved for the one given by the twenty-six-year-old speaker who wasn't even an apostle, Joseph F. Smith: "The spirit and mantle of the prophets was upon him," Wilford wrote.[36]

The next year at a meeting called by President Young with several of the apostles, Joseph F. was there in his capacity as secretary to the Council of the Twelve. The meeting closed and was dispersing when President

Young suddenly called everyone back and announced, "Hold on, shall I do as I feel led? I always feel well to do as the Spirit constrains me. It is my mind to ordain Brother Joseph F. Smith to the Apostleship, and to be one of my counselors."

The proposal was unusual because there was no vacancy in the Council of the Twelve, but it met with the "hearty approval" of all present."[37] By this ordination, done as President Young had been "led by the Spirit" to do, did twenty-seven-year-old Joseph F. become, as Wilford Woodruff noted of the occasion, "a special witness to all nations."[38]

Joseph F. would later say, "I desire to be led by the Spirit of the Lord,"[39] and would counsel the saints,

> We should live so near to the Lord, be so humble in our spirits, so tractable and pliable, under the influence of the Holy Spirit, that we will be able to know the mind and will of the Father concerning us . . . under all circumstances. And when we hear and understand the whisperings of the still, small voice of the Spirit of God, let us do whatsoever that Spirit directs without fear of the consequences.[40]

He also counseled as to how to qualify for that Spirit: "To be a true representative of this cause a man must live faithful to the light that he has; he must be pure, virtuous and upright."[41]

At age thirty-five he was called on his fourth foreign mission, this time to preside over the European mission. The call came during the October 1873 general conference, where he also gave his farewell address, expressing his desire to "prove that I am worthy" and urging his fellow saints to "keep the commandments" and "obey the whisperings of the still small voice in our own hearts. . . . Let our motto be . . . 'The kingdom of God or nothing.'"[42]

While presiding over the European mission, Joseph F. made the following journal entry:

> O! how I thank my God for his protecting, watchful care which has been over me thus far through life; preserving me from the deadly sins

of the world, and many thousand times from my own weakness and proneness to err. . . . O! My Father preserve me in thy holy keeping from the power of temptation . . . and be thou my master.[43]

## Persecution and Presidency

When he returned home from his mission, the Church was experiencing increased opposition over polygamy. With insight like that of the prophet Mormon who, as commander of the embattled Nephite armies, wrote to his son that the real labor facing them was to overcome the enemy of righteousness,[44] Joseph F. explained to the saints that "I do not fear our enemies," for "the labor that is upon us, is to subdue our passions, conquer our inward foes, and see that our hearts are right in the sight of the Lord."[45]

Meanwhile, the outward foes were raging as federal authorities began prosecuting and persecuting Church leaders. Joseph F., who was a polygamist and by now a counselor to President John Taylor, was a marked man. Forced into exile, he was hunted and deprived of normal association with family members whom he dearly loved.

Meanwhile, at the passing of President John Taylor, Wilford Woodruff became President of the Church. President Woodruff already knew, and had years earlier prophesied of the fact, that Joseph F. would one day become President of the Church.[46]

About a year after President Woodruff's Manifesto ended polygamy, the President of the United States issued a pardon to Joseph F., ending his exile. Several years later at the death of Wilford Woodruff, when Lorenzo Snow became President, he called Joseph F. to be his counselor. President Snow confided that the Spirit had whispered to him that Joseph F. would succeed him as President.[47]

Three years later, on October 17, 1901, Joseph F. became the President of the Church, of whose origin he bore powerful witness. "The greatest event that has ever occurred in the world," he declared, "since the resurrection of the Son of God from the tomb and his ascension on high, was the coming of the Father and of the Son to that boy Joseph Smith." Thus, he continued, "I come nearer the possession of the actual knowledge that Jesus is the Christ, the Son of the living God, through the testimony of Joseph Smith." But "Joseph Smith was not the foundation of it. . . . The Lord Almighty has made the promises concerning this work, not Joseph Smith, not Hyrum Smith."[48]

And it was the power of the Almighty which now rested so mightily on President Joseph F. that on various occasions, as witnesses testified, a visible aura of light emanated from him as he taught.[49] He was, in the words of one biographer, "essentially a preacher of righteousness"[50] who bore constant witness of Christ: "We should . . . revere Him in our hearts," and "every moment of our lives we should live so that the desires of our hearts will be a prayer unto God for righteousness, for truth and for the salvation of the human family."[51]

Following his own counsel, he led the Lord's Kingdom as it rolled forth, preaching to the nations of the earth and redeeming the dead. He dedicated the site for the first foreign temple—in Cardston, Canada—and initiated the building of the Hawaii temple in the land where he had served as a missionary.

### Vision and Legacy of Joseph F. Smith

The greatest revelation on record about the Savior's salvation of the human family was given to President Joseph F. Smith. It came one day in October 1918 as he sat in his study "pondering over the scriptures" and "reflecting upon the great atoning sacrifice that was made by the Son of God, for the redemption of the world." Suddenly the "eyes of my understanding were opened, and the Spirit of the Lord rested upon me, and I saw the hosts of the dead, both small and great."[52]

The scene that opened to his view was set at the time of the Crucifixion, just as the Savior was about to enter the spirit world. President Smith saw that in one place were gathered the righteous dead, "filled with joy and gladness, . . . rejoicing together because the day of their deliverance was at hand. They were assembled awaiting the advent of the Son of God into the spirit world, to declare their redemption from the bands of death."[53]

To this vast multitude "the Son of God appeared, declaring liberty to the captives who had been faithful. . . . And the saints rejoiced in their redemption, and bowed the knee and acknowledged the Son of God as their Redeemer and Deliverer from death and the chains of hell. Their countenances shone, and the radiance from the presence of the Lord rested upon them, and they sang praises unto his holy name."[54]

But to the wicked and disobedient spirits, the Savior did not go in person, but "organized his forces and appointed messengers . . . to go forth and carry the light of the gospel to them that were in darkness, even to all the spirits of men; and thus was the gospel preached to the dead."[55]

President Smith further saw that this great missionary labor among the dead is far from over, and that "the faithful elders of this dispensation, when they depart from mortal life, continue their labors in the preaching of the gospel . . . among those who are in darkness." And "the dead who repent will be redeemed" as baptism and other ordinances are vicariously performed for them in the temples.[56]

Within weeks of that glorious vision, President Smith himself passed into that spirit realm to continue his mighty ministry there.

Charles W. Nibley, a fellow Church leader and longtime friend, said of him: "Never was man more moral and chaste and virtuous to the last fiber of his being than he. . . . 'Blessed are the pure in heart,' and . . . he was the very purest."[57]

And with that purity came power, as Nibley further attested: "As a preacher of righteousness, who could compare with him? He was the greatest that I ever heard—strong, powerful, clear, appealing. It was marvelous how the words of living light and fire flowed from him."[58]

President Heber J. Grant similarly described him as "the greatest preacher of righteousness I have ever known."[59] "No man that ever lived had a more powerful testimony of the living God and of our Redeemer than Joseph F. Smith."[60]

Purity and power. These are the legacy of Joseph F. Smith.

One of his successors, President Gordon B. Hinckley, counseled the priesthood of the Church: "Remember Joseph F. Smith's dream. . . . I urge you to be clean."[61]

The words echo those of the Lord Himself who commands His latter-day missionaries: "Be ye clean"[62] in order to "go forth in the power of my Spirit."[63] To do so is to follow Christ Himself, who alone "did no sin"[64] and shed His blood to sanctify all who come unto Him and deny themselves of all ungodliness.[65]

## Legacy of Joseph F. Smith

Riding out of Nauvoo toward Carthage Jail, Hyrum Smith reached down from his horse, picked up his five-year-old son, Joseph F., and kissed him. It was the last time the boy would see his father and his uncle, the Prophet Joseph Smith, alive. Less than a decade later, Joseph F.'s saintly mother died, following which Joseph F., at the tender age of fourteen, was called on a mission to Hawaii. Despite his faithfulness, deep discouragement set in because of his poverty and lowly circumstances, until one night in a dream he learned of the rich blessings that awaited because he had kept himself clean. With this divine assurance and his continued faithfulness, Joseph F. pressed forward to become one of the most powerful preachers of righteousness in history, a beacon for latter-day missionaries who are likewise commanded to be clean.

# CHAPTER 14

# ~ David O. McKay ~
## What E'er Thou Art, Act Well Thy Part

As young Joseph F. Smith and others were sailing westward across the Pacific to preach in the Hawaiian Islands, other missionaries were sailing eastward across the Atlantic to take the gospel to the British Isles. "Hearken ye people from afar," the Lord declares in the opening verse of the Doctrine and Covenants, quoting words He had given to Isaiah, "and ye that are upon the islands of the sea, listen together."[1] Among those who listened were the McKays of Scotland and the Evans of Wales. Both families were converted the same year, and both emigrated to Utah. There a McKay son and an Evans daughter would meet, marry, and raise a son who would learn unforgettable lessons about duty and testimony on his way to becoming one of the Lord's powerful missionaries—David O. McKay.

### Noble Heritage, Loving Home

It was in the Ogden area, some thirty miles north of Salt Lake City, where David's father, also named David, met the girl who changed his life. "David McKay, a lad of fifteen, saw Jennette Evans as she sat on the tongue of the Evans wagon shortly after the family arrived. . . . He said he could not forget the large, brown eyes under her pink sunbonnet."[2] In the next several years they courted, fell in love, and were married by Apostle Wilford Woodruff in the Endowment House in Salt Lake City.

Settling near Ogden in the small town of Huntsville, the McKays farmed and raised a family that would eventually include ten children. Their third child—the first boy—was born September 8, 1873. They named him David Oman McKay.

Huntsville was a boy's paradise, located in a picturesque valley surrounded by mountains, canyons and streams. David's many pets included a dog, a pony, pigeons, rabbits, and a magpie that he tamed and taught to "talk." Farm life also included learning "how to work hard and enjoy the fruits of honest toil."[3] And all this in a small close-knit pioneer community full of friendship, support, and frequent activities like baseball, bonfires, picnics, parades, plays, debates, swimming, singing, and sleighing. It was a good place to grow up.

But "most important of all," recalled one of his sisters, "he grew up in a home full of love, discipline, and sympathetic understanding,"[4] thanks to goodly parents. The story of young David O. McKay vividly illustrates the power of parental influence in preparing children for missionary service, as he would later explain.

> The older I grow the more grateful I am for my parents, for how they lived the gospel in that old country home. . . . Both father and mother lived the gospel. . . . My testimony of the reality of the existence of God dates back to that home when I was a child, and it was through their teachings and their examples that I received then the knowledge of the reality of the spiritual world. . . . That testimony began . . . in the home in my youth because of the example of a father who honored the Priesthood—and his wife, who sustained him and lived it in the home.[5]

Remembering his father, David recounted:

> I thank my earthly father for the lesson he gave to two boys in a hayfield at a time when tithes were paid in kind. We had driven out to the field to get the tenth load of hay, and then over to a part of the meadow where we had taken the ninth load, where there was "wire grass" and "slough grass." As we started to load the hay, father called out, "No, boys, drive over to the higher ground." There was timothy and redtop there. But one of the boys called back (and it was I), "No, let us take the hay as it comes!"
>
> "No, David, that is the *tenth* load, and the best is none too good for God."
>
> That is the most effective sermon on tithing I have ever heard in my life, and it touches, I found later in life, this very principle of the law of sacrifice. You cannot develop character without obeying that law. Temptation is going to come to you in this life. You sacrifice your appetites; you sacrifice your passions for the glory of God; and you gain the blessing of an upright character and spirituality. That is a fundamental truth.[6]

Remembering his mother, David waxed poetic.

> She was frugal yet surprisingly generous, as was father also, in providing for the welfare and education of her children. To make home the most pleasant place in the world for her husband and children was her constant aim, which she achieved naturally and supremely. . . .
>
> Among my most precious soul treasures, is the memory of mother's prayers by the bedside, of her affectionate touch as she tucked the bedclothes around my brother and me and gave each a loving, good-night kiss. We were too young and roguish, then, fully to appreciate such devotion, but not too young to know that mother loved us.
>
> It was this realization of mother's love, with a loyalty to the precepts of an exemplary father, which, more than once during youth, turned my steps from the precipice of temptation. . . .
>
>> My Mother! God bless you!
>> For your purity of soul,
>> Your faith, your tenderness,
>> Your watchful care,
>> Your supreme patience,
>> Your companionship and trust

> Your loyalty to the right,
> Your help and inspiration to father,
> Your unselfish devotion to us children.[7]

Such were, as later described by David's sister, "the tender ties that radiated from a devoted father and loving mother," creating "the dearest, sweetest spot on earth. It [was] only an old country home, but no palace was ever filled with truer love and devotion on the part of parents, brothers, and sisters, than those which pervaded the hearts of the loved ones in that family circle."[8]

## Learning of Prayer and Sacrifice

Even so, boyhood was not without its challenges, one of which arose from young David's concern about Indians. They often showed up in Huntsville, and once an Indian brave had appeared at the McKay house wanting to carry off Jennette as a squaw. From then on, if her husband was away, she would never retire without checking under the beds. One night David dreamed that two Indians came into the yard, and as he turned and ran toward the house, one of them drew his bow and shot the boy in the back. "Only a dream," he later remembered, "but I felt that blow, and I was very much frightened, for in the dream they entered . . . and sneered and frightened mother."

Thereafter, bedtime for David became an ordeal, often a time of great apprehension. Lying in bed one night, he was startled to hear strange noises. His only recourse for safety, he considered, was to pray, which would require him to get out of bed and kneel on the floor—a terrifying prospect. But he had been taught well by parents who faithfully held family prayer and had taught about the Prophet Joseph's first prayer. Little David courageously climbed out of bed, knelt down, and began to plead for protection. His prayer was interrupted when he heard a voice clearly say, "Don't be afraid. Nothing will hurt you."[9] Apprehension was replaced by peace as the boy learned firsthand the power of prayer.

When he was six, severe illness struck his two older sisters and eventually claimed the life of the oldest. On the day of her funeral, the second sister also died. David would never forget the anchor-like faith of his grieving mother, who placed her trust in God at this difficult and tender time.

The next year brought a different kind of challenge, but one the family could choose to avoid. A letter arrived from Salt Lake calling David's father on a mission for at least two and possibly three years. The place to which he was called—his native land of Scotland—seemed right, but the timing of the call appeared to be all wrong. Only recently had the family lost its two oldest children; Jennette was now about to have another baby, her sixth; plans had just been made to enlarge the house; and daily chores needed doing, including animals to be fed and tended, cows milked, wood chopped, and the numerous other demands of farm life. Showing the letter to his wife, and out of concern for her, he assured her that it would be impossible for him to go.

She read the letter, looked at her husband, and stated firmly, "Of course you must accept; you need not worry about me. David O. and I will manage things nicely!"[10] Father made plans to leave in April as his call specified, but this would mean his family would be deprived of his presence just when spring crops needed planting and the new baby would be born. One evening as the family knelt around the supper table for prayer, he suggested that he ask the Church authorities to postpone his call long enough to get his family established for the spring.

Again Jennette showed her willingness to sacrifice. "No," she declared, "your call is for April and you must go." Looking soberly at her two sons, seven-year-old David and five-year-old Thomas, she said, "My little men will see that we get along all right." As one writer noted, "Neither boy ever forgot the thrill of that moment or the solemn promise they made then, 'We'll help you, Mother.'"[11]

On the day in April when their father bid the family goodbye, young David took a major stride toward manhood as he stepped up to fill his father's parting instruction to "take care of mama."[12] Already at this tender age, David was learning about the importance of doing his duty.

Mother's letters to father in far-off Scotland were ever cheerful, never mentioning the challenges and hardships that frequently arose. With faith and hope, she sent nothing but good news and encouragement, managing meanwhile to meet every difficulty with the help of young David and extended family and ward members. In time, the Lord began to prosper this missionary family, blessing them sufficiently for mother to complete the additions to the house that had been planned before the mission call had arrived.

The remodeling was kept a surprise for father. On the night of his return, as the family gathered around the living room to listen to his mission experiences, one of the children asked if he had seen any miracles. He put his arm around his wife and replied, "Your mother is the greatest miracle that one could ever find!"[13]

## A Father's Testimony and a Patriarchal Blessing

There had been other miracles as well, one of which had come in the form of a much-sought-after revelation, as David O. McKay later recalled.

> I was a boy and heard the testimony of my father regarding the revelation that came to him of the divinity of the mission of the Prophet Joseph. . . . When [father] began preaching in his native land [of Scotland], and bore testimony of the restoration of the gospel of Jesus Christ, he noticed that the people turned away from him. They were bitter in their hearts against anything Mormon, and the name of Joseph Smith seemed to arouse antagonism in their hearts. One day he concluded that the best way to reach these people would be to preach just the simple principles, the atonement of the Lord Jesus Christ, the first principles of the gospel, and not bear testimony of the restoration. In a month or so he became oppressed with a gloomy, downcast feeling and he could not enter into the spirit of his work. He did not really know what was the matter; but his mind became obstructed; his spirit

became depressed; he was oppressed and hampered; and that feeling of depression continued until it weighed him down with such heaviness that he went to the Lord and said: "Unless I can get this feeling removed, I shall have to go home. I can't continue my work thus hampered."

The discouragement continued for some time after that, when, one morning, before daylight, following a sleepless night, he decided to retire to a cave, near the ocean, where he knew he would be shut off from the world entirely, and there pour out his soul to God and ask why he was oppressed with this feeling, what he had done, and what he could do to throw it off and continue his work. He started out in the dark towards the cave. He became so eager to get to it that he started to run. As he was leaving the town, he was hailed by an officer who wanted to know what was the matter. He gave some noncommittal but satisfying reply and was permitted to go on. Something just seemed to drive him; he had to get relief. He entered the cave or sheltered opening, and said: "Oh, Father, what can I do to have this feeling removed? I must have it lifted or I cannot continue in this work"; and he heard a voice . . . say: "Testify that Joseph Smith is a Prophet of God."[14]

Back from Scotland, David's father was soon called to serve as bishop, and since Huntsville had no hotel or restaurant, Bishop McKay's home was always open to visitors, including numerous stake officers and general authorities. One of the happiest days in the McKay home came when they were visited by the First Presidency of the Church, President Wilford Woodruff and his counselors, George Q. Cannon and Joseph F. Smith. During the delicious family meal, the McKays' youngest, an infant, was being tended in another room. When the baby was finally brought in, President Woodruff took the child in his arms and gave him a blessing.[15]

One frequent visitor was Church patriarch John Smith, who stayed at the McKay home while giving patriarchal blessings to the saints in the Huntsville area. During one of his visits he gave young David his patriarchal blessing just weeks before the boy turned fourteen. Patriarch Smith declared:

Brother David Oman McKay, thou art in thy youth and need instruction, therefore I say unto thee, be taught of thy parents the way of life and salvation, that at an early day you may be prepared for a responsible position, for the eye of the Lord is upon thee. . . . The Lord has a work for thee to do, in which thou shalt see much of the world, assist in gathering scattered Israel and also labor in the ministry. It shall be thy lot to sit in council with thy brethren and preside among the people and exhort the Saints to faithfulness.[16]

## Seeking Knowledge by Study and Also by Faith

David found it easy, as he later described, "to understand and believe the reality of the visions of the Prophet Joseph" and "to accept his vision, the appearance of God the Father and his Son, Jesus Christ, to the boy praying."[17] He expressed his conviction to his fellow saints, as told in the minutes of one of his Aaronic Priesthood quorum meetings: "David O. McKay bore his testimony and said he felt pleased at coming to meeting."[18]

Even so, he continued to seek for a greater witness, a divine confirmation, for which he "secretly prayed most earnestly on hillside and in meadow."[19] One of those instances he described in detail.

One day in my youth I was [searching for lost] cattle. While climbing a steep hill, I stopped to let my horse rest, and there, once again, an intense desire came over me to receive a manifestation of the truth of the Restored Gospel. I dismounted, threw my reins over my horse's head, and there under a serviceberry bush I prayed that God would declare to me the truth of his revelation to Joseph Smith. . . . I prayed fervently and sincerely and with as much faith as a young boy could muster.

At the conclusion of the prayer, I arose from my knees, threw the reins over my faithful pony's head, and got into the saddle. As I started along the trail again, I remember saying to myself: "No spiritual manifestation has come to me. If I am true to myself, I must say I am just the same 'old boy' that I was before I prayed."[20]

The answer would eventually come, but would require patience and diligence. Meanwhile, David continued to faithfully perform his duties.

These included serving in the Sunday School and in the presidency of the deacons and teachers quorums as they kept the chapel clean and chopped wood for the chapel and the widows of the ward.

He also followed the Lord's command for future missionaries to prepare themselves by learning of things past, present, and even future, "that ye may be prepared in all things when I shall send you."[21] David was a diligent student with "an unquenchable appetite for learning that seemed to foreshadow a career in education. He read and memorized passages from much of the world's great literature, and in later years his sermons and writings were filled with quotations from such literature."[22] His thirst for learning went beyond merely filling the school assignments. While working a summer job that required him to ride a horse some ten hours a day, he used the time to study great literature, particularly the English poets.

David graduated from Huntsville's eighth grade and then continued his education at Weber State Academy in Ogden for two years, whereupon he returned to the Huntsville school as principal. Still he sought higher education, hoping to enroll at the University of Utah, while three of his siblings wanted to do the same. But limited family funds seemed to preclude the possibility for any of them. Just then, Grandmother Evans made a huge financial gift to each of her three children. Jennette's brother and sister urged her to invest her money for future security, but Jennette insisted on a different kind of investment. "Every cent of this," she replied, "goes into the education of our children."[23]

David made the most of the opportunity. Entering the University of Utah at the age of twenty-one, he debated, played on the football team, played the piano in a musical group, and met the girl whom he would later marry, Emma Ray Riggs. When he graduated in four years, it was as president and valedictorian of his class, and the university immediately offered him a teaching position. The offer was a dream come true, for David loved to teach, and he made plans accordingly, knowing that this would provide the opportunity he needed to establish his career, marry his sweetheart, and begin a family.

## Answering the Call and Learning to Be a Missionary

Just when all was in place for this new phase of life, a letter arrived calling him on a mission to Great Britain. As with most missionary calls at that time, his was a surprise; the Church at that time did not ask all young men to prepare to serve missions. David struggled, but knew that no one in his family had ever turned down a call from the Lord. Somehow he already understood the truth that he would eloquently express decades later:

> The most worthy calling in life . . . is that in which man can serve best his fellow man. . . . To no other group of men in all the world is given a better opportunity to engage in the noblest calling in life than that which is afforded the elders in the Church of Jesus Christ of Latter-day Saints. To establish salvation and peace . . . their lives are dedicated; to make the world a better and fitter place for man, their talents and means are consecrated.[24]

Even so, parting from his beloved family was painful. In his journal he recorded his feelings on the day he left his hometown: "The saddest morning ever spent in Huntsville or anywhere else! At eleven o'clock bid my home, dear ones, relatives, and friends goodbye. Sobbed."[25]

Traveling overland with his fellow missionaries, David journeyed via Chicago and Washington, D.C. to New York City. From there they sailed across the Atlantic toward the homeland of his ancestors. Arriving in Liverpool, he was assigned to serve in Scotland—cherished land of his McKay ancestors and of his father's own mission field. This assignment and the subsequent train ride several hours north to Glasgow were intriguing to the new missionary.

But he was still far from home and loved ones, and began to feel discouraged, as reflected in his journal entries over the next several days. "A gloomy-looking place and I was a *gloomy-feeling boy*," he recorded of his arrival at the mission home in Glasgow.[26] Writing the next day about the city's deplorable conditions, he noted that "It is enough to make a person sick."[27] The next day, his first Sunday there, proved happier as he "spent a very pleasant afternoon," followed by "a good meeting" in which he preached.[28]

The small market town of Lanark was his first assigned area, where on his first morning he went tracting and distributed well over a hundred pamphlets. "Although people treated me courteously and with a few exceptions accepted the tracts," he recorded, "yet I never felt so gloomy in my life. I have heaved a *thousand* sighs."[29] He was, as he would later explain, "quite discouraged and downhearted," but "these feelings were removed by humble prayer."[30]

### Pressing Forward in Service

A few days later he spoke for the first time at a street meeting, a willing but worried missionary, as he described in his journal.

> The people stood in their doorways to listen. Some stood in the street one block away. Here, standing in the middle of the street on both sides of which was a long row of whitewashed houses about six feet to the square, I made my first open-air speech. I shall never forget it. The day was cold and cloudy (I had been wishing that it would rain), and the street was dismal and uninviting. Perhaps there were about thirty eager-looking eyes staring wonderingly [into] mine. My remarks were brief and made in fear and trembling!!![31]

Several days later when a returning missionary boarded his ship for America, David was present. "To see him go made me homesick," David recorded, "and thoughts that I would have to stay here two years longer made me sad."[32]

Just over a week later, he wrote that after he and his companion had returned to their lodgings and eaten a "good supper," they "retired to dream of home and happy days gone by; such has been my experience nearly every night since coming here; but with the morning comes disappointment and loneliness."[33]

After another week passed, he made the following journal entry: "At night, I was tired out. My head ached; my muscles ached; my heart ached."[34]

And yet, as David continued to do his duty, there soon came an encouraging experience. It happened at the end of a particularly difficult day in which "the people were bitter. One woman tore a tract in pieces as soon as I gave it to her. Another, finding out what it was, shut the door in my face." But as David and his companion persisted, they "met an estimable old lady who, after hearing who I was and what I was doing, became very much interested." A lengthy conversation ensued, during which the elderly woman expressed her feeling that after being so long in her church, she did not think Christ would forsake her now. Finally, as David was about to leave, she extended her hand and with tears in her eyes said, "God bless ye, for I believe you're doin' a noble work." David was touched, and recorded in his journal: "She did me a *world* of good."[35]

From that point on there is a noticeable change in David's journal entries, which speak less of discouragement and more of better days, increased effectiveness, and greater inspiration. "Was called to speak first," he wrote of a branch meeting. "Enjoyed a good spirit."[36] During Sunday School one day, as one of the revelations to Joseph Smith was read, "the truth flashed upon our minds as clear and distinct as the sun in the cloudless sky. Such instances as this show the divinity of Joseph Smith's mission." Then at a meeting later that day, they "had another feast."[37] In yet another meeting, as David was speaking about the Atonement, he thought he would cite a certain familiar scripture, but suddenly and unexplainably "could not recall a word; everything seemed dark," when suddenly another scripture "flashed before me and I proceeded with my speech. It was a peculiar experience."[38]

David served, studied, preached, prayed, gave priesthood blessings, and grew in his calling, increasingly losing himself in missionary work. Meanwhile, he learned also from the example and counsel of others about the joy of service. One day one of the sisters from the small branch, composed of people of modest means, unexpectedly showed up and handed David and his companion some much-needed warm bedding, including woolen blankets. "Her kind act touched the heart of everyone. It seemed impossible to express our feelings. She was truly happy, for she had done something which filled her benevolent soul with joy. When she was leaving, she said, 'I leave my peace and blessing with you.'"[39]

David was further blessed when he received from his father a long and encouraging letter "full of wisdom and good advice."[40]

## Words in Stone, Message to the Heart

After nearly seven months in Lanark, David was reassigned to work in the city of Stirling, affording him the greatest opportunity yet to appreciate his Scottish heritage. A city of distinguished royal and historic significance, Stirling is home to the grandest of Scottish castles and some of the most important battlegrounds in Scottish history. Here heroes such as William Wallace and Robert the Bruce valiantly fought to preserve Scotland's independence against great odds. Scottish history comes alive at Stirling.

But it was the present that proved difficult for David when, on his very first morning in Stirling, he was "snubbed in tracting" and began to feel "discouraged" and "homesick." That afternoon, on March 26, 1898, he and his companion decided to go sight-seeing. While they were not breaking the rules of their mission, neither were they advancing the Kingdom, and thus "really not doing our duty," as he would later say.[41]

His journal recounts their grand tour, including "old historic Stirling Castle . . . , this rendezvous for so many kings!" They saw the impressive stone statue of King Robert the Bruce, and the field "where the immortal Bruce with 30,000 men defeated the English army of 80,000 men."

They gazed also on the towering stone monument to William Wallace, "reared in commemoration of his worth and honor," and viewed "the battlefield . . . where Wallace regained the castle from the English."

David was moved: "All these places . . . awaken an indescribable interest in and profound respect for the heroes and gallant chiefs of bonny [beautiful] Scotland!"[42] The impression would remain with him; decades later, when visiting this same spot with his children, he would relate in vivid detail Wallace's heroic response to the English judges who tortured and beheaded him.[43]

Thus inspired by the heroes who had done their duty for Scotland, David and his companion began walking home. "As we returned to the town, I saw an unfinished building standing back from the sidewalk several yards. Over the front door was a stone arch, something unusual in a residence, and what was still more unusual, I could see from the sidewalk that there was an inscription chiseled in that arch."[44]

"I said to Elder Johnston, 'I'm going to see what that is.' I was halfway up the graveled walk when there came to my eyesight a striking motto, carved in stone: 'Whate'er thou art, act well thy part.'"[45] "That message struck me,"[46] for it was "as if it came from One in whose service we were engaged."[47]

David's love of drama would have prepared him to take immediate notice of this directive about acting one's part. But the words may have resonated in another way as well, for they are nearly verbatim from Alexander Pope, the greatest English poet of the eighteenth century, whose *An Essay on Man* includes this line: "Act well your part, there all the honour lies."

David had assiduously studied the English poets and would retain a lifelong love of English literature. Many were the passages he had memorized and would later quote, including passages from Pope,[48] who loomed large as one of the most influential authors in early America. In fact, Pope's verse about acting well one's part was known to the American Founding Fathers, who quoted it constantly in their letters.[49] It was probably familiar also to young David O. McKay.

As he and his companion continued walking home, the meaning of the words seemed to unfold.

> We walked quietly, but I said to myself, or the Spirit within me whispered, "You are a member of the Church of Jesus Christ of Latter-day Saints. More than that, you are a representative of the Church." Then I thought what we had done that morning. We had been sightseeing. We had gained historical instruction and information, it is true, and I was thrilled with it. . . . However, that was not missionary work. That afternoon, by the time we found our lodgings, I accepted the message given to me on that stone, and from that moment we tried to do our part as missionaries.[50]

The impression left on David was as permanent as the words on the stone. "The message on this stone changed [him], and it became an important guideline throughout his life,"[51] his "lifelong motto,"[52] and "one of the major factors in [his] growth and development. He referred to it often during his long and productive life."[53]

His journal entries from that time forward reflect his increased tracting efforts[54]—despite the fact that, as he confided in one entry, "Oh, I do dislike tracting; there is nothing pleasant about it."[55] Thus did duty prevail over dislike as he chose to act well his part, and within days he was feeling different about things: "This is the most pleasant tracting day I have experienced," he recorded one evening.[56] One of his favorite sayings in life would become, "Do your duty, that is best; leave unto the Lord the rest."

## Greater Responsibility and Greater Witness

Several weeks later he was handed a letter appointing him to the presidency of the Scottish Conference. Feeling under-qualified and overwhelmed, he "seemed to be seized with a feeling of gloom and fear, lest in accepting this I would prove incompetent. I walked to a secret spot in the wood, just below Wallace's Monument, and there dedicating my services to the Lord, implored him for his divine assistance."[57]

Responding to the letter, David wrote back: "I truly feel weak and unable to fill this position—and if I expressed my own desire, I would say, 'Choose another.' Yet I feel to say, 'Not my will, but thine be done.' And since God, through his servants, has seen fit to place this duty upon me, I shall accept it, depending upon his unerring Spirit for guidance."[58]

He not only accepted but followed through, despite the increased burden. "The responsibility is weighing heavily upon me," he recorded a few days later.[59] The following week he wrote, "The responsibility is growing heavier."[60] Some two weeks later, in a journal entry intended to cover a period of five days, he stated, "Time was spent in attending to a thousand and one little duties in the conference and branch. No time to even write in my diary."[61] In this continuing flurry of activity and service, David was acting well his divinely appointed part.

About a year later, on May 29, 1899, a conference-wide priesthood meeting was held in Glasgow, beginning at ten in the morning and lasting for several hours as the missionaries gave an accounting of their labors and experiences. Several of those in attendance reported on the remarkable event, one missionary calling it "the greatest spiritual feast I ever enjoyed."[62] Another referred to it as "the grandest meeting I ever witnessed in my life."[63] Yet another stated: "Great was the Spirit of God on that occasion."[64]

David himself described "the intensity of the inspiration of that occasion. Everybody felt the rich outpouring of the Spirit of the Lord.

All present were truly of one heart and one mind. Never before had I experienced such an emotion."[65]

> A peaceful heavenly influence pervaded the room. Some of the elders were so affected by it that they had to express their feelings in tears. Just as Brother Young sat down after giving his report, Elder Woolfenden said: "Brethren, there are angels in this room! I see two there by Brother Young . . ." We each felt their presence. Elders wept for joy and could not contain themselves. Sobs came from different parts of the room. . . . All joined with me in a prayer of thanksgiving to the Lord for his blessings and manifestations. President McMurrin then addressed the meeting, saying among other things that the "Lord has accepted our labors and at this time we stand pure before him."[66]

This rare experience brought to David the "spiritual manifestation," as he would later say, "for which I had prayed as a boy in my teens," and it "came as a natural sequence to the performance of duty."[67]

"President . . . McMurrin continued, 'Yes, brethren, there are angels in this room;' and the announcement was not startling, but seemed wholly proper. Designating two of the brethren, he said their guardian angels were present."[68] The mission president then addressed David:

> He turned to me and gave what I thought then was more of a caution than a promise. . . . Paraphrasing the words of the Savior to Peter, he said: "Let me say to you, Brother David, Satan hath desired [to have] you that he may sift you as wheat, but God is mindful of you." Then he added, "If you will keep the faith, you will yet sit in the leading councils of the Church."[69]

David would never be the same.

> His words made an indelible impression upon me. . . . At that moment there flashed into my mind temptations that had beset my path, and I realized even better than President McMurrin, or any other man, how truly he had spoken. . . . With the resolve then and there to keep the faith, there was born a desire to be of service to my fellow men, and with it a realization, a glimpse at least, of what I owed to the elder who first carried the message of the Restored Gospel to my grandfather and grandmother who had accepted the message years before in the north of Scotland, and in South Wales.[70]

David's gratitude would increase when later during his mission he visited his father's native town in northern Scotland, and his mother's native town in Wales. Many years afterwards he came again to Wales, to the house where his mother had lived as a girl.

> I thought, as . . . I stood in that small bedroom, how different life would be now if two humble elders had not knocked at that door a hundred years ago! And how different life would be if my mother's father and mother had not accepted that message! . . . I expressed gratitude, as I sensed it probably never so keenly before, . . . in that little room.[71]

## A Spiritual Giant Acting Well His Part

The unforgettable lessons learned by David in Scotland would shape the rest of his life. He returned home to marry his sweetheart, raise a family, and become an educator. At the young age of thirty-two he was called into the Quorum of the Twelve, and in his first talk as an apostle he emphasized the principle he had learned as a young missionary: "The man who knows what his duty is and fails to perform it, is not true to himself; he is not true to his brethren; he is not living in the light which God and conscience provides. That is where we stand."[72]

His own duties as an apostle included a special assignment as "a missionary to travel around the world." During that memorable global tour, he was repeatedly blessed with the gift of tongues; he dedicated China for the preaching of the gospel; and he received a vision of the Savior whose special witness he was. And while in Hawaii, he with his companions stood on the side of an extinct volcano, where "the veil was thin between us and departed friends, when we stood in prayer . . . and poured our thanksgiving to God for what he had done for President Joseph F. Smith . . . and other missionaries who carried the gospel message to the Hawaiian people."[73]

As President of the Church, David O. McKay emphasized the phrase, "Every member a missionary." It was a concise expression of the truths once taught at the waters of Mormon by Alma, who had asked those about to be baptized if they were ready to "mourn with those that mourn; yea, and comfort those that stand in need of comfort, and to stand as witnesses of God at all times and in all things, and in all places that ye may be in, even until death."[74]

President McKay lived these teachings himself and "wielded a remarkable influence among his fellowmen. . . . His inspiring personality, sense of humor, and sparkling demeanor won many friends for himself and the Church"[75] during his long service as a general authority, longer than anyone else up to that time. During his nearly two decades as President of the Church, from 1951 until 1970, he led the saints and traveled the world while the number of missions doubled, Church membership nearly tripled, and the number of missionaries increased sixfold.

He was a powerful teacher and preacher of righteousness.

> His main religious message concerned the reality of Christ, his Atonement and resurrection, and the restoration of the gospel of Christ through the Prophet Joseph Smith. He taught that Christ's gospel was meant to transform the individual and thus change society. The sanctity of the home, kindness, mercy, tolerance, spirituality, love of freedom, the power of prayer, charity, personal integrity—these were the subjects of his sermons and writings.[76]

His emphasis on the family is enshrined in his saying: "No other success can compensate for failure in the home." As husband, father, friend, and President of the Church, David O. McKay acted well his part.

Upon his passing at age ninety-six, he was mourned by saints and many others the world over. At the funeral, his counselor President N. Eldon Tanner observed: "He was loved and respected and revered by millions of people who now mourn his passing." President Tanner then added, "During his whole life he was a true exemplar of the life of Christ."[77]

President McKay himself had taught that every person's "chief concern in life . . . should be the development of a Christ-like character."[78]

Nothing was more important in his own life in achieving such character than the decision to act well his part, thereby following the example of the Savior Himself. When faced with the overwhelming burden of the world's sins, Jesus did "tremble because of pain" and "bleed at every pore," suffering "both body and spirit—and would that I might not drink the bitter cup, and shrink—nevertheless, glory be to the Father, and I partook and finished my preparations unto the children of men."[79]

Those who come unto Christ, and bring others to Him, must likewise learn to do their duty. To the Savior's Latter-day Saints, all of whom have the duty of standing as His witnesses, He has commanded that each "learn his duty, and to act in the office in which he is appointed, in all diligence."[80]

As Elder Gordon B. Hinckley stated in general conference, "'What e'er thou art, act well thy part' was the motto that President McKay read on a stone in Scotland, and it applies to each of us."[81]

## Legacy of David O. McKay

Born in Utah just decades after the pioneers had arrived, David grew up believing in the testimony of Joseph Smith but wanting to know for sure. As a teenager he knelt in the woods to pray, but no answer came. Years later as a missionary in Scotland, David saw a stone plaque with the inscription, "Whate'er thou art, act well thy part." The words came with power to his heart and changed his life, and shortly thereafter he received the testimony he had sought. David O. McKay became a powerful missionary and prophet, an example for all latter-day missionaries of the importance of acting well one's part.

CHAPTER 15

# ~ Gordon B. Hinckley ~
## Forget Yourself and Go to Work

When Elder David O. McKay was making his world tour as an apostle, Gordon B. Hinckley was a deacon in Salt Lake City. "I was just a normal little boy," he would modestly say of himself decades later. "I have done nothing more than try to do what has been asked of me, and I've tried to do it the best I could."[1] But the entirely selfless and dedicated way in which he went about his work helped him become one of the Lord's most effective missionaries and prophets.

### Learning from Work, Stars, and Books

Gordon learned to work at an early age. "My father had the idea that his boys ought to learn to work," he recalled. In addition to the "immense amount of work to be done constantly" around their large house in the city, Gordon's father bought a farm where his boys could work in the summer. "The chores never seemed to end," Gordon remembered, and "included everything from digging post holes to helping with the irrigating to working our large orchard, where we had apple, peach, cherry, pear, and apricot trees. At harvest time, we were expected to help bring in the fruit." Looking back later, he saw that "the farm provided a fertile environment for a number of lessons, including the fact that we can reap only what we have sown."[2]

After the work was done, Gordon and his brother would sleep out under the stars. Gazing into the night sky, they learned another lesson:

> On those clear, clean summer nights, we would lie on our backs in that old wagon box and look at the myriads of stars in the heavens. We could identify some of the constellations and other stars as they were illustrated in the encyclopedia which was always available in our family library. We identified some of the more visible patterns in the heavens, but our favorite was the North Star. Each night, like many generations of boys before us, we would trace the Big Dipper, down the handle and out past the cup, to find the North Star.
>
> We came to know of the constancy of that star. As the earth turned, the others appeared to move through the night. But the North Star held its position in line with the axis of the earth. Because of those boyhood musings, the polar star came to mean something to me. I recognized it as a constant in the midst of change. It was something that could always be counted on, something that was dependable, an anchor in what otherwise appeared to me a moving and unstable firmament.[3]

The encyclopedia describing the stars was but one of many books with which Gordon became acquainted in the family library of their city home. In that otherwise modest residence, the library stood out as something remarkable, an expression of his parents' ardent love of learning. The room was even adorned with statues of Joseph Smith and Abraham Lincoln, and furnished with a large oak table, comfortable chairs, and a good lamp, all surrounded by shelves filled with over a thousand books, including works of history, literature, and reference.

In this veritable world of words, Gordon began to learn not only of constellations and astronomy—"of things . . . in heaven," as the revelation states—but also of the other things the Lord commands his prospective missionaries to study, "things . . . under the earth; things which have been, things which are, things which must shortly come to pass; things which are at home, things which are abroad; the wars and the perplexities of the nations, and the judgments which are on the land; and a knowledge also of countries and of kingdoms"—in order to "be prepared in all things" when the Lord would send them to fulfill the "mission with which I have commissioned you."[4] Gordon was learning of the vastness of the world, never suspecting that he would one day travel further across the globe than any of God's messengers before him.

## Heritage, Testimony, and Trial

Gordon was also learning of his own heritage and family legacy, including his grandfather Ira Hinckley who had heard Joseph and Hyrum preach in Nauvoo, and had come west with the saints, burying his beloved wife along the trail. Ira later remarried and set down roots, only to receive a call from President Brigham Young to uproot his family and move to southern Utah. "They went where they were asked to go," said Gordon of his grandfather, "and did what they were asked to do, regardless of what it cost in terms of comfort or money or life itself."[5]

Ira's son Bryant continued the heritage of dedication, serving in many civic and Church capacities in Salt Lake City, including as stake president, mission president, and member of a general board. He also worked closely with President Heber J. Grant filling special projects and writing articles, manuals, and books.

After the death of Bryant's first wife, who had borne him several children, he married Ada Bitner. She was a brilliant and lovely woman who, like her husband, "thrived on education and learning."[6] She bore five children, the oldest of whom was Gordon.

Attending his first stake priesthood meeting as a deacon, Gordon sat on the back row of the Tabernacle while his father, a member of the stake presidency, sat on the stand. To open the meeting, all stood and sang the familiar hymn written about the Prophet Joseph Smith:

> Praise to the man who communed with Jehovah!
> Jesus anointed that Prophet and Seer.
> Blessed to open the last dispensation,
> Kings shall extol him, and nations revere.

As young Gordon joined in the singing, he felt a power he had never known before.

> Something happened within me as I heard those men of faith sing. It touched my heart. It gave me a feeling that was difficult to describe. I felt a great moving power, both emotional and spiritual. . . . There came into my heart a conviction that the man of whom they sang was really a prophet of God. I knew then, by the power of the Holy Ghost, that Joseph Smith was indeed a prophet of God.[7]

While Gordon was attending the University of Utah and working his way through school, his mother was diagnosed with cancer. Gordon's father took her to Los Angeles for treatment, and wrote to the children: "She is in the hands of the Lord. He can spare her life and raise her and if it is his will, she will live. If not, all will be well. . . . Go about and do your work and do what is right and all will be well."[8]

Ada was not spared. "We put on a front of bravery and fought back the tears," Gordon recalled. "But inside, the wounds were deep and painful."[9]

### A Mission Call and Means

Other difficulties arose as Gordon expanded his educational horizons and began to think more deeply and question more thoroughly, including "in a slight measure" the faith of his parents. But his father always had a listening ear and open mind, and the testimony that had come to Gordon years earlier would prove to be "a bulwark to which I could cling during those very difficult years."[10]

They were also years of vital preparation as he educated himself for the future. He majored in English and minored in Latin and Greek, reading not only Homer but also the New Testament in the original. His education was rounded out with other courses like economics, sociology, and geology, but language remained his first love, and he was determined to eventually attend the prestigious Columbia School of Journalism in New York City.

Accordingly, when his bishop asked him if he had considered a mission, Gordon was shocked. It was the age of the Great Depression, and missionary service for young men was the exception. But when the bishop asked Gordon if he would go, Gordon agreed, even though he knew it would mean using the savings he had accumulated to attend Columbia.

Shortly thereafter, however, his savings was wiped out by a bank failure, and when Gordon's call arrived assigning him to work in London—the most expensive mission in the world—the problem of expenses loomed large. His father promised to help, as did his brother, but it was still not enough.

Then the family made a remarkable discovery. For years Ada had privately emptied her pocket change into a pot which was now found to contain enough to make up the deficit and allow Gordon to answer the Lord's call. The Lord had provided a way, as the prophet Nephi said, to accomplish what He had commanded, and Gordon was grateful—not only to the Lord, but also to his mother for her quiet sacrifice and inspired foresight.

As Gordon boarded the train to leave Salt Lake City, his father handed him a card that contained just five words, quoting the Savior's command from the New Testament: "Be not afraid, only believe."[11] The card went with him in the mission field, and the five words would guide him throughout the coming decades.[12]

Aboard ship on his Atlantic crossing to England, Gordon read additional words of the Savior, these spoken to him personally in his patriarchal blessing he had received years before: "Thou shalt become a mighty and valiant leader in the midst of Israel. . . . Thou shalt be a messenger of peace; the nations of the earth shall hear thy voice and be brought to a knowledge of the truth by the wonderful testimony which thou shalt bear."[13] Even as he read, the ship was carrying him closer to his first field of labor.

## Discouragement and Its Remedy

His first assignment in England was in historic Preston in Lancashire County, where a century earlier Heber C. Kimball and his colleagues had successfully opened up the work in the British Isles. But times had changed. Anti-Mormon sentiment was strong. And the Depression had left many impoverished and hardened.

On Gordon's first day there, his companion insisted—despite Gordon's reluctance—on holding a street meeting at the marketplace in the public square. The two elders took turns speaking, although Gordon later admitted to being "terrified. I stepped onto that little stand, looked at the crowd of people, and wondered what I was doing there. They were dreadfully poor and looked to have absolutely no interest in religion."[14]

Adding to his trauma was a violent attack of hay fever caused by the heavy pollen in the air. "The day I arrived there I started crying," he recalled.[15] The allergies and tears continued, sapping his energy and diminishing his resolve. Finally, in deep discouragement, Gordon wrote to his father: "I feel I am wasting my time and your money. I don't see any point in my staying here. No one will listen."[16]

Two weeks passed. One morning during scripture study Gordon read the Savior's promise to his apostles as recorded in the New Testament: "For whosoever will save his life shall lose it: and whosoever will lose his life for my sake shall find it."[17] Later that day a letter arrived from Gordon's father. Tearing open the envelope, Gordon hastily unfolded a single sheet of paper that contained these few words:

*Dear Gordon,*

*I have your letter. I have only one suggestion. Forget yourself
and go to work.*

*Love,*

*Dad*

With letter in hand, a subdued Elder Hinckley climbed the stairs to
his bedroom, knelt down, and in response to his earthly father's counsel,
made a life-changing commitment to his Heavenly Father: "Dear Father,
I am sorry. I pledge and covenant that I will try to forget myself and lose
myself in thy service."[18]

As Gordon threw himself into the work with renewed commitment,
something miraculous happened, as he later explained. "The sun began
to shine in my life. I had a new interest. I saw the beauty of this land. I
saw the greatness of the people,"[19] and "there came into my heart a great
consuming love for this work of God and for His Beloved Son, the
Redeemer of the world."[20]

It was that love that motivated Gordon's brief but poignant lament
over the people in Preston who were being offered salvation by two young
missionaries: "Old Preston. . . . When will you put away that unwarranted
pride . . . and accept a word of light that a couple of young fellows are
feebly preaching?"[21]

Transferred to the town of Nelson, still in Lancashire County, Gordon
persisted. "Even when there weren't many who wanted to listen to the
missionaries, he stayed positive," recalled a companion. His accomplish-
ments during his eight months in Lancashire County demonstrate how
well he was carrying out his father's advice: 8,785 pamphlets distributed,
over 400 hours spent with members in missionary work, 191 meetings
attended, and 200 gospel conversations held.[22]

There would come, of course, other challenging days, but parental
influence—even from his departed mother—would continue to strengthen

Gordon. "I experienced times of discouragement on my mission," he would recall, "as does every missionary. On an occasion or two, when the clouds were particularly dark, I felt in a very real but indescribable way the protecting, guiding, encouraging influence of my mother. She seemed very close. I tried then, as I have tried since, to so conduct my life and perform my duty as to bring honor to her name."[23]

## Faith and Service in London

An unexpected transfer took Gordon to the London mission home, where he served for the remainder of his mission. London enthralled him. Forever after he would refer to it as "my town." It was impossible, he observed, to live there without "developing a love for the place."[24]

He also loved his mission president, Apostle Joseph F. Merrill, who called Gordon as an assistant. To work with a member of the Quorum of the Twelve was exhilarating, providing valuable insight into Church administration and missionary work.

Meanwhile, Gordon's proselyting work required him to think quickly and speak deftly in spirited exchanges with hecklers in Hyde Park. At Church, Gordon taught primary children and unruly young adults. As Director of Publicity for the mission, he wrote numerous articles for the *Millennial Star* (the Church magazine in England), and an influential article on the Church's early history for a widely-circulated non-Church magazine. He also learned to utilize the power of media as he played filmstrips introducing the Book of Mormon and key events of the Restoration.

One of his most memorable experiences began one morning in the mission office when President Merrill showed Elder Hinckley several London newspapers containing reviews of a popular book pretending to be a history of the Mormons but painting a false and ugly picture.

"I want you to go down to the publisher," instructed President Merrill, "and protest the publication of this book."

Gordon's first thought was, "Why are you sending *me*? I am just a boy, and you're a distinguished man. Why don't you go yourself?"

But without objection, Gordon accepted the assignment. He immediately went to his room and knelt in prayer, wondering if Moses had experienced the same feeling when he was called to confront Pharaoh.

With a "churning stomach" but with faith in the Lord, Gordon set off to the offices of Skeffington and Son, Ltd. Having no prior appointment, he presented himself and his card to the receptionist, and asked to see Mr. Skeffington. It took just a moment for the receptionist to disappear and return to declare that Mr. Skeffington was too busy, to which Gordon replied that he had come five thousand miles and would be happy to wait.

He took a seat, and after the receptionist made several more trips into her boss's office, she finally announced to Gordon that Mr. Skeffington would see him.

The publisher sat at his desk puffing a large cigar and looking disdainful as young Gordon produced the newspaper reviews and began to explain his position. Skeffington seemed unconvinced and unwilling to help. But as Gordon continued, he sensed a higher power speaking through him. Skeffington began to soften, and Gordon stated, "I am sure that a high-principled man such as yourself would not wish to do injury to a people who have already suffered so much for their religion."

Suddenly, in a move that committed his company to considerable expense, Skeffington agreed to recall all unsold books and add to each a statement that the book was not history but fiction, and that "no offense was intended against the respected Mormon people."

So impressed was Mr. Skeffington with this young Mormon missionary that he thereafter stayed in touch by sending Elder Hinckley an annual Christmas card.

But it was Gordon himself who was most impressed by the experience. "It was a tremendous lesson for me," he later recalled. "I came to know that if we put our faith in the Lord and go forward in trust, he will open the way. . . . I've never forgotten it. That experience left a mark on my life."[25]

Years later, speaking to missionaries, he counseled: "Is there a missionary who has never felt fear? I know of none. . . . All of us experience fear now and again. But God has not given us the spirit of fear. That comes from the adversary. When we recognize that, then we can tell the adversary to get behind us, and we can go forward with courage."[26]

## Finishing His Mission and Traveling Home

In one of Gordon's last assignments as a missionary, he spoke at the first annual British Mission MIA conference. "What a delightful world this would be," he challenged, "if burning in each young heart there was an individual, soul-satisfying testimony that God lives and that Jesus Christ is his son, the Redeemer of the world."[27]

With that testimony burning in his own heart, Gordon left England and his missionary service which had, in the words of biographer Sheri Dew, "literally changed his life."

> He knew that what he had learned, spiritually and otherwise, could not have been duplicated in any other setting—certainly not in the classrooms and ivy-covered passageways of Columbia University. The harvest of baptisms had been sparse for him as well as his associates, but he was unconcerned about his tally of converts, for he was a different person than he had been just twenty-four months before when he had written his father that he might as well come home. "What a blessing it became," he later said, "to set aside my own selfish interests to the greater interests of the work of the Lord."[28]

On his way home in June 1935, Gordon toured Europe. In Germany, Nazi troops were everywhere. He saw Nuremberg draped with Nazi banners and flags just three days after Hitler had staged a large rally. In

Dresden, as Gordon watched an aged woman tearfully place flowers at the Unknown Soldier memorial, he also heard the nearby drums of marching brigades of Hitler Youth. "History is going to repeat itself," he thought. "In a coming day, men and women will kneel at this monument and mourn the loss of the youths marching just a block away."[29] Having just spent two years as a messenger of peace, Gordon was sobered to see the approach of war.

His journey home led him through New York City, where he took time to walk across the campus of Columbia University and inquire about admission. He also went to Rochester and nearby Hill Cumorah, where he attended the annual pageant and the dedication of the statue of Moroni atop the hill.

Arriving at last in Salt Lake City, Gordon felt relieved to be home. "He knew one thing for sure—he had no desire ever to travel again."[30]

As the last remaining item of mission business, Gordon reported to the office of the First Presidency to fulfill his mission president's final assignment of explaining the need for more mission materials. Ushered into the presence of President Heber J. Grant and his counselors, Gordon was told he had fifteen minutes. Over an hour later the First Presidency was still posing questions to him and engaging him in discussion.

When the meeting finally closed, Gordon's mission business was at last completed. He looked ahead to the future and set his sights on the long-deferred degree at Columbia.

### Going Forward with Faith and Courage

But as Elder Neal A. Maxwell observed, that fateful meeting with the First Presidency "in a sense never ended," constituting the commencement of decades of service by Gordon at Church headquarters.[31] Just two days after the meeting, one of President Grant's counselors, David O. McKay, called Gordon and offered him a job as an executive secretary of the Radio, Publicity, and Mission Literature Committee which the First

Presidency had just formed to deal with the needs that Gordon had made known to them.

Gordon accepted. His small salary was supplemented with additional income from teaching a seminary class. It was enough to start a family, which he soon did by marrying Marjorie Pay in the Salt Lake Temple.

As Gordon's service and involvement at Church headquarters expanded, war engulfed the nations of Europe. Hitler conquered country after country and then turned his sights on the island nation where Gordon had served. From his beloved England, where he had once learned his great lesson of selfless service, now came another powerful lesson that Gordon would never forget. On June 4, 1940, London broadcast to the world a much-anticipated speech to Parliament by the new Prime Minister, Winston Churchill. London had been under heavy attack by the German air force, and neither Hitler nor the United States nor even England itself—including its King and Parliament—believed that England could hold out much longer. Everyone expected to hear Prime Minister Churchill plead for a negotiated peace that would allow Hitler to rule the continent.

Gordon was listening intently that day, and he and the rest of the world were surprised by what they heard. Decades later Gordon would tell the Saints:

> If ever there was a man who rallied a nation in its time of deepest distress, it was Winston Churchill. Bombs were then falling on London. The Nazi war machine had overrun Austria, Czechoslovakia, France, Belgium, Holland, and Norway, and was moving into Russia. Most of Europe was in the grasp of tyranny, and England was to be next. In that dangerous hour, when the hearts of many were failing, Churchill spoke: "Do not let us speak of darker days; let us speak rather of sterner days. These are not dark days; these are great days—the greatest days our country has ever lived; and we must all thank God that we have been allowed, each of us according to our stations, to play a part in making these days memorable in the history of our race."

Following the terrible catastrophe at Dunkirk, many prophets of doom foretold the end of Britain. But in that dark and solemn hour this remarkable man said, and I heard him say these words as they were broadcast across America, "We shall not flag or fail. . . . We shall fight in France, we shall fight on the seas and oceans, we shall fight with growing confidence and growing strength in the air, we shall defend our island, whatever the cost may be, we shall fight on the beaches, we shall fight on the landing grounds, we shall fight in the fields and in the streets, we shall fight in the hills; we shall never surrender."

It was this kind of talk, which saw victory distantly through the dark clouds of war, and not the critical faultfinding of cynics, that preserved the people of Britain and saved that nation from catastrophe. . . .

Many of us are troubled with fears concerning ourselves. We are in a period of stress across the world. There are occasionally hard days for each of us. Do not despair. Do not give up. Look for the sunlight through the clouds. Opportunities will eventually open to you.[32]

It was but another way of saying what Gordon had learned from his father: Forget yourself—including your fears and discouragement—and go to work. Gordon himself valiantly continued to do so throughout his decades of service in the callings that came to him. These included Assistant to the Quorum of the Twelve, a member of the Quorum of the Twelve, a counselor to several Church presidents, and—beginning in 1995 at the age of 84—President of the Church. He was already by far the most widely traveled of all his predecessors, despite his dislike of being away from home. "I do not enjoy travel," he once admitted, "but I do enjoy looking into the faces and shaking the hands of faithful Latter-day Saints."[33]

And so he went, with an untiring dedication that was the marvel of all who tried to keep up with him. A much-younger apostle, after accompanying him in a series of meetings throughout Asia, compared the journey to "running a marathon."[34] President Hinckley's service echoes that of Paul's marathon for Christ, and of Nephi's unwearyingness in his missionary labors.

Through his selfless work, President Hinckley reached further than anyone before in extending the blessings of gospel, not only to those in mortality but also to those in the spirit world: some seventy-five new temples were built while he served as President. As he mightily rolled forth the latter-day work, he urged his fellow saints to do likewise.

> The progress of the Church in our day is truly astounding. The God of heaven has brought to pass this latter-day miracle, and what we have seen is but a foretaste of greater things yet to come. . . . With our charge divinely given, with blessings divinely promised, let us go forward in faith. . . . The stone cut out of the mountain without hands will continue to roll forth until it has filled the whole earth. . . . This is God's work that we do, and with his blessing we shall not fail.[35]

Appropriately, the title chosen for the most comprehensive biography ever written about President Hinckley was *Go Forward with Faith*.

### Selfless Love and the Savior

His biography might also have been titled *Go Forward with Love*, for so he did. His "brotherly love and humility," noted President Boyd K. Packer after one of his many trips with the Prophet, were "always apparent whether he was with the laborers on a dusty road or a banquet in a presidential palace."[36] Wherever he went, President Hinckley was equally at home with the poor and the powerful, the famous and the common. In his multitude of meetings held throughout the earth, "time and again, he expressed to members of the Church . . . his love for them," and they in return—as had happened in the ministries of the Apostle Paul and the Apostle Wilford Woodruff—shed many tears[37] in "great outpourings of love."[38]

Visiting England after he became the President of the Church, he explained the genesis of that love: "Please accept the testimony of an old British missionary who came to this land in the dark days of the world Depression in 1933, and here learned to love the people and to love the Lord in a way that I had not known before."[39]

On various occasions he would refer to that event as the watershed experience of his life. "Something happened inside of me in England that was so significant and deep-rooted that I have never gotten over it. It is the same thing I have seen happen to thousands of other young men and women who commit themselves to the Lord, and their faith in Him becomes their anchor."[40]

Referring specifically to the arrival of the life-changing letter from his father, President Hinckley would ever call it "my day of decision,"[41] for "everything that has happened to me since, that's been good, I can trace to that decision made in that little house in Preston, Lancashire."[42] And recalling the commitment he made to his Heavenly Father to go forward and forget himself in service, he told a colleague near the end of his life, "I have been doing that ever since."[43]

In the process, he became ever more like the Savior whom he served. As described by a missionary who had been blessed by his kindness, "Gordon B. Hinckley was a great and good man, tireless in his testimony of Christ and faithful in his work for the gospel. He was certainly a man who knew Christ, and it radiated from him almost as a real light."[44]

President Hinckley's tireless work changed not only himself but also the world, from which he departed at the age of 97 as the oldest president of the Church. At his funeral, a fellow general authority observed:

> The Hinckley era evokes the image of missionary work to all the world. In the almost 13 years of President Hinckley's presidency, over 400,000 missionaries have been called, representing over 40 percent of all missionaries ever called since the Church was organized. Almost one-third of all members today were baptized since President Hinckley became our prophet. President Hinckley's challenge to increase our missionary efforts and our retention of new converts remains a charge we are still working to achieve.[45]

Speaking at the first general conference after being called as the Prophet, President Hinckley urged: "We have work to do, you and I, so very much of it. Let us roll up our sleeves and get at it, with a new commitment, putting our trust in the Lord."[46] It is another way of saying what the Lord Himself commands his missionaries: to forget themselves "with an eye single to the glory of God," and to go to work with all their "heart, might, mind and strength."[47]

To do so is to follow the greatest example of self-forgetting, by Him who in His atoning hour of agony subjected Himself to the will of His Father: "O my Father, if it be possible, let this cup pass from me: nevertheless not as I will, but as thou wilt."[48] His was, in the words of President Hinckley, "an offering beyond comprehension."[49]

## Legacy of Gordon B. Hinckley

Education and work were key components of Gordon B. Hinckley's pioneer heritage and upbringing. With the onset of the Depression, Gordon was surprised to receive a mission call, but he accepted and went as assigned to England. Discouragement soon overtook him, and he wrote home saying it was pointless to continue, as he was wasting his time and his father's money. The reply letter urged him simply to forget himself and go to work. As Gordon did so, a new day seemed to dawn. The inspired instruction became Gordon's reigning principle as he grew into one of the most productive missionaries and prophets in history. His compelling example of selfless work led the Kingdom of God to expand further than ever before and to shine forth as a light to the nations.

CHAPTER 16

# ~ *Thomas S. Monson* ~
## *Lift up the Hands Which Hang Down*

W hen Elder Gordon B. Hinckley was serving his mission in England, a boy by the name of Tommy Monson was growing up in Salt Lake City. His was a heart and heritage of unusual compassion, a trait that would become the hallmark of his powerful ministry in which, like his forefather Abraham, he would "succor the weak, lift up the hands which hang down, and strengthen the feeble knees"[1] as he followed his Lord and Savior.

### The Leisure and Lessons of Boyhood

Born on Sunday, August 21, 1927, in Salt Lake City, Tommy was the second of six children in a strong Latter-day Saint family whose ancestors had sacrificed valiantly for the restored gospel. "From all of them," he later said, "I received a legacy of total dedication to the gospel of Jesus Christ."[2] A close-knit family, the Monsons lived in the "Terrace," a cluster of houses built by Grandfather Condie for himself and each of his four daughters and their husbands.

It was the age of the Great Depression, and times were tough. Tommy later remembered the bitter cold of his bedroom during winter time, but also the warm glow of family relationships. "These were joyful days filled with frequent family get-togethers"[3] in the Terrace, where young Tommy never felt the need to knock on a door. There were also occasional visits to the Condie family farm outside the city.

In addition, Grandfather Condie owned a cabin on the Provo River at Vivian Park where the families spent weeks together every summer. There with his cousins and relatives, Tommy fished, swam, hiked, played softball, shot arrows, had mud fights, and at night "slept on a screened porch and took in the sounds of the woods."[4]

There he also learned to fish, a hobby that became a lifelong love of this future fisher of men. Fishing especially afforded him the opportunity to quietly contemplate the Creator's handiwork. "I would sit on the bank for hours and look at the mountainside across the river," he recalled.[5] And as had happened with Abraham and Wilford Woodruff and others, the majesty of creation drew Tommy Monson to seek the Creator. "He'd pray an awful lot," remembered one of Tommy's boyhood buddies, "and I noticed him many times take a hat off and say a prayer even when he was out on the stream fishing."[6]

His love of nature included a fascination with birds, and at age ten he became president of the Audubon Society at school. Young Tommy also loved to read, and walked several times each week to the library "where he found a world opened to him beyond his own neighborhood."[7]

But it was what he learned from his family that most determined the course of his life. One of the homes built by Grandfather Condie stood vacant and came to be occupied in an unusual way, as Tommy later described when he recalled a visit from an elderly man known as "Old Bob."

He was a widower in his eighties when the house in which he was living was to be demolished. I heard him tell my grandfather his plight as the three of us sat on Grandfather's old front porch swing. With a plaintive voice, he said to Grandfather, "Mr. Condie, I don't know what to do. I have no family. I have no place to go. I have no money." I wondered how Grandfather would answer. Slowly Grandfather reached into his pocket and took from it that old leather purse from which, in response to my hounding, he had produced many a penny or nickel for a special treat. This time he removed a key and handed it to Old Bob. Tenderly he said, "Bob, here is the key to that house I own next door. Take it. Move your things in there and stay as long as you like. There will be no rent to pay and nobody will ever put you out again."

Tears welled up in the eyes of Old Bob, coursed down his cheeks, then disappeared in his long, white beard. Grandfather's eyes were also moist. I spoke no word, but that day my grandfather stood ten feet tall. I was proud to bear his given name. Though I was but a boy, I learned a great lesson on love that day.[8]

Tommy's mother did her part as well to care for Old Bob. Sunday dinner in the Monson home never began until Tommy had first delivered a hot plate to Old Bob, who gratefully and at times tearfully responded, "God bless you, my boy. You have a wonderful mother."[9] Nor did she turn away the hungry souls who streamed in from the railroad tracks, not far from the Terrace, and knocked at the back door during those Depression years. She went out of her way to make a fresh sandwich and pour a glass of milk for each famished visitor.

It was not only from his mother's side of the family that Tommy learned compassion.

My own father, a printer, worked long and hard practically every day of his life. I'm certain that on the Sabbath he would have enjoyed just being at home. Rather, he visited elderly family members and brought cheer into their lives.

One such family member was his uncle, who was crippled by arthritis so severe that he could not walk or care for himself. On a Sunday afternoon Dad would say to me, "Come along, Tommy. Let's take Uncle Elias for a short drive." Boarding the old 1928 Oldsmobile, we would proceed to Eighth West, where, at the home of Uncle Elias,

I would wait in the car while Dad went inside. Soon he would emerge from the house, carrying in his arms like a china doll his frail and crippled uncle. I would then open the door and watch how tenderly and with such affection my father would place Uncle Elias in the front seat so that he would have a fine view while I occupied the rear seat.

The drive was brief and the conversation limited, but oh, what a legacy of love! Father never read to me from the Bible about the good Samaritan. Rather, he took me with him and Uncle Elias in that old 1928 Oldsmobile and provided a living example I have always remembered.[10]

That example of Tommy's parents proved contagious. One Christmas day while the holiday dinner was being prepared in the Monson home, Tommy was playing outside with a friend. Smelling the sweet aroma, the friend asked what they were having for dinner.

"Turkey," Tommy responded.

"What does turkey taste like?" his friend asked.

"Oh, about like chicken tastes," replied Tommy.

"What does chicken taste like?"

Realizing that his friend had never eaten either, Tommy asked him what he was having for dinner.

There was silence and a downward glance, and finally the words, "I dunno. There's nothing in the house."

Tommy's mind raced. He had neither turkey nor chicken to offer, nor any money. Then he remembered his two pet rabbits, "the pride of my life," he would recall, his beautiful New Zealand whites. A large breed prized as pets for their beautiful white fur and gentle temperament, they are also raised for their excellent meat. "You come with me," Tommy told his friend, "because I've got something for your dinner." Walking to the rabbit hutch, he took out his cherished pets and put them in a box. "You take these home, and your dad will know what to do with them. They taste a whole lot like chicken."

As he closed the empty hutch, tears came to Tommy's eyes, not out of sadness for his loss but from a sudden "warmth, a feeling of indescribable joy" that filled his heart. "My friend later said that had been the best holiday dinner they had ever had."[11]

## Work, Miracles, and Education

Another thing Tommy learned from his father was the value of hard work. "To know my brother Tom," his younger brother would say years later, "you have to know our father. He was a quiet man—quieter than Tom," but "whatever assignment he accepted, he saw it through to completion. He believed that if you did a job, you did it all the way. He always gave 100 percent."[12]

Tom had ample opportunity to observe this trait, especially beginning at age twelve when he began to work with his father in the printing trade every day after school. Circumstances required his involvement, even though it prevented him from participating in school sports.

No wonder that when he made his first visit to Temple Square in that same year, he contemplated how the nickels and dimes might be extracted from the bottom of the reflecting pool. Even so, the visit impressed him deeply, particularly the pioneer monument to the miracle of the seagulls eating the crickets. Not long afterwards when called upon to give his first talk in Church, it was that event about which he spoke.

But it was a personal experience that impressed upon him how the Lord uses mortals to help accomplish His miracles. One summer while floating down the Provo River in an inner tube, he suddenly happened upon a desperate scene: a teenage girl was floundering in a whirlpool and gasping for breath while her frantic parents yelled from the shore. Tom happened to be floating right past the girl, whose head bobbed out of the water just within his reach. He grabbed her hair and lifted her partially across his lap, and then paddled to shore and delivered her to her parents. Weeping for joy, they embraced and kissed their daughter, and then embraced and kissed Tom. As he continued on his way, Tom felt gratitude.

> I realized I had participated in saving a human life. Heavenly Father had permitted me, a deacon, to float by at precisely the time I was needed. That day I learned that God, our Heavenly Father, knows each one of us and permits us to share His divine power to save.[13]

Little did he know that the experience portended his future ministry of salvation, a ministry described in the patriarchal blessing he received at age sixteen:

> The Holy Ghost has been conferred upon you to be your inspiration and your guide, to direct you in your labors, and to bring to your mind the things that have passed and to show unto you things to come. . . . You shall be indeed a leader among your fellows. . . . You shall have the privilege of going into the world to proclaim the message of the gospel . . . and you shall have the spirit of discernment. . . . Seek the Lord in humility to guide and direct you, that you might know the proper course to pursue . . . in the high and holy callings unto which you shall be called.[14]

Naturally expecting to be called on a mission, Tom did all he could to prepare, including graduating from high school and enrolling in the University of Utah. But the Depression years had turned into the War years, with America being brought into the global conflict when its Pacific naval fleet was bombed at Pearl Harbor. No missionary call seemed possible in the foreseeable future.

## Serving God and Country

But duty did call, loud and clear. In 1945, eighteen-year-old Tom Monson enlisted to defend his country. Among the forty-two who signed up that day, forty-one chose the regular Navy with a fixed four-year commitment and a promise of discharge, whether the war was over or not. It seemed the prudent course, since it looked like the conflict would drag on for many years. But there was another option: the Naval Reserve, with a commitment for the duration of the war plus six months.

Not sure what to do, Tom said a silent prayer. The answer came to his mind to ask two older men standing nearby. When both said they had chosen the Naval Reserve, Tom did also. Decades later at a temple dedication as President of the Church, he observed that he probably wouldn't be standing there if those many years earlier he had chosen the regular Navy.[15] Tom Monson guided his life by prayer.

Shortly before leaving for the Navy, Tom was ordained an elder. As he departed from the Salt Lake train station, among the well wishers was a bishopric member who handed him the *Missionary Handbook*. Tom laughed and commented that he wasn't going on a mission.

"Take it anyway," came the reply. "It may come in handy."

Tom tucked it away in the bottom of his bag and forgot about it.

His tour of duty began in San Diego with the rigors of basic training. On the night before Christmas leave, as Tom and his colleagues were settled in their bunks and falling asleep, the silence was broken by moaning. It came from the nearby bunk of a Latter-day Saint friend. "I'm sick!" he cried out in pain. "I'm sicker than I've ever been."

Tom suggested a trip to the infirmary, but his friend declined, saying that if he did, he would be kept there and not be allowed to return home for Christmas. The moaning continued until Tom heard his friend call out for him again.

"Monson, aren't you an elder? Will you give me a blessing?"

Tom was caught by surprise. "I thought to myself, 'I've never given a blessing. I've never received a blessing. I don't know that I've ever seen anyone receive a blessing.'"[16] Tom said a silent prayer for help.

The answer came: "Look in the bottom of the sea bag." Thus, at two A.M. I emptied on the deck the contents of the bag. I then took to the night-light that hard, rectangular object, the *Missionary Handbook*, and read how one blesses the sick. With many curious sailors looking on, I proceeded with the blessing.[17]

By the time Tom said "Amen," his friend was sleeping peacefully. The next morning as all assembled to go on leave, his friend remarked, "Monson, I'm glad you hold the priesthood."

"I'm glad I do too,"[18] Tom replied.

Such spiritual sensitivity would become one of Tom's most prominent characteristics. "No one can understand [him]," a fellow apostle observed many years later, "who does not understand the frequency, the repetition of those kinds of spiritual promptings in his life and his absolute loyalty in responding to them."[19]

### On the Lord's Errand

The influence of the Spirit in Tom's young life soon became apparent also in the decision he had made to choose the Naval Reserve over the regular Navy, as Elder Jeffrey R. Holland explained:

> Within just a few weeks of his joining, there was an armistice in Europe and only a few months later came peace in the Pacific. Less than a year after he began his active duty, Ensign Thomas S. Monson returned home to graduate with honors from the University of Utah, just one quarter behind those members of his class who had not given military service. The impressions of the Spirit had spared him three years of post-war military duty. Little did he know that even then he was being fitted with "the whole armour of God" (Eph. 6:11) for quite a different kind of battle and a much longer tour of duty. He was "on the Lord's errand" and time was of the essence.[20]

And already during his military tour of duty, Ensign Monson had been an unofficial but persuasive missionary. At least two men ended up joining the Church because of his example and teaching.[21]

Pursuing his studies at the University of Utah, Tom was, as described by his department head, "an outstanding student" who "got straight A's in everything he did."[22] In 1948 he graduated with honors in business. But it was by no means the end of his venture of learning. Years later, even after being called as a general authority, he would earn his Masters of Business Administration degree from Brigham Young University.

Meanwhile, the new graduate turned down job offers from prominent companies across the country to accept an offer from the Salt Lake City newspaper, the *Deseret News.*

Not long afterwards, he married Frances Johnson in the Salt Lake Temple. They had met before his naval service, and at his first meeting with her parents it was discovered that Tom's great uncle had helped convert the Johnson family in Sweden. "Tears filled the eyes of Franz and Hildur Johnson as they embraced their future son-in-law. Although the incident was tinged with mild embarrassment for Frances, who hardly anticipated such a reception for her young boyfriend, she and Tom reflected later that the relationship of their Swedish ancestors may have portended more than mere coincidence."[23]

Life was busy for the new husband. His career as an advertising executive was demanding, but he had also rejoined the Naval Reserve with the goal of receiving a commission as an officer. Shortly after the letter arrived offering him the commission, he was called to serve as a counselor in the bishopric. The time commitment required to serve as an officer would have made his service in the bishopric impossible, and he sought the advice of Apostle Harold B. Lee, Tom's former stake president. Elder Lee counseled him to decline the commission and seek a discharge from the Naval Reserve. "Your future is not with the military," he told Tom.

Tom struggled with the decision but chose to follow the counsel. He was released from the Naval Reserve in the last group processed before the outbreak of the Korean War, to which Tom surely would have been called had he accepted the commission.

### Bishop Tom Monson

Tom's future, as prophetically referred to by Elder Lee, began to unfold quickly. Those who knew him described him as "a born leader," with "energy that is beyond belief, and enthusiasm that was just contagious. . . . I don't know of anybody that Tom Monson dealt with that didn't love him. . . . He just had the ability to reach out and touch hearts."[24]

At the age of twenty-two, Tom was called to serve as bishop. With over a thousand members, including some eighty-five widows, the ward constituted the largest welfare challenge of any in the Church. "The magnitude of the calling was overwhelming and the responsibility frightening," he later recalled. "My inadequacy humbled me."[25] How could he meet the challenge? He put up in his office a beautiful painting by artist Heinrich Hofmann of the Savior as a reminder that His example would show the way.

On one occasion, though, the way was shown by one of the Savior's chosen Twelve, Elder Spencer W. Kimball, who called with a request.

> He said, "Brother Monson, in your ward is a trailer court, and in a little trailer in that court—the smallest trailer of all—is a sweet Navajo widow, Margaret Bird. She feels unwanted, unneeded, and lost. Could you and the Relief Society presidency seek her out, extend to her the hand of fellowship, and provide for her a special welcome?" This we did. A miracle resulted. Margaret Bird blossomed in her newly found environment. Despair disappeared. The widow in her affliction had been visited. The lost sheep had been found. Each who participated in the simple human drama emerged a better person.[26]

Decades later, Tom would still "often think of the quiet manner in which President Spencer W. Kimball served his God. . . . No one ever knew all he did in serving his Heavenly Father, for he did it in the true spirit of the Savior, many times not letting the right hand know what the left was doing."[27]

So also did Bishop Monson, who took a week of his personal vacation time every Christmas season to pay a personal visit to all eighty-five widows, presenting each with a plump chicken that he himself had raised and dressed out. Nor did the personal visits stop after Tom was released as bishop. Every Christmas thereafter, for as long as they lived, every one of the surviving widows received a visit and gift from Tom Monson at Christmas time.

> One night during the Christmas holidays . . . President Monson was making his customary rounds to "his" widows, leaving gifts purchased from his own pocket, including plump dressed chickens that were, in the early years, raised in his own coops. In one of the many Salt Lake City rest homes he has come to know so intimately, he found one of his ward members, alone and silent in the darkened room of a world made even darker by the onset of blindness. As President Monson made his way to this sweet sister's side, she reached out awkwardly, groping for the hand of the only visitor she had received in the whole of the Christmas season. "Bishop, is that you?" she inquired. "Yes, dear Hattie, it is I." "Oh, Bishop," she wept through sightless eyes, "I knew you would come." They all knew he would come, and he always did.[28]

He also spoke at their funerals, all their funerals. "Perhaps no one in the . . . leadership of the Church has spoken at so many funerals—he once had three services in one day—and always very personal remarks [were] given."[29]

### Ministering to the Nations

After serving several years as bishop, Tom was called as a counselor in the stake presidency. Meanwhile his career was progressing as he rose to Assistant General Manager of the Deseret News Press. With the increased salary, the family built a new home on an acre lot in the suburbs.

Not long afterwards he was called to preside over the Canadian Mission headquartered in Toronto and covering a vast area. As thus promised in his patriarchal blessing, the nations of the earth began to hear his voice, a voice directed first to the missionaries over whom he presided—although he was not much older than they were. "His main focus was the missionaries. He quickly learned their names, taught and counseled them regularly, and encouraged each one to become his best self."[30]

Nor did his heavy responsibilities cause him to neglect his greatest responsibility, his family. Every night when his son would march upstairs to say goodnight to Dad, President Monson would set aside his work to play a game of checkers.

Back home in Salt Lake City after completing his mission, Tom found that his missionary service was not over. He was soon called to the Church's priesthood missionary committee, another opportunity among many that would come his way. Years later after Tom was sustained as President of the Church, one of his fellow apostles observed that "President Monson has been a great missionary all his life. His personal missionary effort, his supervisory work of the Missionary Department, and his calling and training of mission presidents have been undertaken with enthusiasm. He made significant contributions to the new missionary guide, *Preach My Gospel.* . . . He is indeed a great missionary."[31]

Tom's professional career continued to escalate as he was appointed General Manager of the Deseret Press. Suddenly in October 1963, at the age of thirty-six, his life changed forever when he was called by President David O. McKay to serve in the Quorum of the Twelve. Minutes after being sustained in October general conference, Elder Monson walked to the pulpit. In the audience and sitting three rows back near the center were two priesthood leaders from Arizona. Watching intently as the new apostle gave his brief address, the two men witnessed a remarkable transfiguration. One—who would later be called as a patriarch—leaned over to the other and said, "Did you see what I saw?" The other responded, "Joseph Smith." Yes, nodded the first. These men knew that this new apostle would one day stand as successor to the Prophet Joseph Smith.[32]

Decades later when that had became a reality, as President Monson was speaking in general conference he recalled something that had impressed *him* in that earlier conference. "In the October 1963 general conference—the conference at which I was sustained as a member of the Quorum of the Twelve Apostles—President David O. McKay made this statement: 'Man's greatest happiness comes from losing himself for the good of others.'"³³

President McKay's insight was not lost on Elder Monson. Moving into his office as a new apostle, he placed on the wall his prized picture of the Savior, whose selfless example of service Elder Monson sought to follow. And follow he did, as a brilliant administrator and energetic leader with a keen intellect, amazing memory, unflagging energy, and a gift of speaking. "A genius in Church government" is how fellow apostle Bruce R. McConkie referred to him, while President Spencer W. Kimball called him "truly a 'do it' man"—one "who acts promptly and resolutely."³⁴

As Nephi of old, Elder Monson readily responded to the Lord's instructions, which came in a constant flow: "Throughout [his] ministry, there have been regular, recurring, dramatic experiences in answering the whispered beckonings of the Spirit."³⁵ These have guided him while serving in numerous leadership capacities both in and out of the Church.³⁶

In 1985 he was called as a counselor in the First Presidency, serving first with President Ezra Taft Benson and later with President Howard W. Hunter and finally President Gordon B. Hinckley. When President Hinckley passed away in 2008, the Savior called Thomas S. Monson—this model of serving the Savior by serving the least of His brethren³⁷—to be His representative to all mankind as the President of the Church of Jesus Christ of Latter-day Saints.

## Meeting Temporal and Spiritual Needs

But President Monson's legacy is not in the prominence of his high callings, but rather in his response to the calling given to all saints everywhere, to "follow Jesus"³⁸ and "bear one another's burdens," to "mourn with those that mourn," and "comfort those that stand in need of comfort, and to stand as witnesses of God."³⁹

Even in overseeing the Church's global humanitarian efforts that reached out to millions suffering from the devastation of flood, fire, famine, earthquake, and poverty, "his concern is not abstract," emphasized fellow apostle Jeffrey R. Holland. "He has been known to literally give the clothes off his back to members in need who had no opportunity to buy new clothing. His service is often given out of the public eye. 'So much has taken place privately,' says his daughter, Ann. Frequently, individuals will share those experiences with his sons or daughter. 'Not even we children know all he has done,' she says."[40]

But what *is* publicly known of his compassionate work has drawn worldwide attention. In 1981 he was appointed by U.S. President Ronald Reagan to serve on the President's Task Force for Private Sector Initiatives, and in 1998 he and Sister Monson were presented with the Continuum of Caring Humanitarian Award by the Sisters of Charity of St. Joseph Villa, a worldwide Roman Catholic women's order dedicated to spreading the love of Christ through service to the needy.

Among the needy that came to Elder Monson's attention as a young apostle were the East German Saints who, having experienced the devastation of World War II, now found themselves behind the Iron Curtain. As he later described after visiting, "The Communist party's hammer-and-sickle flag was displayed in each window of the ancient and war ravaged hotel where I stayed. Church meetings were watched and monitored by the secret police. . . . The feeling in East Germany was one of overwhelming oppression."[41]

One evening in November 1968 following meetings with the East German members, Elder Monson recorded in his journal:

> I was touched by the sincerity of these wonderful Saints. I was humbled by their poverty. They have so little. My heart was filled with sorrow because they have no patriarch, they have no wards or stakes—just branches, [and] they have few teaching materials. They cannot receive temple blessings, neither endowments nor sealings. They are forbidden to leave their country. Yet they trust in the Lord with all their hearts and lean not unto their own understanding.

I stood at the pulpit with tear-filled eyes and a voice choked with emotion and made a promise to the people: "If you will remain true and faithful to the commandments of God, every blessing any member of the Church enjoys in any other country will be yours." . . .

This evening in my hotel room, as I realized the full impact of the promise I had made . . . , I dropped to my knees and said to my Heavenly Father, "Father, I am on Thy errand, this is Thy Church. I have spoken words that came not from me, but from Thee and Thy Son. Wilt Thou, therefore, fulfill the promise in the lives of this noble people." There coursed through my mind the words from the Psalm, "Be still, and know that I am God" (Psalm 46:10).[42]

In the ensuing years, Elder Monson labored tirelessly to help bring to pass the marvelous promise he had pronounced. His efforts to bring a temple to East Germany were accompanied by miracles as he was led by the Spirit to overcome the daunting political and bureaucratic obstacles that had made the task appear impossible.

In 1975 on a hillside near the Elbe River, he offered a dedicatory prayer for the land of East Germany, and in 1983 in Frieberg, another dedicatory prayer on the site of the future temple. Two years later when the completed temple was dedicated by President Hinckley, Elder Monson was called upon to be the first speaker at the first dedicatory session. In his journal entry for that day, he noted: "It was difficult for me to control my emotions as I spoke, for racing through my mind were examples of the faith of the devoted Saints in this part of the world. . . . All honor and glory belong to our Heavenly Father, for it is only through his divine intervention that these events have taken place."[43]

So spoke the man who had valiantly served as the Lord's primary mortal instrument in bringing succor to the oppressed saints in East Germany. Thanks to Elder Monson's compassion, faith, and persistence, the hands that there had long hung down were now lifted up in praise and worship in the House of the Lord.

## Concern for the One

President Monson's concern for the German Saints was not merely collective. Once while visiting Hamburg in West Germany to preside over a regional conference, he asked about a certain Brother Panitsch, a patriarch who had been one of the pioneer Saints in Germany.

The local leader assigned to accompany President Monson was Dieter Uchtdorf, who replied that Brother Panitsch was seriously ill. President Monson asked if they could please visit him. As recounted later by Elder Uchtdorf:

> I knew that shortly before his trip to Hamburg, President Monson had undergone foot surgery and that he could not walk without pain. I explained that Brother Panitsch lived on the fifth floor of a building with no elevators. We would have to climb the stairs to see him.
>
> But President Monson insisted. And so we went.
>
> I remember how difficult it was for President Monson to climb those stairs. He could take only a few at a time before needing to stop and rest. He never uttered a word of complaint, and he would not turn back. Because the building had high ceilings, the stairs seemed to go on forever, but President Monson cheerfully persevered until we arrived at the apartment of Brother Panitsch on the fifth floor.
>
> Once there, we had a wonderful visit. President Monson thanked him for his life of dedicated service and cheered him with a smile. Before we left, he gave him a wonderful priesthood blessing.
>
> No one but Brother Panitsch, the immediate family, and myself ever saw that act of courage and compassion.
>
> President Monson could have chosen to rest between our long and frequent meetings. He could have asked to see some of the beautiful sights of Hamburg. I have often thought of how remarkable it was that of all the sights in that city, the one he wanted to see more than any other was a feeble and ailing member of the Church who had faithfully and humbly served the Lord.
>
> President Monson came to Hamburg to teach and bless the people of a country, and that is what he did. But at the same time, he focused on the one, name by name.[44]

Whether abroad or at home, President Monson sought out those in need. "On any given day at a handful of nursing homes in Salt Lake City," noted one writer, "a buoyant yet distinguished gentleman can be seen talking, laughing and listening to the residents. Despite his heavy load of religious assignments, Thomas S. Monson, the president of The Church of Jesus Christ of Latter-day Saints, is the self-appointed chaplain for these facilities. Fellow Church leader President Boyd K. Packer said, 'He visits them anytime his busy schedule permits, and sometimes even when it doesn't permit.'"[45]

Nor in all his service did President Monson neglect his own family. On a fishing trip once with his son Clark, as they sat in the boat, President Monson suddenly asked him to reel in the line. "In about five minutes your brother Tom will be sitting down to take the bar exam admitting him to the practice of law. He has worked hard through three years of law school for this and he will be a little apprehensive. Let's just kneel here in the boat. I'll offer a prayer for him, and then you offer one."[46] Clark was deeply touched by the tender thoughtfulness and faith of his father.

A long-time friend called him "a man of the common people, the champion of the underdog,"[47] while a colleague in the Quorum of the Twelve noted that "he has reached out to those in need in a remarkable and personal way. . . . His personal ministry has been Christlike and has given comfort and peace to countless numbers of people. . . . His effort to personally minister to those who are sick and afflicted has been extraordinary."[48] In the words of Church member Maurine Proctor,

> His has been a ministry to the lost battalions of the faltering, the lonely, the sick, the struggling, the forgotten, the widow, the uncared for, those who fall by the wayside. His has been a call captured in this scripture: "Wherefore, be faithful; stand in the office which I have appointed unto you; succor the weak, lift up the hands which hang down, and strengthen the feeble knees." (D&C 81:5).

Among his countless compassionate visits, as Maurine further recounts, was the one made to her relative suffering from a disfiguring cancer.

The face we had loved was distorted, unrecognizable, and his suffering nearly incomprehensible. The bright red of the now-enormous tumor, which seemed to grow daily, looked angry, burning. His torso was covered with dime and nickel-sized sores. Radiation treatments were attempted but only burned his body, making the pain even more intense. We could not have recognized Keith as anyone familiar except for the affectionate tone in his voice, while he could still mumble out a few sentences.

Keith did not live far from President Monson. In fact, at one time they had been in the same ward, before boundaries had been redrawn. President Monson got word about Keith's illness and called immediately, wondering if he could come by that very early evening to cheer him and give him a blessing on his way home from work.

I don't know what else might have been on President Monson's schedule that day—surely many pressing things, a desk full of urgencies. Yet, nothing is so urgent for President Monson as the soul of the distressed. It calls to his sympathies; it stirs his love.

We had been visiting Keith that day before President Monson arrived. He was surrounded by his wife, a son and daughters who loved him, but the situation was so grim, it was hard to be anything but teary. Life just seemed too hard if someone like Keith could be so afflicted and we struggled to say anything besides a pitiful, "I'm so sorry, so sorry." We felt heavy, grayed over with the burden.

Then, at the appointed moment, President Monson arrived, and it was like the sun came up on a new day. It was not only that the Spirit was with him, which we all felt immediately; it was that his very presence was buoyant. A tangible sense of joy and assurance had entered the room. . . .

He didn't look surprised or shocked to see Keith's condition. He didn't put on a long face in sympathy. He smiled that large, warming smile and with enthusiasm said, "Keith it is good to see you." President Monson then began to give Keith what he needed most. It was the same thing any very sick person needs, whose once energetic and perfect body has been ravaged by an illness until he can't recognize himself anymore. President Monson gave him back his identity, and a sense of himself.

"Keith," he said, "Do you remember when you were in the bishopric and I had just moved into the ward and you assigned me to head up the committee to build a new meetinghouse? I told you that I didn't know anyone in the ward, and you said, 'That's OK. Just call them Gunderson and you'll be right 40% of the time.'"

At that Keith laughed out of the corner of his mouth not yet smothered by cancer. We all laughed, our laughter cascading through the sick room like a blessed relief. President Monson continued the banter about everything he knew about Keith, a heartening conversation about how dedicated and committed Keith had always been. We were swept away by a series of delightful memories. Each one drove the gray and gloom further and further from our hearts.

Then President Monson did a remarkable thing. He changed the subject to something even lighter. (How completely delightful for a sick person to finally get to hear something besides how sorry all the rest of us are and how sick they are.)

He started to tell us the story about when he recently went to lunch with the chairman of the board of Parker Brothers who said that Monopoly was still their best-selling game, and he had asked, jokingly, if President Monson could remember the names of any of the properties of the game. He told him that he could indeed remember them—all of them—IN ORDER. We were all laughing then, and President Monson, with his perfect memory, named them all—right there beside the sick bed—Mediterranean, Baltic, Reading Railroad and continuing all the way around, he ended with Park Place and Boardwalk.

With all of us now in a happy mood, he said gently, "Now, Keith, let's give you a blessing. Scot, will you anoint?" The Spirit continued to illuminate our hearts.

Then he laid hands upon Keith's head and gave him a blessing of power and comfort, promising him in a powerful voice that, "This is only temporary." (And it would be. Keith died ten days later.)

The joy that filled the room, the Spirit comforting every wounded heart, was tangible.[49]

## Following the Savior to Succor, Lift, and Strengthen

President Monson was described by those close to him as "absolutely without guile,"[50] and towering "like a pine tree—the top is high and ascending to heaven but the branches are broad, low to the ground, and protective of all who need shelter there."[51]

It is no coincidence that this image is the same used anciently to depict Father Abraham, whose loving-kindness changed the world and through whose covenant all nations are now being blessed. Extending the blessings of Abraham further than ever before, President Monson did so from the start with the loving-kindness of Abraham—and of Christ. "Love," said President Monson, "is the catalyst that causes change. Love is the balm that brings healing to the soul. . . . True love is a reflection of Christ's love."[52]

Regarding the painting of the Christ in President Monson's office, he stated, "I love that painting. I feel strength in having it near me. Look at the kindness in those eyes. Look at the warmth of expression. When facing difficult situations, I often look at it and ask myself, 'What would He do?'"[53] The painting suggested the answer: "The Master could be found mingling with the poor, the downtrodden, the oppressed, and the afflicted. He brought hope to the hopeless, strength to the weak, and freedom to the captive."[54]

No one ever followed the Master better than President Monson in seeking out the sick and afflicted, the downhearted and downtrodden, and all those in need of a helping hand and a kind word. His genius in Church government did not blind him to the needs of the downtrodden; his passion, stated President Boyd K. Packer, was always humanitarian concerns.[55]

President Dieter F. Uchtdorf described President Monson as "a man who focuses on the one, but has a heart for the whole world."[56]

Elder Quentin L. Cook noted that "President Monson has done his very best to 'succor the weak, lift up the hands which hang down, and strengthen the feeble knees.'"[57]

According to Elder Jeffrey R. Holland, "President Thomas S. Monson's life has been devoted to helping people succeed spiritually and temporally. . . , lifting up heavy hands, and strengthening feeble knees."[58]

President Monson himself attested to the satisfaction for so doing. "Of all the blessings I have had in my life, one of the sweetest is that feeling the Lord provides when I know that He has answered the prayer of another through me."[59] That Latter-day Saints may obtain these blessings is the counsel of President Monson:

> The Master frequently spoke of hand and heart. In a revelation given through the Prophet Joseph Smith at Hiram, Ohio, in March 1832, he counseled: ". . . be faithful; stand in the office which I have appointed unto you; succor the weak, lift up the hands which hang down, and strengthen the feeble knees. And if thou art faithful unto the end, thou shalt have a crown of immortality, and eternal life in the mansions which I have prepared in the house of my Father." (D&C 81:5–6.)
>
> As I ponder his words, I can almost hear the shuffle of sandaled feet, the murmurs of astonishment from listeners as they echoed from Capernaum's peaceful scene. Here multitudes crowded around Jesus, bringing the sick to be healed. A palsied man picked up his bed and walked, and a Roman centurion's faith restored his servant's health. . . .
>
> The beloved apostles noted well his example. He lived not so to be ministered unto, but to minister; not to receive, but to give; not to save his life, but to pour it out for others. . . .
>
> Time passes. Circumstances change. Conditions vary. Unaltered is the divine command to succor the weak and lift up the hands which hang down and strengthen the feeble knees.[60]
>
> Today there are hearts to gladden, there are deeds to be done—even precious souls to save. The sick, the weary, the hungry, the cold, the injured, the lonely, the aged, the wanderer, all cry out for our help.[61]
>
> We can dry the tear of the weeping. We can comfort the dying by sharing the promise of eternal life. If we lift one weary hand which hangs down, if we bring peace to one struggling soul, if we give as did the Master, we can—by showing the way—become a guiding star. . . . May we resolve from this day forward to fill our hearts with love. May

we go the extra mile to include in our lives any who are lonely or downhearted or who are suffering in any way.[62]

## Legacy of Thomas S. Monson

From his boyhood, Tom Monson felt compassion for the less fortunate, and he reached out in love even as he had seen his family do so often and so well. The coming of World War II made a mission call impossible, but Tom left to serve his country and discovered for himself the power of the priesthood he held. Not long after returning home, he was overwhelmed to be called as bishop of a huge ward that included eighty-five widows. To guide him in his heavy responsibility, he placed in his office a beautiful painting of the Savior; and as He had ministered to the downhearted and downtrodden, so did His servant Tom Monson. President Monson's Abrahamic ministry of succoring the weak and lifting up the hands that hang down is an invitation for all Latter-day Saints to follow the Savior in extending His love to all mankind.

# NOTES

## Introduction

[1] Mosiah 18:9.

[2] Benson, *Witness and Warning*, 11.

[3] Benson, *Come Unto Christ*, 93.

[4] Galbraith, *Scriptural Teachings of Prophet Joseph Smith*, 261–262.

[5] Thomas S. Monson, "Models to Follow," *Ensign* 32:11 [Nov. 2002], 60.

[6] Galbraith, *Scriptural Teachings of Prophet Joseph Smith*, 133.

## Chapter 1 • Enoch

[1] See D&C 107:40–57.

[2] Moses 6:23.

[3] VanderKam, *Enoch*, 11–12; Westermann, *Genesis 1–11*, 326–327; Wenham, *Genesis 1–15*, 111, 127; Sarna, *Genesis*, 36.

[4] Kvanvig, *Roots of Apocalyptic*, 41–42; Botterweck, *Theological Dictionary of the Old Testament* 5:19–20; Skinner, *Commentary on Genesis*, 116.

[5] Moses 6:31.

[6] Enoch received his patriarchal ordination at age 25. In contrast, Seth had been 69, Enos 134, Cainan 87, Mahalaleel 496, and Jared 200. D&C 107:41–48.

[7] Moses 6:27–29.

[8] 1 Enoch 9:9, in *Old Testament Pseudepigrapha* 1:17.

[9] Toorn, *Dictionaries of Deities and Demons*, 344.

[10] Moses 8:18.

[11] Moses 6:30.

[12] Moses 6:31.

[13] Moses 6:32, 34.

[14] Moses 6:35–36.

[15] Moses 6:37–39. Enoch's walking with God is mentioned also in Gen. 5:21, 24 and Moses 7:69.

[16] Moses 6:40.

[17] See Nibley, *Enoch the Prophet*, 277–278.

[18]Book of the Giants, 4Q530, in Vermes, *The Complete Dead Sea Scrolls*, 516–517; Milik, *The Books of Enoch*, 305–307.

[19]Moses 6:42.

[20]Moses 6:43–46.

[21]Moses 6:47.

[22]Moses 6:48–49.

[23]Moses 6:50–52.

[24]Moses 6:57.

[25]Moses 6:59–61.

[26]Moses 6:64–66.

[27]Moses 7:11.

[28]Ginzberg, *Legends of the Jews* 1:128.

[29]*Journal of Discourses* 26:89.

[30]Galbraith, *Scriptural Teachings of Prophet Joseph Smith*, 344.

[31]*Journal of Discourses* 18:303.

[32]2 Enoch [J] 51:4, in Charlesworth, *Old Testament Pseudepigrapha* 1:178.

[33]Moses 7:13.

[34]Abr. 2:7.

[35]The "very deep roots" of Isaiah, according to one scholar, are in the ancient traditions that gave rise to the Enoch literature. Barker, *The Older Testament*, 137, 125–137, 161–180.

[36]Isa. 51:16; and see 59:21. See also commentary on these verses in Motyer, *Isaiah*, 412–413, 492–493, and Westermann, *Isaiah 40–66*, 244.

[37]Moses 7:16–19.

[38]Moses 7:19.

[39]Galbraith, *Scriptural Teachings of Prophet Joseph Smith*, 194–195.

[40]Moses 7:24.

[41]See 3 Ne. 28:36–40.

[42]Moses 7:24.

[43]Moses 7:25–26.

[44]Moses 7:28.

[45]Moses 7:37.

[46]Moses 7:41–44.

[47]Moses 7:47.

[48]Moses 7:58–59.

[49]Moses 7:60–62.

[50]Bateman, Merrill J. "Truth and Righteousness Will Sweep the Earth." Talk given at the 2000 Brigham Young University Women's Conference, online at http://ce.byu.edu/cw/womensconference/archive/2000/bateman_merill.htm.

[51]D&C 71:1; and see 24:12; 28:16; 30:5.

[52]D&C 31:3.

[53]D&C 30:11.

[54]D&C 33:8, 10.

[55]*Journal of Discourses* 10:306.

[56]Ibid., 17:113.

[57]D&C 6:6.

[58]Neal A. Maxwell, "O, Divine Redeemer," *Ensign* 11:11 [Nov. 1981], 8–9.

[59]Moses 7:63–64.

[60]Henry B. Eyring, "Our Hearts Knit as One," *Ensign* 38:11 [Nov. 2008], 68–71.

## Chapter 2 • *Noah*

[1]Moses 8:2.

[2]Based on the chronology in Moses 6:10–25; 8:1–9, Zion was translated in the year 1052, and Noah was born in 1056.

[3]Moses 7:48.

[4]Sarna, *Genesis*, 43; and so also, for example: Westermann, *Genesis 1–11*, 44; Wenham, *Genesis 1–15*, 127; Brown, *Hebrew and English Lexicon*, 628–630; Harris, *Theological Wordbook*, 562–563.

[5]Galbraith, *Scriptural Teachings of Prophet Joseph Smith*, 297; D&C 107:52.

[6]Book of Yashar (Jasher) 4:15, in Noah, *The Book of Yashar*, 10.

[7]The Conflict of Adam and Eve with Satan, book 3, chapter 1, in Malan, *Conflict of Adam*, 142 (standardizing "wilfully" to "willfully").

[8]1Q20, Genesis Apocryphon, col. 6, English translation in Machiela, *The Dead Sea Genesis Apocryphon*.

[9]Gen. 6:11 (corresponding to Moses 8:28).

[10]Moses 7:48.

[11]Lewis, *Interpretation of Noah and the Flood*, 123, citing rabbinic sources.

[12]Ibid., 130, citing rabbinic sources.

[13]Moses 8:17, which is Joseph Smith's inspired translation of Gen. 6:3.

[14]2 Pet. 2:5; also Josephus, and other early sources. See Ginzberg, *Legends of the Jews* 1:139 and corresponding footnotes.

[15]Moses 8:19–20.

[16]Moses 8:16.

[17]Moses 6:23.

[18]Gen. 6:9.

[19]The King James "just" of Gen. 6:9 reads "righteous" in most modern translations. The Hebrew is *zadik*, from *zedek*, the word for "righteousness" (which occurs, for example, in the name *Melchizedek*). Even so, according to one Old Testament scholar, "We have no satisfactory English word for th[is] theologically significant [Hebrew] word." Rad, *Genesis*, 120.

The King James "perfect" of Gen. 6:9 reads "blameless" in many modern translations. The Hebrew is *tamim*, derived from the verb *tam*, "to be complete or finished," and is likewise without an entirely adequate English equivalent. *Tamim* describes something or someone who is complete, whole, sound, unimpaired, innocent, or having integrity. Brown, *Hebrew and English Lexicon*, 1070–1071; Harris, *Theological Wordbook*, 973–974. The most frequent occurrence of the word in the Old Testament is in sacrificial contexts, where it describes a sacrificial animal without blemish, and when used of persons "connot[es] 'unblemished' by moral fault—hence a person of unimpeachable integrity." Sarna, *Genesis*, 50.

[20]Enoch 65:11, in Charlesworth, *Old Testament Pseudepigrapha* 1:45.

[21]Sibylline Oracles 1:125–126, in Charlesworth, *Old Testament Pseudepigrapha* 1:338.

[22]Philo, On the Virtues 201, in *Philo VIII,* 287.

[23]Lactantius, Div. inst. ii.13, in Lewis, *Interpretation of Noah and the Flood*, 159.

[24]Josephus, Jewish Antiquities I. iii. 2, 8, in *Josephus IV*, 35, 49.

[25]Moses 7:47, and see 6:57.

[26]1 Pet. 1:19, translation in Lattimore, *New Testament*, 501; see also translation in *New Jerusalem Bible*: "a blameless and spotless lamb." King James has "a lamb without blemish and without spot."

[27]Moses 8:19.

[28]Moses 7:1; and see 6:68.

[29]Moses 8:27 says that Shem, Ham, and Japeth "walked with God."

[30]Moses 8:20.

[31]Moses 8:24.

[32]Moses 8:23–24.

[33]Leibowitz, *Studies in Bereshit*, 70–71, quoting Midrash Tanhuma.

[34]Ibid.

[35]Culi, *Torah Anthology* 1:337.

[36]The Conflict of Adam and Eve with Satan, book 3, chapter 4, in Malan, *Conflict of Adam*, 146.

[37]Sefer Ha-Aggadah 2:120, in Bialik, *Book of Legends*, 27.

[38]Sibylline Oracles 1:171–172, in Charlesworth, *Old Testament Pseudepigrapha* 1:339.

[39]Moses 6:38.

[40]Qur'an 11:26, 32, in Cragg, *Qur'an*, 114.

[41]Moses 8:18.

[42]Moses 8:26, 18.

[43]The First Epistle of Clement to the Corinthians VII, in *Ante-Nicene Fathers* 1:7.

[44]Moses 7:27.

[45]Book of Yashar (Jasher) 6:11–12, in Noah, *Book of Yashar*, 13.

[46]D&C 88:89–91.

[47]D&C 43:20–22.

⁴⁸Moses 7:28.

⁴⁹JST Gen. 9:21–23.

⁵⁰JS—M 1:41; cf. Matt. 24:37.

⁵¹JS—M 1:30.

⁵²JS—M 1:31.

⁵³Galbraith, *Scriptural Teachings of Prophet Joseph Smith*, 380.

⁵⁴D&C 1:17–18, 23.

⁵⁵D&C 63:37.

⁵⁶D&C 5:19.

⁵⁷D&C 100:16.

⁵⁸D&C 4:2.

## Chapter 3 • Abraham

¹Abr. 1:5–11.

²Recognitions of Clement 1.32, in *Ante-Nicene Fathers* 8:86.

³Ginzberg, *Legends of the Jews* 1:185.

⁴Jubilees 11:17, in VanderKam, *Book of Jubilees*, 67.

⁵Green, *Devotion and Commandment*, 43–44.

⁶Clark, *Blessings of Abraham*, 39–44. Jubilees specifies Abraham's age when he began to pray.

⁷Clark, *Blessings of Abraham*, 43–44.

⁸Abr. 1:5–7.

⁹See Abr. 1:31, and Clark, *Blessings of Abraham*, 68–79.

¹⁰Abr. 1:2.

¹¹Abr. 2:11.

¹²Levner, *Legends of Israel* 1:82.

¹³*On Abraham* 42, in *Philo VI*, 121.

¹⁴See Clark, *Blessings of Abraham*, 59–60.

¹⁵Ibid., 82.

¹⁶Moro. 8:26.

¹⁷Warren Zev Harvey, "Grace or Loving-Kindness," in Cohen, *Contemporary Jewish Religious Thought*, 302.

¹⁸Abr. 2:6.

¹⁹Abr. 2:15.

²⁰Buxbaum, *Hillel*, 126.

²¹Qur'an 19:49–50, in Asad, *Qur'ān*, 462. For clarity, I have unbracketed the words "unto others," which are bracketed in the original.

²²Knappert, *Islamic Legends* 1:73.

[23]Klinghoffer, *Discovery of God*, 31, quoting Maimonides.

[24]Levy, *A Faithful Heart*, 54, quoting the Zohar.

[25]Midrash Rabbah on the Song of Songs 1:3:3, in Freedman, *Song of Songs,* 39.

[26]Tuchman, *Passions of the Matriarchs*, 5.

[27]Munk, *Call of the Torah* 1:262.

[28]Ginzberg, *Legends of the Jews* 1:205, citing Yashar.

[29]Book of Yashar (Jasher) 13:2, in Noah, *Book of Yashar* 36.

[30]Ginzberg, *Legends of the Jews* 1:205, citing Yashar.

[31]Nibley, *Teachings of the Pearl of Great Price*, Lecture 24, 10–11.

[32]Chavel, *Encyclopedia of Torah Thoughts*, 31.

[33]Ginzberg, *Legends of the Jews* 5:382, n. 4.

[34]Ibid., 5:259, n. 274.

[35]Klinghoffer, *Discovery of God*, 36, quoting Maimonides.

[36]Culi, *Torah Anthology* 2:166.

[37]Montefiore, *Rabbinic Anthology*, 564.

[38]Clark, *Blessings of Abraham*, 108–110.

[39]1QapGen xix.25, in Martinez, *Dead Sea Scrolls* 1: 41. See Clark, *Blessings of Abraham*, 115.

[40]Clark, *Blessings of Abraham*, 105–122.

[41]Abr. 3, and see verse 15.

[42]Petersen, *Abraham*, 53.

[43]Al-Rabghūzī, *Stories of the Prophets* 2:114; Pitron 6:24, in Gaster, *Asatir*, 233.

[44]Wacholder, Ben Zion. "How Long Did Abraham Stay in Egypt?" *Hebrew Union College Annual* 35 (1964), 43.

[45]Hugh Nibley, "A New Look at the Pearl of Great Price, part 9, continued: Setting the Stage: The World of Abraham," *Era* 73:1 [Jan. 1970], 57.

[46]Matthews, *Armenian Commentary on Genesis*, 81 (see Clark, *Blessings of Abraham*, 275, note 6).

[47]Testament of Abraham (Recension A) 1:2, in Charlesworth, *Old Testament Pseudepigrapha* 1:882 (parenthesis in original).

[48]Ginzberg, *Legends of the Jews* 1:241; 5:248, n. 223.

[49]Zohar, Vayera 102b, in Sperling, *Zohar* 1:328–329.

[50]Gen. 18:23–33.

[51]Kasher, *Encyclopedia of Biblical Interpretation* 3:46.

[52]Nibley, *Abraham in Egypt*, 204–205.

[53]Kasher, *Encyclopedia of Biblical Interpretation* 3:46.

[54]Hershon, *Rabbinical Commentary on Genesis*, 103.

[55]As many translations render Isa. 41:8. See Clark, *Blessings of Abraham*, 19.

[56]Noble, *Great Men of God*, 61–63.

[57] Bezah 32b, in Epstein, *Babylonian Talmud*.

[58] Galbraith, *Scriptural Teachings of Prophet Joseph Smith*, 270.

[59] Clark, *Blessings of Abraham*, 191–195.

[60] Ginzberg, *Legends of the Jews* 1:270–271.

[61] Levner, *Legends of Israel* 1:82.

[62] Rappoport, *Ancient Israel* 1:276–277.

[63] Levner, *Legends of Israel* 1:82.

[64] Rappoport, *Ancient Israel* 1:276–277.

[65] See Clark, *Blessings of Abraham*, 207–221, on Abraham's offering of Isaac.

[66] Gen. 22:1.

[67] Morgenstern, *Jewish Interpretation of Genesis*, 145, capitalizing "his."

[68] Matt. 3:17.

[69] As reported by John Taylor in *Journal of Discourses* 24:264.

[70] See Galbraith, *Scriptural Teachings of Prophet Joseph Smith*, 15.

[71] Jacob 4:5.

[72] John 3:16.

[73] Ether 12:33.

[74] Nibley, *Abraham in Egypt*, 203–204.

[75] According to Maimonides, the leading Jewish scholar of the Middle Ages. Soloveitchik, *Man of Faith in the Modern World*, 83.

[76] Clark, *Blessings of Abraham*, 233 (footnotes omitted).

[77] Crothers, *Abraham the First Missionary*, 25.

[78] *Journal of Discourses* 24:125–126.

[79] David A. Bednar, "Becoming a Missionary," *Ensign* 35:11 [Nov. 2005], 44–45.

[80] D&C 132:32.

[81] Spencer W. Kimball, "The Example of Abraham," *Ensign* 5:6 [June 1975], 7.

[82] D&C 12:8.

## Chapter 4 • Isaiah

[1] Isa. 51:1–2.

[2] Or, "is the source of," or perhaps "has granted," "salvation" or "help." See Wildberger, *Isaiah 1–12*, 4–5; Young, *Isaiah 1–3*; Brown, *Hebrew and English Lexicon*, 446–448; Harris, *Theological Wordbook* 1:414–416; Botterweck, *Theological Dictionary of the old Testament* 6:441–463.

[3] King Amaziah. Megillah 10b, 15b, in Epstein, *Hebrew English Talmud*; Ginzberg, *Legends of the Jews* 6:357.

[4] For the proposition that Isaiah is most likely describing an event that actually occurred at the temple, or at least that began at the temple (as opposed to a visionary event in heaven), see: *Encyclopaedia Judaica* 9:47; Seitz, *Isaiah 1–39*, 54; Wildberger, *Isaiah 1–12*, 263–270.

[5]The King James "LORD" in all capital letters is the reverential rendering of the sacred name of Israel's God, Yahweh, or as the King James transliterates it in a handful of passages, Jehovah.

[6]Isa. 6:1–4.

[7]Isa. 6:5.

[8]Isa. 6:7.

[9]*NIV Study Bible: New International Version* Isa. 6:7.

[10]See, for example, Wildberger, *Isaiah 1–12*, 270.

[11]*Encyclopaedia Judaica* 5:1382.

[12]For a convenient description of the elaborate ceremony, see *Encyclopaedia Judaica* 5:1382.

[13]Mosiah 4:2.

[14]Isa. 6:8.

[15]Watts, *Isaiah 1–33*, 72–73.

[16]Isa. 6:8.

[17]Abr. 3:27.

[18]Abr. 3:27.

[19]Isa. 1:4, 7.

[20]Isa. 1:16–17.

[21]1 Ne. 20:1, quoting Isa. 48:1 concerning those who "come forth out of the waters of Judah"—but adding, "or out of the waters of baptism."

[22]Isa. 1:18.

[23]Isa. 9:6.

[24]Isa. 7:14, and same translation in: *NIV Study Bible: New International Version*; *Holy Bible: New King James Version*; and *New American Standard Bible*; and is the marginal reading in: Metzger, *New Revised Standard Version*; and *New Jerusalem Bible*.

[25]Isa. 53:3–5.

[26]Sawyer, *Fifth Gospel*, 21. For summaries of Isaiah usage in the New Testament, see *ibid.* 26–28, and Hastings, *Dictionary of Christ and Gospels* 1:839.

[27]Sawyer, *Fifth Gospel*, 1.

[28]Motyer, *Isaiah*, 13.

[29]2 Ne. 11:2.

[30]1 Ne. 11:13–33.

[31]Galbraith, *Scriptural Teachings of Prophet Joseph Smith*, 172.

[32]Sparks, *Apocryphal Old Testament*, 775–778; Charlesworth, *Old Testament Pseudepigrapha* 2:149–150.

[33]Ascension of Isaiah 10–11, in Charlesworth, *Old Testament Pseudepigrapha* 2:172–176, and in Sparks, *Apocryphal Old Testament*, 806–812.

[34]Ascension of Isaiah 3.13, in Sparks, *Apocryphal Old Testament*, 789.

[35]Ascension of Isaiah 3:13, in Charlesworth, *Old Testament Pseudepigrapha* 2:160.

[36] Ascension of Isaiah 3.14–17, in Sparks, *Apocryphal Old Testament*, 789–790.

[37] Ibid., 4.20, in Sparks, *Apocryphal Old Testament*, 793.

[38] See, for example, Moses 1:41, and also verses 6, 16–20, 32–33; Moses 4:1–4.

[39] Compared to the extensive editorial changes that befell the original first chapters of Genesis (as restored through Joseph Smith in the Book of Moses), the changes of substance made to the original book of Isaiah (as it appears in the Book of Mormon and in the Joseph Smith Translation) appear to be remarkably few. In fact, the only Isaiah chapter to undergo significant alteration was the one that prophesies the coming forth of the Book of Mormon itself (see JST Isa. 29). But the majestic messianic passages remained almost untouched.

[40] See Mosiah 14–15.

[41] See Matt. 3:1–6.

[42] For summaries, see Hastings, *Dictionary of Apostolic Church* 1:621 (a discussion of Paul's extensive use of Isaiah); and Dunn, *Theology of Paul*, 764–765 (a list of the Isaiah passages mentioned in Dunn's book). Among the numerous citations of Isaiah by Paul, see, for example: Acts 13:47 (see Isa. 49:6); Rom. 10:15 (see Isa. 52:7); 1 Cor. 1:19 (see Isa. 29:14); Philip. 2:9–11 (see Isa. 45:23).

[43] Isa. 6:9.

[44] Isa. 53:1 ("message" in *NIV Study Bible: New International Version*).

[45] Alma 4:19.

[46] Ginzberg, *Legends of the Jews* 6:359.

[47] 2 Kgs. 17:5–6.

[48] Isa. 28:1–4.

[49] Josephus, Jewish Antiquities IX.xiv.1, in *Josephus VI*, 149.

[50] Ludlow, *Isaiah*, 2. That they carried at least some of their scriptural records with them may be implied in the account of 2 Esdras telling of their later determination—when the opportunity presented itself to travel northward to uninhabited regions—to "keep their statutes that they had not kept in their own land." Metzger, *New Revised Standard Version* 2 Esdras 13:42.

[51] 2 Kgs. 21:2.

[52] Ascension of Isaiah 11:43, in Sparks, *Apocryphal Old Testament*, 812.

[53] Ascension of Isaiah 3:13–17, in Sparks, *Apocryphal Old Testament*, 789–790.

[54] 1 Ne. 1:19–20.

[55] Sparks, *Apocryphal Old Testament*, 775, citing the Palestinian Talmud, *Sanhedrin* x.2.

[56] Ascension of Isaiah 5:11, in Sparks, *Apocryphal Old Testament*, 794. Isaiah's death by being sawn asunder is attested in numerous sources. See generally: Ginzberg, *Legends of the Jews* 6:374–375; Charlesworth, *Old Testament Pseudepigrapha* 2:150–151; and Sparks, *Apocryphal Old Testament*, 775–778.

[57] Ginzberg, *Legends of the Jews* 4:263.

[58] 3 Ne. 23:2.

[59] 3 Ne. 23:1.

[60]3 Ne. 20:30.

[61]3 Ne. 20:40, quoting (with slight variation) Isa. 52:7.

[62]JS—H 1:19; cf. Isa. 29:13: "this people draw near me with their mouth, and with their lips do honour me, but have removed their heart far from me."

[63]D&C 1:1; see Isa. 49:1: "Listen, O isles, unto me; and hearken, ye people, from far."

[64]D&C 4:3; and see 6:3; 11:3; 12:3; 14:3.

## Chapter 5 • Abinadi

[1]2 Chr. 36:16.

[2]Mosiah 11:20

[3]Mosiah 29:17–18.

[4]See Mosiah 11–12.

[5]Mosiah 11:20–21.

[6]Mosiah 11:26.

[7]Mosiah 11:27–28.

[8]See, e.g., Isa. 10:12–19; and 14:4–23.

[9]Mosiah 12:1–12.

[10]Mosiah 12:9–19.

[11]Might it have been Alma?

[12]Mosiah 12:20.

[13]Mosiah 12:21–24, quoting Isa. 52:7–10.

[14]North, *Second Isaiah*, 220–221.

[15]Mosiah 12:25–27.

[16]Mosiah 12:29–30.

[17]Mosiah 12:31–37.

[18]Mosiah 13:1.

[19]Mosiah 13:2–24.

[20]Mosiah 13:27–33.

[21]Mosiah 13:34–35.

[22]Mosiah 14:3–5, quoting Isa. 53:3–5.

[23]Mosiah 15:1, 8–9.

[24]Mosiah 15:14–15.

[25]Mosiah 15:16–17.

[26]Mosiah 15:18.

[27]Mosiah 15:19–27.

[28]Mosiah 15:28–31, quoting and explaining Isa. 52:8–9.

[29]Mosiah 16:1–15.

[30]Mosiah 16:1–4.

[31] Mosiah 17:20.

[32] Mosiah 14:3–4, quoting Isa. 53:3–4.

[33] Mosiah 17:20.

[34] Hanson, *Isaiah 40–66*, 149.

[35] Mosiah 15:18.

[36] 3 Ne. 11:15–17.

[37] 3 Ne. 11:19.

[38] 3 Ne. 17:10.

[39] 3 Ne. 20:30.

[40] 3 Ne. 20:40; emphasis added.

[41] Mosiah 15:28.

[42] D&C 128:19.

## Chapter 6 • *Alma the Younger*

[1] Mosiah 27:8.

[2] Mosiah 27:8–10.

[3] Mosiah 27:10–12; and see Alma 36:6–7.

[4] Mosiah 27:14–15.

[5] Mosiah 27:16.

[6] Alma 36:9; Mosiah 27:16.

[7] Alma 36:11.

[8] Alma 36:12–16.

[9] D&C 19:15.

[10] Mosiah 26:27.

[11] Mosiah 16:2.

[12] Mosiah 27:20–22.

[13] Alma 36:17–18.

[14] Jeffrey R. Holland, "Alma, Son of Alma," *Ensign* 7:3 [March 1977], 79.

[15] Alma 36:19–22.

[16] Mosiah 27:24.

[17] Mosiah 27:28; Alma 36:24.

[18] Mosiah 27:25–26.

[19] Mosiah 18:21–22 (Mormon's summary of Alma's preaching).

[20] Mosiah 15:10–13.

[21] Moses 6:59–68.

[22] D&C 93:15; and see John 1:32.

[23] Mosiah 27:32.

[24] Mosiah 27:35.

[25]Alma 36:24.

[26]Mosiah 27:36.

[27]Mosiah 27:32.

[28]Mosiah 29:42.

[29]Alma 1–3.

[30]See, for example, Alma 4:4–5.

[31]Alma 4:18–19.

[32]Alma 5:14.

[33]Alma 5:26.

[34]Alma 5:21.

[35]Alma 5:48.

[36]Alma 7:7, 10–13.

[37]Alma 33:22.

[38]Alma 32:21.

[39]Alma 9:26–27.

[40]Alma 5:33.

[41]Alma 13:27.

[42]Alma 5:62.

[43]Alma 32:16.

[44]Alma 13:28.

[45]Alma 5:54.

[46]Alma 33.

[47]Alma 32:40–43; 33:23.

[48]Alma 33:14–15.

[49]Alma 5:8–10.

[50]Alma 32:28–42; 33:23.

[51]Alma 5:46.

[52]Alma 8:10.

[53]Alma 43:1.

[54]Alma 45:18.

[55]Alma 29:1–2.

[56]See Clark, *Fathers and Sons in the Book of Mormon*, 147–148.

[57]Alma 45:19.

[58]Mosiah 27:25–26.

[59]D&C 1:2.

[60]D&C 5:16.

## Chapter 7 • Ammon

[1] Mosiah 28:4.

[2] Alma 17:2–3.

[3] Mosiah 27:35–36.

[4] Jarom 1:7.

[5] Ammon is listed first among the sons (Mosiah 27:34), just as Mosiah had been listed first among his brothers (Mosiah 1:2). Later is it said that Ammon was "chief among" Mosiah's sons (Alma 17:18). In ancient Israel, "normally the eldest son was expected to succeed, but the king had the right to choose his heir." *Encyclopaedia Judaica* 10:1015.

[6] Jacob 7:24; and see Enos 1:20.

[7] Alma 26:23.

[8] Alma 26:24–25.

[9] Alma 17:14–15.

[10] Mosiah 28:3.

[11] Mosiah 28:2.

[12] Alma 17:6.

[13] Mosiah 28:7.

[14] Alma 19:23. Here the specific promise about Ammon is reported.

[15] Alma 17:6.

[16] Mosiah 28:1; Alma 17:12.

[17] Alma 17:9.

[18] Alma 17:5.

[19] Alma 26:27.

[20] Alma 26:28–31.

[21] Alma 17:25.

[22] Alma 17:29.

[23] Alma 17:33.

[24] Alma 18:2.

[25] Alma 18:4.

[26] Alma 18:10–11.

[27] Alma 18:20–21.

[28] Alma 18:34–35.

[29] Alma 18:38–39.

[30] Mosiah 3:5–10.

[31] Mosiah 3:5. See also Luke 22:27: "I am among you as he that serveth."

[32] Alma 18:40–41.

[33] Alma 19:12–13.

[34] Alma 19:13.

[35]Alma 19:29.
[36]Alma 19:30–36.
[37]Alma 26:9.
[38]Alma 26:1, 3
[39]Alma 26:15.
[40]Alma 26:4.
[41]Alma 26:16.
[42]Alma 26:37.
[43]Luke 22:27.
[44]See, for example, D&C 1:6, 38; 45:25; 84:36; 112:1; 133:8.
[45]D&C 93:46.

## Chapter 8 • Nephi, Son of Helaman

[1]Hel. 3:37.
[2]Hel. 4:14.
[3]Hel. 4:15–26; 5:1–3.
[4]Hel. 5:4.
[5]Hel. 5:5.
[6]Hel. 5:6–7.
[7]D&C 33:8.
[8]Hel. 5:8.
[9]Hel. 5:9–11.
[10]See Moses 7:53.
[11]See Isa. 8:14.
[12]Hel. 5:12.
[13]Hel. 5:14.
[14]Hel. 5:17–19.
[15]Hel. 5:17.
[16]Hel. 5:19.
[17]Hel. 5:21–25.
[18]Hel. 5:26.
[19]Hel. 5:27–33.
[20]Hel. 5:34–41.
[21]Hel. 5:42–49.
[22]Hel. 5:50.
[23]Hel. 6:5.
[24]Hel. 7:2–3.
[25]Hel. 6:17.

²⁶Hel. 6:23.

²⁷Hel. 7:5.

²⁸Hel. 7:6–12.

²⁹Hel. 7:13–17.

³⁰Hel. 7:18–28.

³¹Hel. 8:22.

³²Hel. 8:24.

³³Hel. 8:27–28.

³⁴Hel. 9:1–9.

³⁵Hel. 9:10–20.

³⁶Hel. 9:21–36.

³⁷Hel. 9:37–41; 10:1.

³⁸Hel. 10:1–3.

³⁹Hel. 10:4–5.

⁴⁰Hel. 10:5–10.

⁴¹Hel. 10:11.

⁴²Hel. 10:12.

⁴³Hel. 10:15–17.

⁴⁴Hel. 13–15.

⁴⁵3 Ne. 1:3.

⁴⁶Benson, *Witness and Warning*, 37.

⁴⁷D&C 64:33.

⁴⁸D&C 64:25.

⁴⁹D&C 4:2.

⁵⁰Coffin, *Creed of Jesus*, 258.

## Chapter 9 • John the Baptist

¹1 Ne. 10:7–9.

²See Hel. 5:6.

³Alma 34:14.

⁴*Encyclopaedia Judaica* 10:984.

⁵Bock, *Luke 1:1–9:50*, 79.

⁶The King James "Zacharias" transliterates the Greek form of the Aramaic "Zechariah," the latter of which is used in nearly all modern English translations.

⁷Either "My God is the one by whom I swear" or "My God is fortune." Fitzmeyer, *Luke I–IX*, 322; Darrell L. Bock, *Luke 1:1–9:50*, 76–77.

⁸Luke 1:6.

⁹As pointed out in Fitzmeyer, *Luke I–IX*, 322.

[10]Kittel, *Theological Dictionary of New Testament* 4:1.

[11]Bock, *Luke 1:1–9:50*, 79.

[12]Wigoder, *Encyclopedia of Judaism*, 363.

[13]See Levine, *Leviticus*, 100.

[14]The glory of the angel is not mentioned in Luke, but is perhaps implied by Zacharias' fear at seeing the angel (Luke 1:12). It is from Joseph Smith that we know that this angel appeared in great glory: Joseph Smith's identification of this angel as a righteous spirit necessarily means, according to Joseph Smith, that the spirit appeared in "flaming fire and glory." Galbraith, *Scriptural Teachings of Prophet Joseph Smith*, 366.

[15]Fitzmeyer, *Luke I–IX*, 325.

[16]Luke 1:14–17.

[17]Luke 1:19.

[18]Galbraith, *Scriptural Teachings of Prophet Joseph Smith*, 178.

[19]The original Greek word in Luke 1:36 does not specify the degree of kinship (Fitzmeyer, *Luke I–IX*, 352), so that most modern translations render the word as "relative" rather than the King James "cousin."

[20]Nephi, who saw her centuries before in vision, described her as "most beautiful and fair above all other virgins." 1 Ne. 11:15.

[21]Luke 1:27 in: Metzger, *New Revised Standard Version; New American Standard Bible*; and Fitzmeyer, *Luke I–IX*, 334.

[22]Luke 1:36.

[23]Luke 1:38. The word translated in King James as "handmaid" appears as "maid-servant" in *Holy Bible: New King James Version*, and as "servant" in: Metzger, *New Revised Standard Version; NIV Study Bible: New International Version; Revised English Bible*; and *New Jerusalem Bible*.

[24]Luke 1:46–47.

[25]JST Luke 1:75–76; cf. Luke 1:76–77.

[26]D&C 84:28.

[27]Galbraith, *Scriptural Teachings of Prophet Joseph Smith*, 294.

[28]For example, the Protevangelium of James 22–24, in Hennecke, *New Testament Apocrypha* 1:387–388.

[29]Budge, *Book of the Bee*, 86.

[30]Galbraith, *Scriptural Teachings of Prophet Joseph Smith*, 294.

[31]Ibid.; and see Matthews, *A Burning Light*, 24–26.

[32]JST Luke 1:79 (compare Luke 1:80).

[33]Matthews, *A Burning Light*, 27–28. The most famous Jewish desert community was the Essene community at Qumran, who were known, according to the historian Josephus, to adopt "other men's children, while yet pliable and docile . . . and mold them according to their own ways." Josephus, *Jewish Wars* 2.8.2 §120, cited in Fitzmeyer, *Luke I–IX*, 389. The Qumran community perceived its own mission in the desert to be that described by Isaiah 40:3: "In the wilderness, Prepare ye the way of the Lord." Raymond E. Brown, "The Dead Sea Scrolls and the New Testament," in Charlesworth, *John and the Dead Sea Scrolls*, 4.

³⁴D&C 84:27.

³⁵D&C 13.

³⁶John's statement to the effect that "he that sent me to baptize with water" (John 1:33) seems to imply that he had been sent by an angel.

³⁷JST Matt. 3:26.

³⁸*Eerdmans Bible Dictionary*, 588; see Matt. 3:4; Mark 1:6.

³⁹*Encyclopaedia Judaica* 11:816; 13:1176, citing Yoma 9b of the Babylonian Talmud: "After the later prophets Haggai, Zechariah, and Malachi died, the Holy Spirit departed from Israel." Yoma 9b, Epstein, *Hebrew English Talmud*.

⁴⁰JST Matt. 3:28–29; cf. Matt. 3:2–3, which instead of "For I am he who . . ." reads "For this is he that was . . ."

⁴¹Motyer, *Isaiah*, 300; and see Hanson, *Isaiah 40–66*, 21.

⁴²Hastings, *Dictionary of Christ and Gospels* 1:863; see Matt. 3:5–10; Luke 3:7–14; John 1:19, 35–51.

⁴³Young, *Isaiah* 3:28–29, commenting on Isa. 40:3, and noting that John the Baptist did correctly bring out "the fundamental meaning of the prophecy," that is, that the way to prepare for the Lord is to repent.

⁴⁴Most modern English translations.

⁴⁵Fitzmeyer, *Luke I–IX*, 463.

⁴⁶Luke 3:10–14.

⁴⁷Mark 1:4.

⁴⁸JST Matt. 3:32; emphasis added; cf. Matt. 3:6.

⁴⁹JST Matt. 3:38; cf. Matt. 3:11.

⁵⁰John 1:29, 36.

⁵¹Matt. 3:14.

⁵²Most modern English translations.

⁵³Matt. 3:15.

⁵⁴Matt. 3:13–17; and see Mark 1:9–11; Luke 3:21–22.

⁵⁵D&C 93:15–17, from a larger section comprising verses 6–17, from "the record of John" (verse 18). That this is John the Baptist rather than John the author of the fourth Gospel is suggested by comparing the above quoted section with JST Matt. 3:44–46, showing that it was John the Baptist who saw the Spirit descend and heard the voice from heaven—and showing in turn that the record of John in D&C 93 is the record of John the Baptist, which was incorporated by the apostle John as a prologue to his Gospel. For a discussion of the independent nature of the prologue and its relationship to the rest of the Gospel of John, see Brown, *The Gospel According to John*, 18–21.

⁵⁶John 5:35.

⁵⁷Luke 7:27–28.

⁵⁸John 10:41.

⁵⁹"The greatest miracles I see today are not necessarily the healing of sick bodies, but the greatest miracles I see are the healing of sick souls." Harold B. Lee, "Stand Ye in Holy Places," *Ensign* 3:7 [July 1973], 123.

⁶⁰See, e.g., John 1:19–52; Acts 18:24–28; 19:1–7.

⁶¹*Eerdmans Bible Dictionary,* 588, citing Mark 6:14–29.

⁶²John 3:28–30.

⁶³JST John 3:34–36; cf. John 3:34–36.

⁶⁴JST Luke 3:3–11; cf. Luke 3:4–6.

⁶⁵D&C 13.

⁶⁶D&C 34:5–6.

⁶⁷D&C 39:20.

⁶⁸D&C 33:10–11.

⁶⁹D&C 59:2. See also D&C 106:8.

## Chapter 10 • Paul the Apostle

¹Smith, *Life and Letters of Saint Paul,* 20–21.

²See Hawthorne, *Dictionary of Paul,* 504; and Bruce, *Paul,* 41.

³Bruce, *Paul,* 32–36.

⁴Ibid., 38.

⁵Philip. 3:5.

⁶Hammer, *Jerusalem Anthology,* 115.

⁷Ps. 137:5, translation in Metzger, *New Revised Standard Version.*

⁸*Encyclopaedia Judaica* 8:482.

⁹Bruce, *Paul,* 51.

¹⁰Ibid., 49, quoting Shabbat 31a.

¹¹Gal. 1:14; and see Smith, *Life and Letters of Saint Paul,* 29–33.

¹²Acts of Paul and Thecla, in Hennecke, *New Testament Apocrypha* 2:353–354

¹³Galbraith, *Scriptural Teachings of Prophet Joseph Smith,* 205.

¹⁴Gen. 49:27, see translation in Metzger, *New Revised Standard Version.*

¹⁵Smith, *Life and Letters of Saint Paul,* 34.

¹⁶Bruce, *Paul,* 71.

¹⁷Acts 6:5.

¹⁸Acts 6:8.

¹⁹Acts 6:10.

²⁰Acts 6:15.

²¹Acts 7:54.

²²Smith, *Life and Letters of Saint Paul,* 43.

²³Acts 7:56.

[24]Smith, *Life and Letters of Saint Paul*, 43–44.

[25]Acts 22:20.

[26]Philip. 3:6.

[27]Acts 8:1–3; 22:19.

[28]Bruce, *Paul*, 71.

[29]Acts 9:1.

[30]See Bruce, *Paul*, 72–73.

[31]Philip. 3:12, translation in Bruce, *Paul*, 74. See other translations: Christ "took hold of me." *NIV Study Bible: New International Version; Revised English Bible; New Jerusalem Bible.*

[32]Acts 26:13.

[33]See Acts 9:17, and Bruce, *Paul*, 74, discussing 1 Cor. 9:1 and 15:8.

[34]Acts 22:9; JST Acts 9:7.

[35]Acts 26:14, in Johnson, *Gospel of Luke*, 430.

[36]Acts 26:14; and see 9:4. Or, as in most modern translations, kick against the "goads," which are cattle prods.

[37]Johnson, *Gospel of Luke*, 435.

[38]Acts 26:15.

[39]Acts 22:10.

[40]Acts 26:16–18.

[41]Abr. 2:6.

[42]Tillemont, *Ecclesiastical Memoirs* 1:159.

[43]Acts 22:10.

[44]Plural, in Acts 9:12 in modern translations like: Metzger, *New Revised Standard Version; NIV Study Bible: New International Version;* and *Revised English Bible.*

[45]Acts 9:11.

[46]The word is translated as "vessel" in the King James, and as "instrument" in modern translations like: Metzger, *New Revised Standard Version;* and *NIV Study Bible: New International Version.*

[47]Acts 9:15–16.

[48]Acts 9:17.

[49]Boardman, *Oxford History of the Classical World*, 11.

[50]Bruce, *Paul*, 29.

[51]Athanasius, "Ad Dracontium," *Nicene and Post Nicene Fathers* 4:559.

[52]See Rom. 15:28; Hawthorne, *Dictionary of Paul*, 661; Bruce, *Paul*, 314–316, 444–450; Smith, *Life and Letters of Saint Paul*, 612–613.

[53]John 4:35.

[54]Acts 16:9.

[55]Gal. 5:16, 25.

[56]Rom. 8:14; Gal. 5:18 ("led of the Spirit").

[57]Philip. 3:14 in *Revised English Bible*. The King James translation reads: "I press toward the mark for the prize of the high calling of God in Christ Jesus."

[58]2 Cor. 12:7–9.

[59]2 Cor. 6:4–5; 11:23.

[60]2 Cor. 11:24–27 in *Revised English Bible*.

[61]2 Cor. 4:8–9.

[62]2 Cor. 12:10.

[63]Philip. 4:13.

[64]Rom. 8:32 follows precisely the Greek text of Gen. 22:16. Dunn, *Theology of Paul* 224–225.

[65]Rom. 8:31–32.

[66]Rom. 5:3.

[67]Philip. 1:12, in *NIV Study Bible: The New International Version*.

[68]Philip. 3:10.

[69]Philip. 3:8–9.

[70]1 Cor. 2:2. See Hawthorne, *Dictionary of Paul*, 499.

[71]Orr, *I Corinthians*, 162.

[72]1 Cor. 1:18.

[73]1 Cor. 2:4.

[74]Acts 16:16–26.

[75]Acts 14:8–11.

[76]Acts 19:11, in Metzger, *New Revised Standard Version*.

[77]Acts 19:11–12.

[78]1 Cor. 13:4–7. The language is similar to how the prophet Mormon would later describe it in Moro. 7:45–47.

[79]Rom. 8:35, 38–39; and see 5:5.

[80]Rom. 13:8.

[81]Eph. 4:32.

[82]Paul Beasley-Murray, "Paul as Pastor," in Hawthorne, *Dictionary of Paul*, 655, internal scriptural references omitted.

[83]Gal. 4:14.

[84]Hastings, *Dictionary of Apostolic Church* 2:155, referring to Acts 20:36–38.

[85]Athanasius, Letter XI, in *Nicene and Post Nicene Fathers* 4:532.

[86]Galbraith, *Scriptural Teachings of Prophet Joseph Smith*, 15, 172, 194; D&C 76:67.

[87]Apocalypse of Paul 20, in Hennecke, *New Testament Apocrypha* 2:771–772.

[88]1 Cor. 2:9; and see D&C 76:10.

[89]Rom. 10:14–15.

[90]Acts 20:23, in Metzger, *New Revised Standard Version*.

[91]Acts 20:22-24.

[92]Acts 9:15–16.

[93]Acts 26:28.

[94]Philem. 1:1.

[95]Martyrdom of the Holy Apostle Paul 1–7, in Hennecke, *New Testament Apocrypha* 2:383.

[96]Tillemont, *Ecclesiastical Memoirs* 1:242–243.

[97]Ibid., 1:241.

[98]Ibid., 1:242.

[99]Martyrdom of the Holy Apostle Paul 1–7, in Hennecke, *New Testament Apocrypha* 2:384–385 (omitting the parentheses around the word "now"; capitalizing the word "for" after the word "service!"; and adding paragraph indentions ).

[100]2 Tim. 4:7–8.

[101]John 19:30.

[102]Tillemont, *Ecclesiastical Memoirs* 1:159.

[103]Martyrdom of the Holy Apostle Paul 1–7, in Hennecke, *New Testament Apocrypha* 2:383–387.

[104]1 Clement 5:5–6(7). First three segments quoted are from the Lightfoot translation, online at http://en.wikisource.org/wiki/1_Clement_(Lightfoot_translation); last segment quoted is translation from Hawthorne, *Dictionary of Paul*, 692.

[105]D&C 66:12.

[106]Galbraith, *Scriptural Teachings of Prophet Joseph Smith*, 59.

[107]Ibid., 77–78 (omitting dash after "death").

## Chapter 11 • Joseph Smith

[1]2 Thes. 2:3.

[2]2 Thes. 2:3, in Vaughan, *Twenty-Six Translations*, 3:951.

[3]Jessee, *Papers of Joseph Smith*, 5, spelling and capitalization normalized.

[4]JS—H 1:10.

[5]Jessee, *Papers of Joseph Smith*, 5–6, spelling and capitalization normalized.

[6]James 1:5 (see JS—H 1:11).

[7]JS—H 1:12.

[8]JS—H 1:14.

[9]Zohar, Lech Lecha 88a, in Sperling, *Zohar* 1:293.

[10]JS—H 1:15.

[11]JS—H 1:16; and see Acts 26:13.

[12]Orson Pratt's account, in Backman, *Joseph Smith's First Vision*, 172.

[13]Warren Cowdery's account, in Backman, *Joseph Smith's First Vision*, 159.

[14]JS—H 1:17; and see Jessee, *Papers of Joseph Smith*, 6.

[15]Galbraith, *Scriptural Teachings of Prophet Joseph Smith*, 365.

[16]JS—H 1:26.

[17]Although there are several men named James in the New Testament, James the brother of Jesus is, according to Raymond E. Brown, "the only truly plausible candidate" for author of the epistle of James. Brown, *Introduction to the New Testament*, 725.

[18]Thomson, *The Praying Christ*, 34.

[19]Ibid.

[20]Jessee, *Papers of Joseph Smith*, 7.

[21]JS—H 1:23.

[22]JS—H 1:24–25.

[23]Galbraith, *Scriptural Teachings of Prophet Joseph Smith*, 148, echoing Philem. 1: 1,9.

[24]D&C 127:2.

[25]Galbraith, *Scriptural Teachings of Prophet Joseph Smith*, 28.

[26]Evans, *Joseph Smith*, 422.

[27]Smith, *History of the Church* 6:346.

[28]Gibbons, *Joseph Smith*, 1.

[29]JS—H 1:29.

[30]Snow, *Biography and Family Record of Lorenzo Snow*, 138–140, quoting Oliver Cowdery.

[31]Galbraith, *Scriptural Teachings of Prophet Joseph Smith*, 220.

[32]Enos 1:11–18.

[33]3 Ne. 18:15, 18.

[34]3 Ne. 18:20.

[35]For example, see: 2 Ne. 4:35; Enos 1:15; 3 Ne. 27:28–29; Morm. 9:21.

[36]Galbraith, *Scriptural Teachings of Prophet Joseph Smith*, 305–306 (capitalizing the instance of the word "gospel" that is not capitalized).

[37]D&C 65:1–2, 6.

[38]*Teachings of the Presidents of the Church: Joseph Smith*, 90.

[39]Smith, *History of the Church* 1:78.

[40]D&C 21:7

[41]Hartshorn, *Joseph Smith*, 15–16.

[42]Galbraith, *Scriptural Teachings of Prophet Joseph Smith*, 133.

[43]Briggs, *Brother Joseph*, 103–104.

[44]Joseph B. Wirthlin, "The Example of Joseph Smith," in *The Prophet and His Work*, 92.

[45]Hartshorn, *Joseph Smith*, 17–18.

[46]Galbraith, *Scriptural Teachings of Prophet Joseph Smith*, 139.

[47]See *Journal of Discourses* 3:66–67.

[48]Robinson, "George Washington Taggart."

[49]*Journal of Discourses* 8:206.

[50]Parley P. Pratt, *Autobiography*, 32.

[51]Flake, *Mighty Men of Zion*, 11.

[52]Ibid.

[53]Madsen, *Joseph Smith*, 90.

[54]Ibid.

[55]*Teachings of the Presidents of the Church: Joseph Smith*, 150.

[56]D&C 42:14.

[57]Leonard J. Arrington, "Joseph Smith," in Arrington, *Presidents of the Church*, 24.

[58]*Teachings of the Presidents of the Church: Joseph Smith*, 246–247.

[59]Ibid., 127.

[60]*Journal of Discourses* 24:55.

[61]Smith, *History of the Church* 1:109–110.

[62]*Teachings of the Presidents of the Church: Joseph Smith*, 131.

[63]Moro. 7:48.

[64]Galbraith, *Scriptural Teachings of Prophet Joseph Smith*, 350.

[65]Ibid., 355.

[66]Ibid., 269.

[67]Andrus, *Joseph Smith*, 42.

[68]Ibid.

[69]Ibid.

[70]Ibid.

[71]Galbraith, *Scriptural Teachings of Prophet Joseph Smith*, 104.

[72]Ibid., 199.

[73]Hartshorn, *Joseph Smith*, 15, quoting D&C 15:6, a passage repeated in 16:6.

[74]D&C 39:6.

[75]Moses 7:62; and see Benson, *Witness and Warning*, vii.

[76]Ludlow, *Encyclopedia of Mormonism* 1:107.

[77]Benson, *Witness and Warning*, 11.

[78]Hinckley, *Teachings of Gordon B. Hinckley*, 367–368.

[79]Cannon, *Life of Joseph Smith*, 160.

[80]Briggs, *Brother Joseph*, 98.

[81]Barrett, *Joseph Smith and the Restoration*, 344.

[82]Whitney, *Heber C. Kimball*, 132.

[83]Galbraith, *Scriptural Teachings of Prophet Joseph Smith*, 362.

[84]Gibbons, *Joseph Smith*, 260.

[85]D&C 4:4; 11:3; 12:3; 14:3; 33:3.

[86]Bushman, *Joseph Smith*, 410.

[87]Smith, *History of the Church* 5:139.

[88]Thomas S. Monson, "The Prophet Joseph Smith: Teacher by Example," in *The Prophet and His Work*, 15.

[89]Galbraith, *Scriptural Teachings of Prophet Joseph Smith*, 129.

[90]Ibid., 57.

[91]Ibid., 326.

[92]Ibid., 93.

[93]Ibid., 92.

[94]Ibid., 57.

[95]Benson, *Come unto Christ*, 17, quoting *Manuscript History of Brigham Young*, February 23, 1847.

[96]Galbraith, *Scriptural Teachings of Prophet Joseph Smith*, 57.

[97]Ibid., 156-157.

[98]D&C 4:7, and, with at times minor variation: 6:5; 11:5; 12:5; 14:5.

[99]D&C 33:17.

[100]D&C 30:6.

[101]D&C 103:36.

[102]D&C 65:2, 5.

[103]See, e.g., Smith, *History of the Church* 4:231, 568, 599; 5:151.

[104]McConkie, *Joseph Smith*, xxiv.

[105]D&C 121:1–4.

[106]Smith, *History of the Church* 3:293–294 (punctuating the scripture as it appears in D&C 121:7–8).

[107]D&C 121:34–46.

[108]Briggs, *Brother Joseph*, 104–105.

[109]Galbraith, *Scriptural Teachings of Prophet Joseph Smith*, 432.

[110]Bushman, *Joseph Smith*, 550.

[111]Heb. 11:38.

[112]D&C 135:3.

[113]*Journal of Discourses* 24:54.

[114]Barrett, *Joseph Smith and the Restoration*, 633.

[115]D&C 46:7.

[116]Galbraith, *Scriptural Teachings of Prophet Joseph Smith*, 61.

[117]Smith, *History of the Church* 4:540.

## Chapter 12 • Wilford Woodruff

[1]Cowley, *Wilford Woodruff: Fourth President*, 5–9.

[2]Ibid., 5.

[3]Kenney, *Wilford Woodruff's Journal* 1:5 (all quotations from this journal have, when necessary, been normalized for spelling, grammar, and punctuation).

[4]Dean C. Jessee, "Wilford Woodruff," in Arrington, *Presidents of the Church*, 117.

[5]Ibid., 119.

[6]Kenney, *Wilford Woodruff's Journal* 1:5.

[7]Dean C. Jessee, "Wilford Woodruff," in Arrington, *Presidents of the Church*, 120.

[8]Ibid., 121.

[9]Ibid., 121–122.

[10]Ibid., 122.

[11]Cowley, *Wilford Woodruff: Fourth President*, 18.

[12]Gibbons, *Wilford Woodruff: Wondrous Worker*, 6.

[13]Kenney, *Wilford Woodruff's Journal* 1:5. Cf. Rom. 8:14: "For as many as are led by the Spirit of God, they are the sons of God," and Gal. 5:18: "But if ye be led of the Spirit, ye are not under the law."

[14]Woodruff, *Leaves from My Journal*, 2.

[15]Ibid., 2–3.

[16]Cowley, *Wilford Woodruff: Fourth President*, 33, capitalizing "spirit" in this and subsequent passages from this source.

[17]Kenney, *Wilford Woodruff's Journal* 1:6.

[18]Cowley, *Wilford Woodruff: Fourth President*, 34.

[19]Ibid., 35.

[20]Ibid.

[21]Durham, *Discourses of Wilford Woodruff*, 5.

[22]*Journal of Discourses* 13:157.

[23]Ludlow, *Latter-day Prophets Speak*, 285.

[24]*Teaching of the Presidents of the Church: Wilford Woodruff*, 46.

[25]Cowley, *Wilford Woodruff: Fourth President*, 17–18.

[26]Durham, *Discourses of Wilford Woodruff*, 67.

[27]Lundwall, *The Vision*, 12.

[28]Dean C. Jessee, "Wilford Woodruff," in Arrington, *Presidents of the Church*, 126.

[29]Durham, *Discourses of Wilford Woodruff*, 38.

[30]Ibid., 38–39.

[31]Kenney, *Wilford Woodruff's Journal* 1:9.

[32]Ibid., 1:9–10.

[33]*Journal of Discourses* 13:158.

[34]See Rom. 12:1 and 2 Cor. 6:8.

[35]Kenney, *Wilford Woodruff's Journal* 1:3.

[36]Durham, *Discourses of Wilford Woodruff*, 133–134.

[37]Cowley, *Wilford Woodruff: Fourth President*, 46–47 (capitalizing "spirit").

[38]Kenney, *Wilford Woodruff's Journal* 1:17.

[39]Dean C. Jessee, "Wilford Woodruff," in Arrington, *Presidents of the Church*, 139.

[40]Cowley, *Wilford Woodruff: Fourth President*, 47.

[41]Ibid., 50.

[42]Ibid., 55–56.

[43]Gibbons, *Wilford Woodruff: Wondrous Worker*, 17.

[44]Cowley, *Wilford Woodruff: Fourth President*, 63.

[45]D&C 42:14.

[46]Gibbons, *Wilford Woodruff: Wondrous Worker*, 22.

[47]Kenney, *Wilford Woodruff's Journal* 1:74–75.

[48]Gibbons, *Wilford Woodruff: Wondrous Worker*, 23.

[49]Ibid.; Alexander, *Things in Heaven and Earth*, 40.

[50]Gibbons, *Wilford Woodruff: Wondrous Worker*, 23.

[51]Kenney, *Wilford Woodruff's Journal* 1:54.

[52]Alexander, *Things in Heaven and Earth*, 42.

[53]Kenney, *Wilford Woodruff's Journal* 1:171.

[54]Ibid., 1:171 ("God" is in all caps in original).

[55]Ibid., 1:174.

[56]Ibid., 1:175.

[57]Ibid.

[58]Ibid., 1:176–177.

[59]Ibid., 1:193.

[60]Ibid., 1:402.

[61]Ibid., 1:405.

[62]*Journal of Discourses* 15:283.

[63]Ibid., 17:249.

[64]Kenney, *Wilford Woodruff's Journal* 1:408.

[65]Ibid., 1:411–412.

[66]Ibid.

[67]Ibid., 1:413.

[68]Ibid., 1:409 (adding a comma after "had").

[69]Ibid., 1:408.

[70]Ibid., 1:411.

[71]*Journal of Discourses* 15:343.

[72]Cowley, *Wilford Woodruff: Fourth President,* 116.

[73]Kenney, *Wilford Woodruff's Journal* 1:423.

[74]Ibid.

[75]Gibbons, *Wilford Woodruff: Wondrous Worker,* 53.

[76]*Journal of Discourses* 15:343.

[77]Gibbons, *Wilford Woodruff: Wondrous Worker,* 53.

[78]*Journal of Discourses* 15:343.

[79]Cowley, *Wilford Woodruff: Fourth President,* 117.

[80]Ibid.

[81]Kenney, *Wilford Woodruff's Journal* 1:423–424.

[82]Cowley, *Wilford Woodruff: Fourth President,* 117.

[83]Ibid., 118.

[84]Kenney, *Wilford Woodruff's Journal* 1:426.

[85]Ibid., 1:431.

[86]Ibid., 1:433.

[87]Cowley, *Wilford Woodruff: Fourth President,* 119.

[88]Dean C. Jessee, "Wilford Woodruff," in Arrington, *Presidents of the Church,* 127 (I have here capitalized the word "Pentecost").

[89]Cowley, *Wilford Woodruff: Fourth President,* 119–120.

[90]Kenney, *Wilford Woodruff's Journal* 1:520.

[91]Ibid., 2:69 (reading "word" for "work").

[92]Ibid., 1:483.

[93]Cowley, *Wilford Woodruff: Fourth President,* 141.

[94]Ibid., 142.

[95]Ibid., 120.

[96]Ibid., 149.

[97]Ibid., 18.

[98]Durham, *Discourses of Wilford Woodruff,* 147.

[99]Ibid., 74.

[100]*Journal of Discourses* 16:37.

[101]Ibid., 23:130.

[102]Ludlow, *Latter-day Prophets Speak,* 385.

[103]Thomas S. Monson, "Wilford Woodruff," in Hinckley, *Heroes of the Restoration,* 214.

[104]Durham, *Discourses of Wilford Woodruff,* 54.

[105]Ludlow, *Latter-day Prophets Speak,* 389.

[106]D&C 42:6.

[107]For example, when He was "led up of the Spirit, into the wilderness, to be with God." JST Matt. 4:1.

## Chapter 13 • Joseph F. Smith

[1]Kenney, *Wilford Woodruff's Journal* 5:316–317.

[2]Scott Kenney, "Joseph F. Smith," in Arrington, *Presidents of the Church*, 185.

[3]Smith, *Gospel Doctrine*, 493.

[4]Gibbons, *Joseph F. Smith*, 9.

[5]Ibid., 10.

[6]Smith, *Gospel Doctrine*, 491.

[7]Ibid., 490–491.

[8]D&C 135:3.

[9]Smith, *History of the Church* 5:107–108.

[10]Smith, *History of Joseph Smith by His Mother*, 309.

[11]D&C 124:15.

[12]Smith, *History of the Church* 2:338.

[13]Gibbons, *Joseph F. Smith*, 3.

[14]Smith, *Gospel Doctrine*, 96.

[15]Smith, *Life of Joseph F. Smith*, 132–133.

[16]Gibbons, *Joseph F. Smith*.

[17]Smith, *Joseph F. Smith*, 159.

[18]Gibbons, *Joseph F. Smith*, 26.

[19]*Journal of Discourses* 6:273 (Americanizing the spelling of "labour").

[20]Smith, *Joseph F. Smith*, 176.

[21]Ibid., 177.

[22]Ibid., 180–181.

[23]Scott Kenney, "Joseph F. Smith," in Arrington, *Presidents of the Church*, 185.

[24]Smith, *Doctrines of Salvation* 3:110–111.

[25]Gibbons, *Joseph F. Smith*, 40 (adding a hyphen in "mid-teens").

[26]Scott Kenney, "Joseph F. Smith," in Arrington, *Presidents of the Church*, 185.

[27]Smith, *Joseph F. Smith*, 445.

[28]Ibid., 445–447.

[29]Ibid., 173–179.

[30]*Journal of Discourses* 19:21.

[31]Smith, *Joseph F. Smith*, 188.

[32]Smith, *Gospel Doctrine*, 89.

[33]Ibid., 188–189.

[34]Smith, *Joseph F. Smith*, 220.

[35] Gibbons, *Joseph F. Smith*, 235.

[36] Kenney, *Wilford Woodruff's Journal* 6:241.

[37] Gibbons, *Joseph F. Smith*, 83; Smith, *Life of Joseph F. Smith*, 227.

[38] Kenney, *Wilford Woodruff's Journal* 6:241.

[39] *Journal of Discourses* 15:325.

[40] Smith, *Gospel Doctrine*, 59.

[41] *Journal of Discourses* 12:329–330.

[42] Gibbons, *Joseph F. Smith*, 94.

[43] Ibid., 101.

[44] Moro. 9:6.

[45] *Journal of Discourses* 18:90.

[46] Cowley, *Wilford Woodruff: Fourth President*, 535–536.

[47] Smith, *Joseph F. Smith*, 324.

[48] Smith, *Gospel Doctrine*, 495.

[49] Gibbons, *Joseph F. Smith*, 236.

[50] Ibid., 259.

[51] Ibid., 236.

[52] D&C 138:1–2, 11.

[53] D&C 138:15–16.

[54] D&C 138:18, 23–24.

[55] D&C 138:30.

[56] D&C 138:57–58.

[57] Smith, *Gospel Doctrine*, 524–525.

[58] Gibbons, *Joseph F. Smith*, 235.

[59] Grant, *Gospel Standards*, 227.

[60] Flake, *Mighty Men of Zion*, 38.

[61] Gordon B. Hinckley, "Be Ye Clean," *Ensign* 26:5 [May 1996], 48–49.

[62] D&C 38:42; 133:5; and see 88:74.

[63] D&C 42:6.

[64] D&C 45:4; 1 Peter 2:22.

[65] Moro. 10:30–33.

## Chapter 14 • David O. McKay

[1] D&C 1:1, quoting Isa. 49:1.

[2] Morrell, *Highlights*, 10.

[3] Ibid., 17.

[4] Ibid., 17, 22–23.

[5] Conference Report, Oct.1960, 85–86, quoted in *Presidents Student Manual*, 147.

[6]Middlemiss, *Cherished Experiences*, 19 (rendering "Father" as uncapitalized, and repositioning the last comma in the first paragraph).

[7]McKay, *Home Memories*, 5.

[8]Morrell, *Highlights*, 31.

[9]McKay, *Pathways to Happiness*, 227–228.

[10]McKay, *Home Memories*, 5.

[11]Reading, *Shining Moments*, 63–64.

[12]Morrell, *Highlights*, 23.

[13]McKay, *Home Memories*, 6.

[14]Middlemiss, *Cherished Experiences*, 22–23.

[15]Morrell, *Highlights*, 27–28.

[16]Ibid., 26.

[17]Conference Report, Oct. 1951, 182–83, quoted in *Presidents Student Manual*, 147.

[18]Allen, "David O. McKay," in Arrington, *Presidents of the Church*, 280.

[19]Morrell, *Highlights*, 38.

[20]Middlemiss, *Cherished Experiences*, 16.

[21]D&C 88:78–80.

[22]Allen, "David O. McKay," in *Utah History Encyclopedia*.

[23]Morrell, *Highlights*, 31–32.

[24]McKay, *Gospel Ideals*, 133–134.

[25]Larson, *What E'er Thou Art*, 4.

[26]Ibid., 11.

[27]Ibid.

[28]Ibid., 12.

[29]Ibid., 13.

[30]Ibid., 13, n. 29.

[31]Ibid., 15.

[32]Ibid., 16.

[33]Ibid., 21.

[34]Ibid., 24.

[35]Ibid. (changing the original "your" to "you're").

[36]Ibid., 25.

[37]Ibid., 28.

[38]Ibid., 31.

[39]Ibid., 30.

[40]Ibid., 40.

[41]Ibid., 274.

[42]Ibid., 78–79.

[43]McKay, *Home Memories*, 166.

[44]Middlemiss, *Cherished Experiences*, 174, reading "What E'er" as two words for consistency with other reported accounts.

[45]McKay, *"My Young Friends . . ."*, 39.

[46]Larson, *What E'er Thou Art*, xxxv.

[47]Middlemiss, *Cherished Experiences*, 174, reading "What E'er" as two words for consistency with other reported accounts.

[48]See, for example, McKay, *Gospel Ideals*, 113.

[49]David McCullough, Speech on May 1, 2008, at Montpelier Station, Virginia, replayed on BookTV, CSpan2.

[50]McKay, *"My Young Friends . . ."*, 39.

[51]Larson, *What E'er Thou Art*, xxxvi.

[52]Allen, "David O. McKay," in *Utah History Encyclopedia*.

[53]Gibbons, *David O. McKay*, 46.

[54]See, for example, the journal entries for March 29, April 4, 5, 6, and 14, 15, 18, 19, 21, 22, in Larson, *What E'er Thou Art*, 81–88.

[55]Larson, *What E'er Thou Art*, 81.

[56]Ibid., 87.

[57]Ibid., 103.

[58]Ibid., 103, n. 153.

[59]Ibid., 103.

[60]Ibid., 104.

[61]Ibid., 105.

[62]Joseph H. Mitchell, in Larson, *What E'er Thou Art*, 241, n. 352.

[63]Thomas A. Kerr, in Larson, *What E'er Thou Art*, 241, n. 352.

[64]William S. Gould, in Larson, *What E'er Thou Art*, 240, n. 348.

[65]Allen, "David O. McKay," in Arrington, *Presidents of the Church*, 282–283.

[66]Larson, *What E'er Thou Art*, 239–241.

[67]Middlemiss, *Cherished Experiences*, 16.

[68]Morrell, *Highlights*, 38.

[69]Allen, "David O. McKay," in Arrington, *Presidents of the Church*, 283.

[70]Ibid.

[71]Middlemiss, *Cherished Experiences*, 26.

[72]Conference Report, Oct. 1906, 113, quoted in *Presidents Student Manual*, 149.

[73]McKay, *Cherished Experiences*, 134.

[74]Mosiah 18:9.

[75]Anderson, *Prophets I Have Known*, 122.

[76]James B. Allen, "David O. McKay," in Ludlow, *Encyclopedia of Mormonism* 2:874.

77 Allen, "David O. McKay," in Arrington, *Presidents of the Church*, 313.

78 Anderson, *Prophets I Have Known*, 133.

79 D&C 19:18–19.

80 D&C 107:99.

81 Hinckley, *Teachings of Gordon B. Hinckley*, 128.

## Chapter 15 • Gordon B. Hinckley

1 Dew, *Go Forward with Faith*, 9.

2 Hinckley, *Standing for Something*, 79–80.

3 Jeffrey R. Holland, "President Gordon B. Hinckley: 'Stalwart and Brave He Stands,'" *Ensign* 25:6 [June 1995], 2.

4 D&C 88:79–80.

5 Jeffrey R. Holland, "President Gordon B. Hinckley: 'Stalwart and Brave He Stands,'" *Ensign* 25:6 [June 1995], 6.

6 McCune, *Gordon B. Hinckley*, 104.

7 Dew, *Go Forward with Faith*, 35–36.

8 Ibid., 51.

9 Ibid., 51.

10 Ibid., 46–47.

11 Quoting Mark 5:36. Dew, *Go Forward with Faith*, 59.

12 Dell Van Orden, "President Hinckley notes his 85th birthday, reminisces about life," *Church News* 65:25 [June 24, 1995], 6.

13 Dew, *Go Forward with Faith*, 60.

14 Ibid., 62.

15 Ibid., 64.

16 McCune, *Gordon B. Hinckley*, 200.

17 Matthew 16:25; and see Mark 8:35. McCune, *Gordon B. Hinckley*, 200; Dew, *Go Forward with Faith*, 64.

18 McCune, *Gordon B. Hinckley*, 200.

19 Ibid.

20 Ibid., 201.

21 Ibid., 66.

22 Ibid., 68–69.

23 Hinckley, *Wondrous Power of a Mother*, 1–2.

24 Dew, *Go Forward with Faith*, 69, 78.

25 Ibid., 74; McCune, *Gordon B. Hinckley*, 209.

26 Hinckley, *Teachings of Gordon B. Hinckley*, 221.

27 Dew, *Go Forward with Faith*, 76.

28 Ibid., 78.

[29]Ibid., 80; McCune, *Gordon B. Hinckley*, 212.

[30]Dew, *Go Forward with Faith*, 83.

[31]Neal A. Maxwell, "President Gordon B. Hinckley: The Spiritual Sculpturing of a Righteous Soul," *Ensign* 12:1 [Jan. 1982], 13.

[32]Hinckley, *Faith*, 75.

[33]"President Hinckley Traveled the Globe Greeting Throngs," *Church News* 66:52 [Dec. 28, 1996], 3.

[34]Dew, *Go Forward with Faith*, 555.

[35]Hinckley, *Faith*, 57.

[36]Boyd K. Packer, "This Gentle Prophet," *Ensign* Supplement 38:3 [March 2008 Supplement], 25.

[37]"Prophet Goes to Islands of the Pacific," *Church News* 67:43 [Oct. 25, 1997], 3–4.

[38]"An Outpouring of Love for Prophet," *Church News* 67:5 [Feb. 1, 1997], 3, 8.

[39]Mike Cannon, "Prophet Returns to 'Beloved England,'" *Church News* 65:35 [Sept. 2, 1995], 4.

[40]Dew, *Go Forward with Faith*, 547.

[41]"President Gordon B. Hinckley," *Ensign* Supplement 38:3 [March 2008 Supplement], 5.

[42]McCune, *Gordon B. Hinckley*, 200.

[43]Henry B. Eyring, "Things Will Work Out," *Ensign* Supplement 38:3 [March 2008 Supplement], 27.

[44]Paul McNabb, "An Experience with Gordon B. Hinckley," online at http://gordonhinckley.com/59/elder-gordon-hinckley-makes-personal-phone-calls-to-the-parents-of-hundreds-of-missionaries.

[45]Earl C. Tingey, "Footprints on the Sands of Time," *Ensign* Supplement 38:3 [March 2008 Supplement], 22.

[46]Gordon B. Hinckley, "We Have a Work to Do," *Ensign* 25:5 [May 1995], 87.

[47]D&C 4:2, 5.

[48]Matt. 26:39.

[49]Dew, *Go Forward with Faith*, 557.

## Chapter 16 • *Thomas S. Monson*

[1]D&C 81:5.

[2]Thomas S. Monson, "Looking Back and Moving Forward," *Ensign* 38:5 [May 2008], 88–89.

[3]Jeffrey R. Holland, "President Thomas S. Monson: Finishing the Course, Keeping the Faith," *Ensign* 24:9 [Sept. 1994], 12.

[4]Carrie A. Moore, "President Monson recalls influence of family on his life," *Deseret Morning News* [Salt Lake City], Feb. 4, 2008.

[5]*On the Lord's Errand: The Life of Thomas S. Monson* (video), The Church of Jesus Christ of Latter-day Saints, Intellectual Reserve 2008.

[6]Ibid.

[7]Carrie A. Moore, "President Monson recalls influence of family on his life," *Deseret Morning News* [Salt Lake City], Feb. 4, 2008.

[8]Monson, *Inspiring Experiences*, 11–12.

[9]Francis M. Gibbons, "President Thomas S. Monson," *Ensign* 25:7 [July 1995], 6.

[10]Monson, *Inspiring Experiences*, 8.

[11]Ibid., 7.

[12]Jeffrey R. Holland, "President Thomas S. Monson: Finishing the Course, Keeping the Faith," *Ensign* 24:9 [Sept. 1994], 12.

[13]*On the Lord's Errand: The Life of Thomas S. Monson* (video), The Church of Jesus Christ of Latter-day Saints, Intellectual Reserve 2008.

[14]Jeffrey R. Holland, "President Thomas S. Monson: Man of Action, Man of Faith, Always 'on the Lord's Errand,'" *Ensign* 16:2 [Feb. 1986], 10.

[15]As told by President Monson at the first session of the Arizona Gila Valley Temple Dedication, May 23, 2010.

[16]*On the Lord's Errand: The Life of Thomas S. Monson* (video), The Church of Jesus Christ of Latter-day Saints, Intellectual Reserve 2008.

[17]Monson, *Inspiring Experiences*, 67–68.

[18]*On the Lord's Errand: The Life of Thomas S. Monson* (video), The Church of Jesus Christ of Latter-day Saints, Intellectual Reserve 2008.

[19]Ibid.

[20]Jeffrey R. Holland, "President Thomas S. Monson: Man of Action, Man of Faith, Always 'on the Lord's Errand,'" *Ensign* 16:2 [Feb. 1986], 10.

[21]As mentioned by President Monson at the first session of the Arizona Gila Valley Temple Dedication, May 23, 2010.

[22]Jeffrey R. Holland, "President Thomas S. Monson: Man of Action, Man of Faith, Always 'on the Lord's Errand,'" *Ensign* 16:2 [Feb. 1986], 10.

[23]Francis M. Gibbons, "President Thomas S. Monson," *Ensign* 25:7 [July 1995], 6.

[24]*On the Lord's Errand: The Life of Thomas S. Monson* (video), The Church of Jesus Christ of Latter-day Saints, Intellectual Reserve 2008. First comment by President Monson's brother; others by Elder Russell M. Ballard.

[25]Thomas S. Monson, "Yellow Canaries with Gray on Their Wings," *Ensign* 27:8 [Aug. 1997], 2.

[26]Monson, *Inspiring Experiences*, 32.

[27]Thomas S. Monson, "How Do We Show Our Love," *Ensign* 28:1 [Jan. 1998], 2.

[28]Jeffrey R. Holland, "President Thomas S. Monson: Man of Action, Man of Faith, Always 'on the Lord's Errand,'" *Ensign* 16:2 [Feb. 1986], 10.

[29]Ibid.

[30]Francis M. Gibbons, "President Thomas S. Monson," *Ensign* 25:7 [July 1995], 6.

[31]Quentin L. Cook, "Give Heed Unto the Prophet's Words," *Ensign* 38:5 [May 2008], 49.

[32] As told to the author, with permission to use herein, by E. Arthur Patterson, who had leaned over and asked the question to Jim Sorenson. Brother Patterson was then serving as a counselor to Bishop Sorenson.

[33] Thomas S. Monson, "What Have I Done for Someone Today?" *Ensign* 39:11 [Nov. 2009], 84.

[34] Jeffrey R. Holland, "President Thomas S. Monson: Man of Action, Man of Faith, Always 'on the Lord's Errand,'" *Ensign* 16:2 [Feb. 1986], 10.

[35] Jeffrey R. Holland, "President Thomas S. Monson: In the Footsteps of the Master," *Ensign* 32:18 [June 2008], 2–16.

[36] Among his many Church assignments were: Chairman of the Adult Correlation Committee; Advisor to the Young Men's and Young Women's organizations; Chairman of the Church Leadership Committee; Chairman of the Scripture Publication Committee; Area Supervisor for Missionary Work for the Western United States; Supervisor of the missions of the South Pacific; member of the Missionary Executive Committee; and Area Advisor of Europe and Europe West mission areas. He also served on various corporate boards, as president of the Deseret News Publishing Company, and as a member of the Utah Board of Regents, a trustee of the Freedoms Foundation at Valley Forge, and on the National Executive Board of the Boy Scouts of America—an organization that awarded him their highest honors.

[37] See Matt. 25:40.

[38] 2 Ne. 31:10.

[39] Mosiah 18:8–9.

[40] Jeffrey R. Holland, "President Thomas S. Monson: In the Footsteps of the Master," *Ensign* 32:18 [June 2008], 2–16.

[41] Monson, *Faith Rewarded*, vii.

[42] Ibid., 5, 7.

[43] Ibid., 104.

[44] Dieter F. Uchtdorf, "Faith of Our Father," *Ensign* 38:5 [May 2008], 69–70.

[45] "President Thomas S. Monson: On the Lord's Errand," 4 Feb. 2008, Newsroom, Church of Jesus Christ of Latter-day Saints, online at http://www.news room.lds.org/ldsnewsroom/eng/search/president-thomas-s-monson-on-the-lord-s-errand.

[46] Jeffrey R. Holland, "President Thomas S. Monson: Man of Action, Man of Faith, Always 'on the Lord's Errand,'" *Ensign* 16:2 [Feb. 1986], 10.

[47] Wendell J. Ashton, quoted in Jeffrey R. Holland, "President Thomas S. Monson: Man of Action, Man of Faith, Always 'on the Lord's Errand,'" *Ensign* 16:2 [Feb. 1986], 10.

[48] Quentin L. Cook, "Give Heed Unto the Prophet's Words," *Ensign* 38:5 [May 2008], 50.

[49] Maurine Proctor, "President Thomas S. Monson: The Pure Love of Christ," Meridian Magazine, May 15, 2008, online at http://www.ldsmag.com/churchupdate/080206monson.html.

[50] *On the Lord's Errand: The Life of Thomas S. Monson* (video), The Church of Jesus Christ of Latter-day Saints, Intellectual Reserve 2008. Remark by President Boyd K. Packer.

[51]Wendell J. Ashton, quoted in Jeffrey R. Holland, "President Thomas S. Monson: Man of Action, Man of Faith, Always 'on the Lord's Errand,'" *Ensign* 16:2 [Feb. 1986], 10.

[52]Thomas S. Monson, "The Doorway of Love," *Ensign* 26:10 [Oct. 1996], 2.

[53]Jeffrey R. Holland, "President Thomas S. Monson: In the Footsteps of the Master," *Ensign* 32:18 [June 2008], 2–16.

[54]Thomas S. Monson, "Yellow Canaries with Gray on Their Wings," *Ensign* 27:8 [Aug. 1997], 2.

[55]Boyd K. Packer, remarks in special broadcast to 88 Arizona stake conferences, Nov. 2, 2008.

[56]*On the Lord's Errand: The Life of Thomas S. Monson* (video), The Church of Jesus Christ of Latter-day Saints, Intellectual Reserve 2008.

[57]Quentin L. Cook, "Give Heed Unto the Prophet's Words," *Ensign* 38:5 [May 2008], 50.

[58]Jeffrey R. Holland, "President Thomas S. Monson: Finishing the Course, Keeping the Faith," *Ensign* 24:9 [Sept. 1994], 12–13.

[59]Monson, *Live the Good Life*, 114.

[60]Monson, *Pathways to Perfection*, 220.

[61]Thomas S. Monson, "Your Jericho Road," *Ensign* 27:5 [May 1977], 71.

[62]Thomas S. Monson, "May We So Live," *Ensign* 38:8 [Aug. 2008], 7–9.

# BIBLIOGRAPHY

Alexander, Thomas G. *Things in Heaven and Earth: The Life and Times of Wilford Woodruff, a Mormon Prophet.* Salt Lake City: Signature Books, 1991.

Allen, James B. "David O. McKay." *Utah History Encyclopedia* (online at http://historytogo.utah.gov/people/davidomckay.html).

Al-Rabghūzī. *The Stories of the Prophets: Qiṣaṣ al Anbiyā, An Eastern Turkish Version.* 2 vols.; Leiden: Brill, 1995.

Anderson, Joseph. *Prophets I Have Known.* Salt Lake City: Deseret Book Company, 1973 [1974].

Andrus, Hyrum L. *Joseph Smith, the Man and the Seer.* Salt Lake City: Deseret Book, 1960.

*The Ante-Nicene Fathers: Translations of The Writings of the Fathers down to A.D. 325.* 10 vols. Edinburgh: T&T Clark; and Grand Rapids, Michigan: Wm. B. Eerdmans Publishing Company, 1985–1986 [reprint].

Arrington, Leonard J., ed. *The Presidents of the Church: Biographical Essays.* Salt Lake City: Deseret Book Company, 1986.

Asad, Muhammad. *The Message of the Qur'ān.* Gibraltar: Dar Al-Andalus, 1980.

Backman, Milton V., Jr. *Joseph Smith's First Vision: The First Vision in Its Historical Context.* Salt Lake City: Bookcraft, Inc., 1971.

Barker, Margaret. *The Older Testament: The Survival of Themes from the Ancient Royal Cult in Sectarian Judaism and Early Christianity.* London: SPCK, 1987.

Barrett, Ivan J. *Joseph Smith and the Restoration: A History of the Church to 1846.* rev. ed. Provo, Utah: Brigham Young University Press, 1973.

Benson, Ezra Taft. *A Witness and a Warning: A Modern-day Prophet Testifies of the Book of Mormon.* Salt Lake City, Utah: Deseret Book Company, 1988.

———. *Come unto Christ.* Salt Lake City: Deseret Book Co., 1983.

Bialik, Hayim Nahman and Yehoshua Hana Ravnitzky, eds. *The Book of Legends: Sefer Ha-Aggadah.* New York: Schocken Books, 1992.

Boardman, John, Jasper Griffin, and Oswyn Murray, eds. *The Oxford History of the Classical World.* Oxford: Oxford University Press, 1986 [1988].

Bock, Darrell L. *Luke, Volume 1, 1:1–9:50.* Baker Exegetical Commentary on the New Testament. Grand Rapids, Michigan: Baker Books, 1994.

Botterweck, G. Johannes, Helmer Ringgren, and Heinz-Josef Fabry, eds. *Theological Dictionary of the Old Testament*. 15 vols. Grand Rapids, Michigan: William B. Eerdmans Publishing Company, 1977–2006.

Briggs, Kay W. *Brother Joseph: Stories and Lessons from the Life of the Prophet*. Salt Lake City: Bookcraft, 1994.

Brown, Francis, S. R. Driver, and Charles A. Briggs. *A Hebrew and English Lexicon of the Old Testament*. Oxford: Clarendon Press, 1980.

Brown, Raymond E. *An Introduction to the New Testament*. New York: Doubleday, 1997.

_____. *The Gospel According to John (i-xii)*. The Anchor Bible 29. Garden City, New York: Doubleday & Company, Inc. 1966.

Bruce, F. F. *Paul: Apostle of the Heart Set Free*. Grand Rapids: William B. Eerdmans Publishing Company, 1977.

Budge, Ernest A. Wallis, ed. *The Book of the Bee*. Anecdota Oxoniensia, Semitic Series, vol. I, pt. II. Oxford: The Clarendon Press, 1886.

Bushman, Richard Lyman. *Joseph Smith: Rough Stone Rolling*. New York: Alfred A. Knopf, 2005.

Buxbaum, Yitzhak. *The Life and Teachings of Hillel*. Lanham, Maryland: Rowman & Littlefield Publishers, Inc., 1994 [2004].

Cannon, George Q. *Life of Joseph Smith the Prophet*. Salt Lake City: Deseret Book Company, 1967.

Charlesworth, James H., ed. *John and the Dead Sea Scrolls*. New York: Crossroad, 1990.

_____. *The Old Testament Pseudepigrapha*. 2 vols. Garden City, New York: Doubleday & Company, Inc., 1983–1985.

Chavel, Charles B. *Encyclopedia of Torah Thoughts*. New York: Shilo Publishing House, Inc., 1980.

Clark, E. Douglas. *The Blessings of Abraham: Becoming a Zion People*. American Fork, Utah: Covenant Communications, Inc., 2005.

Clark, E. Douglas, and Robert S. Clark. *Fathers and Sons in the Book of Mormon*. Salt Lake City: Deseret Book Company, 1991.

Cragg, Kenneth. *Readings in the Qur'an*. London: Collins, 1988.

Coffin, Henry Sloane. *The Creed of Jesus and Other Sermons*. New York: Charles Scribner's Sons, 1907.

Cohen, Arthur A., and Paul Mendes-Flohr, eds. *Contemporary Jewish Religious Thought: Original Essays on Critical Concepts, Movements, and Beliefs*. New York: The Free Press, 1987.

Cowley, Matthias F. *Wilford Woodruff: Fourth President of the Church of Jesus Christ of Latter-day Saints: History of His Life and Labors as Recorded in His Daily Journals*. Salt Lake City: Bookcraft, 1964 [1974].

Crothers, Samuel. *Abraham the First Missionary*. Chillicothe, Ohio: Ely & Allen, 1847.

Culi, Yaakov, Yitzchok Magriso, and Yitzchok Behar Argueti. *The Torah Anthology: MeAm Lo'ez*. 17 vols. New York: Maznaim Publishing Corporation, 1977–1984.

Dew, Sheri L. *Go Forward with Faith: The Biography of Gordon B. Hinckley*. Salt Lake City: Deseret Book Co., 1996.

Dunn, James D. G. *The Theology of Paul the Apostle*. Grand Rapids, Michigan: William B. Eerdmans Publishing Company, 1998.

Durham, G. Homer, ed. *The Discourses of Wilford Woodruff: Fourth President of the Church of Jesus Christ of Latter-day Saints*. Salt Lake City: Bookcraft Inc., 1946 [1969].

*The Eerdmans Bible Dictionary*. Grand Rapids: William B. Eerdmans Publishing Company, 1987.

*Encyclopaedia Judaica*, corrected ed. 17 vols. Jerusalem: Keter Publishing House.

Epstein, I., ed. *Hebrew English Edition of the Babylonian Talmud*, new ed. London: The Soncino Press, 1987–1990.

Evans, John Henry. *Joseph Smith: An American Prophet*. Salt Lake City: Deseret Book Company, 1961.

Fitzmeyer, Joseph A. *The Gospel According to Luke I–IX*. The Anchor Bible, vol. 28. Garden City, New York: Doubleday & Company, Inc., 1981.

Flake, Lawrence R. *Mighty Men of Zion: General Authorities of the Last Dispensation*. Salt Lake City: Karl D. Butler, 1974.

Freedman, H., ed. *Midrash Rabbah: Song of Songs*, 3rd ed. London: The Soncino Press, 1983.

Galbraith, Richard C. and Joseph Fielding Smith, eds. *Scriptural Teachings of the Prophet Joseph Smith*. Salt Lake City: Deseret Book Company, 1993.

Gaster, Moses, ed. *The Asatir*. London: The Royal Asiatic Society, 1927.

Gibbons, Francis M. *David O. McKay: Apostle to the World, Prophet of God*. Salt Lake City: Deseret Book Co., 1986.

_____. *Joseph Smith: Martyr, Prophet of God*. Salt Lake City: Deseret Book Company, 1977.

_____. *Joseph F. Smith: Patriarch and Preacher, Prophet of God*. Salt Lake City: Deseret Book, 1984.

_____. *Wilford Woodruff: Wondrous Worker, Prophet of God*. Salt Lake City: Deseret Book Company, 1988.

Grant, Heber J. *Gospel Standards*. 9th ed. Salt Lake City: The Improvement Era, 1943.

Ginzberg, Louis. *The Legends of the Jews*. 7 vols. Philadelphia: The Jewish Publication Society of America, 1912–1938.

Gove, Philip Babcock, ed. *Webster's Third New International Dictionary of the English Language Unabridged*. Springfield, Massachusetts: Merriam-Webster Inc., Publishers, 1981.

Green, Arthur. *Devotion and Commandment: The Faith of Abraham in the Hasidic Imagination*. Cincinnati: Hebrew Union College Press, 1989.

Hammer, Reuven. *The Jerusalem Anthology: A Literary Guide*. Philadelphia: The Jewish Publication Society, 1995.

Hanson, Paul D. *Isaiah 40–66*. Interpretation: A Bible Commentary for Teaching and Preaching. Louisville: John Knox Press, 1995.

Harris, R. Laird, Gleason L. Archer, Jr., and Bruce K. Waltke, eds. *Theological Wordbook of the Old Testament*. 2 vols. Chicago: Moody Press, 1980.

Hartshorn, Leon R. *Joseph Smith: Prophet of the Restoration*. Salt Lake City: Deseret Book Company, 1973.

Hastings, James, ed. *A Dictionary of Christ and the Gospels*. 2 vols. Edinburgh: T.&T. Clark, 1906.

_____. *Dictionary of the Apostolic Church*. 2 vols. New York: Charles Scribner's Sons, 1916.

Hawthorne, Gerald F. and Ralph P. Martin, eds. *Dictionary of Paul and His Letters*. Downers Grove, Illinois: InterVarsity Press, 1993.

Hennecke, Edgar. *The New Testament Apocrypha*. 2 vols. Philadelphia: The Westminster Press, 1963.

Hinckley, Gordon B. *Faith: The Essence of True Religion*. Salt Lake City: Deseret Book Co., 1989.

Hinckley, Gordon Bitner, et al. *Heroes of the Restoration*. Salt Lake City: Bookcraft, 1997.

Hinckley, Gordon B. *Standing for Something*. New York: Random House, 2000.

_____. *Teachings of Gordon B. Hinckley*. Salt Lake City: Deseret Book Company, 1997.

_____. *The Wondrous Power of a Mother*. Salt Lake City: Deseret Book Company, 1989.

*Holy Bible: The New King James Version*. Nashville: Thomas Nelson Publishers, 1982.

Jessee, Dean C., ed. *The Papers of Joseph Smith: Volume 1: Autobiographical and Historical Writings*. Salt Lake City: Deseret Book Company, 1989.

_____. *The Personal Writings of Joseph Smith*. Salt Lake City: Deseret Book, 1984.

Johnson, Luke Timothy. *The Gospel of Luke*. Sacra Pagina Series 3. Collegeville, Minnesota: The Liturgical Press, 1991.

*Josephus IV*. Loeb Classical Library 261. Cambridge, Massachusetts: Harvard University Press, 1978.

_____. The Loeb Classical Library 326. Cambridge, Massachusetts: Harvard University Press, 1937 [1987].

*Journal of Discourses*. 26 vols. London: Latter-day Saints Book Depot, 1854–1886.

Kenney, Scott G., ed. *Wilford Woodruff's Journal, 1833–1898: Typescript*. 9 vols. Midvale, Utah: Signature Books, 1983–1985.

Kittel, Gerhard and Gerhard Friedrich, eds. *Theological Dictionary of the New Testament.* 10 vols. Grand Rapid, Michigan: Wm. B. Eerdmans Publishing Company, 1964–1976.

Klinghoffer, David. *The Discovery of God: Abraham and the Birth of Monotheism.* New York: Doubleday, 2003.

Knappert, Jan. *Islamic Legends: Histories of the Heroes, Saints and Prophets of Islam.* Religious Texts Translation Series, vol. 15:1–2. 2 vols. Leiden: Brill, 1985.

Kvanvig, Helge S. *Roots of Apocalyptic: The Mesopotamian Background of the Enoch Figure and of the Son of Man.* Wissenschaftliche Monographien zum Alten und Neuen Testament. Neukirchen-Vluyn: Neukirchener Verlag, 1988.

Larson, Stan and Patricia, eds. *What E'er Thou Art Act Well Thy Part: The Missionary Diaries of David O. McKay.* Salt Lake City: Blue Ribbon Books, 1999.

Lattimore, Richmond, translator. *The New Testament.* New York: North Point Press, 1996.

Leibowitz, Nehama. *Studies in Bereshit (Genesis),* 7th rev. ed. Jerusalem: World Zionist Organization, 1985.

Levine, Baruch A. *Leviticus: The JPS Torah Commentary.* Philadelphia: The Jewish Publication Society, 1989.

Levner, J. B. *The Legends of Israel.* 2 vols. London: James Clarke & Co., Limited, 1946, 1956.

Levy, Benjamin. *A Faithful Heart: Preparing for the High Holy Days. A Study Based on the Midrash Maaseh Avraham Avinu.* New York: UAHC Press, 2001.

Lewis, Jack P. *A Study of the Interpretation of Noah and the Flood in Jewish and Christian Literature.* Leiden: Brill, 1968 [1978].

Ludlow, Daniel H., ed. *Encyclopedia of Mormonism.* 5 vols. New York: Macmillan Publishing Company, 1992.

———. *Latter-day Prophets Speak.* Salt Lake City: Bookcraft, 1951 [1969].

Ludlow, Victor L. *Isaiah: Prophet, Seer, and Poet.* Salt Lake City, Utah: Deseret Book Company, 1982.

Lundwall, N.B. *The Vision.* Salt Lake City: Bookcraft Publishing Co., n.d.

Machiela, Daniel A. *The Dead Sea Genesis Apocryphon: A New Text and Translation with Introduction and Special Treatment of Columns 13–17.* Studies on the Texts of the Desert of Judah. Leiden: Brill, 2009.

Madsen, Truman G. *Joseph Smith the Prophet.* Salt Lake City: Bookcraft, 1989.

Malan, S. C., ed. *The Book of Adam and Eve, also called The Conflict of Adam and Eve with Satan.* London: Williams and Norgate, 1882.

Martinez, Florentino Garcia and Eibert J. C. Tigchelaar. *The Dead Sea Scrolls Study Edition.* 2 vols. Leiden: Brill, 1997–1998.

Matthews, Edward G., Jr., translator. *The Armenian Commentary on Genesis Attributed to Ephrem the Syrian.* Corpus Scriptorum Christianorum Orientalium, vol. 573, Scriptores Armeniaci, tomus 24. Lovanii: In Aedibus Peeters, 1998.

Matthews, Robert J. *A Burning Light: The Life and Ministry of John the Baptist.* Provo, Utah: Brigham Young University Press, 1972.

McConkie, Joseph Fielding and Robert L. Millet. *Joseph Smith: The Choice Seer.* Salt Lake City: Bookcraft, 1996.

McCune, George M. *Gordon B. Hinckley: Shoulder for the Lord.* Salt Lake City: Hawkes Publishing Inc., 1996.

McKay, David O. *Gospel Ideals.* Salt Lake City: Deseret Book Company, 1953 [1976].

_____. *"My Young Friends . . ."* Salt Lake City: Bookcraft, 1973.

_____. *Pathways to Happiness.* Salt Lake City: Bookcraft, 1957.

McKay, Llewelyn R. *Home Memories of President David O. McKay.* Salt Lake City: Deseret Book Co., 1956.

Metzger, Bruce M. and Roland E. Murphy *The New Oxford Annotated Bible: New Revised Standard Version.* New York: Oxford University Press, 1991.

Middlemiss, Clare, ed. *Cherished Experiences from the Writings of President David O. McKay.* Salt Lake City: Deseret Book Co., 1955.

Milik, J. T. *The Books of Enoch: Aramaic Fragments of Qumrân Cave 4.* Oxford: Clarendon Press, 1976.

Millet, Robert L. *Joseph Smith: Selected Sermons and Writings.* Sources of American Spirituality. New York: Paulist Press, 1989.

Monson, Thomas S. *Faith Rewarded: A Personal Account of Prophetic Promises to the East German Saints.* Salt Lake City: Deseret Book Company, 1994.

_____. *Inspiring Experiences That Build Faith: From the Life and Ministry of Thomas S. Monson.* Salt Lake City: Deseret Book Company, 1994.

_____. *Live the Good Life.* Salt Lake City: Deseret Book Company, 1988.

_____. *Pathways to Perfection.* Salt Lake City: Deseret Book Company, 1973.

Montefiore, C. G. and H. Loewe. *A Rabbinic Anthology.* New York: Shocken Books, 1974.

Morgenstern, Julian. *A Jewish Interpretation of the Book of Genesis.* Cincinnati: Union of American Hebrew Congregations, 1919.

Morrell, Jeanette McKay. *Highlights in the Life of President David O. McKay.* Salt Lake City: Deseret Book Co., 1966.

Motyer, J. Alec. *The Prophecy of Isaiah: An Introduction & Commentary.* Downers Grove, Illinois: InterVarsity Press, 1993.

Munk, Elie. *The Call of the Torah.* 2 vols. Jerusalem: Feldheim Publishers, 1980.

*New American Standard Bible.* Nashville: Holman Bible Publishers, 1981.

*The NIV Study Bible: New International Version.* Grand Rapids, Michigan: Zondervan, 1985. *The New Jerusalem Bible.* Garden City, New York: Doubleday & Company, Inc., 1985.

Nibley, Hugh. *Abraham in Egypt,* 2nd ed. The Collected Works of Hugh Nibley, vol. 14. Salt Lake City: Deseret Book Company, and Provo, Utah: Foundation for Ancient Research and Mormon Studies at Brigham Young University, 2000.

_____. *Enoch the Prophet.* The Collected Works of Hugh Nibley, vol. 2. Salt Lake City: Deseret Book Company, and Provo, Utah: Foundation for Ancient Research and Mormon Studies at Brigham Young University, 1986.

_____. *Teachings of the Pearl of Great Price.* Provo, Utah: Foundation of Ancient Research and Mormon Studies, 1986.

*Nicene and Post Nicene Fathers of the Christian Church.* Second Series, 14 vols. Grand Rapids: Wm. B. Eerdmans Publishing Company, 1980–1900.

Noah, Mordecai Manuel, ed. *The Book of Yashar.* New York: Hermon Press, 1972.

Noble, W. F. P. *The Great Men of God: Biographies of Patriarchs, Prophets, Kings and Apostles.* New York: Nelson and Phillips, 1876.

North, Christopher R. *The Second Isaiah: Introduction, Translation and Commentary to Chapters XL–LV.* Oxford: Clarendon, 1964.

Orr, William F. and James Arthur Walther. *I Corinthians.* The Anchor Bible, vol. 32. New York: Doubleday, 1976.

Petersen, Mark E. *Abraham: Friend of God.* Salt Lake city: Deseret Book Company, 1979.

*Philo VIII.* The Loeb Classical Library 341. Cambridge, Massachusetts: Harvard University Press, 1939 [1968].

*Philo VI.* The Loeb Classical Library 289. London: William Heinemann Ltd, 1935 [1966].

*Presidents of the Church: Student Manual, Religion 345.* Salt Lake City: The Church of Jesus Christ of Latter-day Saints, 2004.

*The Prophet and His Work: Essays from General Authorities on Joseph Smith and the Restoration.* Salt Lake City: Deseret Book Company, 1996.

Rad, Gerhard von. *Genesis: A Commentary,* rev. ed. The Old Testament Library. Philadelphia: The Westminster Press, 1972.

Rappoport, Angelo S. *Ancient Israel: Myths and Legends, 3 volumes in 1.* New York: Bonanza Books, 1987.

Reading, Lucile C. *Shining Moments: Stories for Latter-day Saint Children, vol. 2.* Salt Lake City: Deseret Book Company, 1987.

*The Revised English Bible with the Apocrypha.* Oxford: Oxford University, and Cambridge: Cambridge University, 1989.

Robinson, Eileen Taggart. "George Washington Taggart: A Biography and Tribute." Online at http://www.taggartfamily.org/GWT%20by%20Eileen%20Robinson.htm.

Sarna, Nahum M., *Genesis*. The JPS Torah Commentary. Philadelphia: The Jewish Publication Society, 1989.

Sawyer, John F.A. *The Fifth Gospel: Isaiah in the History of Christianity*. Cambridge: Cambridge University Press, 1996.

Seitz, Christopher R. *Isaiah 1–39*. Interpretation: a Bible Commentary for Teaching and Preaching. Louisville: John Knox Press, 1993.

Skinner, John. *A Critical and Exegetical Commentary on Genesis, 2nd ed.* The International Critical Commentary. Edinburgh: T. & T. Clark Ltd, 1930.

Smith, David. *The Life and Letters of Saint Paul.* New York: Harper & Brothers, n.d.

Smith, Joseph. *History of the Church of Jesus Christ of Latter-day Saints.* 2nd ed. rev. 7 vols. Salt Lake City: Deseret Book Company, 1932–1951.

Smith, Joseph F. *Gospel Doctrine: Selections from the Sermons and Writings of Joseph F. Smith.* Salt Lake City: Deseret Book Co., 1939 [1968].

Smith, Joseph Fielding. *Doctrines of Salvation.* 3 vols. Salt Lake City: Bookcraft, 1954.

_____. *Life of Joseph F. Smith: Sixth President of the Church of Jesus Christ of Latter-day Saints.* 2nd ed. Salt Lake City: Deseret Book Company, 1969.

Smith, Lucy Mack. *History of Joseph Smith by His Mother.* Salt Lake City: Bookcraft, 1958.

Snow, Eliza R. *Biography and Family Record of Lorenzo Snow.* Salt Lake City: Deseret News Company, 1884.

Soloveitchik, Joseph B. *Man of Faith in the Modern World: Reflections of the Rav.* vol. 2. Hoboken, New Jersey: Ktav Publishing House, Inc., 1989.

Sparks, H. F. D., ed. *The Apocryphal Old Testament.* Oxford: Clarendon Press, 1984.

Sperling, Harry, and Maurice Simon, translators. *The Zohar,* 2nd ed., 5 vols. London: The Soncino Press, 1984.

*Teachings of the Presidents of the Church: Joseph Smith.* Salt Lake City: The Church of Jesus Christ of Latter-day Saints, 2007.

Thomson, James G. S. S. *The Praying Christ: A Study of Jesus' Doctrine and Practice of Prayer.* Grand Rapids, Michigan: Wm. B. Eerdmans Publishing Company, 1959.

Tillemont, Le Nain de. *Ecclesiastical Memoirs of the Six First Centuries,* 2 vols. London, 1733–1735.

Toorn, Karel van der; Bob Becking; and Pieter W. van der Horst. *Dictionaries of Deities and Demons in the Bible,* 2nd ed. Leiden: Brill, 1999.

Tuchman, Shera Aranoff and Sandra E. Rapoport. *The Passions of the Matriarchs.* Jersey City, New Jersey: KTAV Publishing House, Inc., 2004.

VanderKam, James C. *Enoch: A Man for All Generations.* Studies on Personalities of the Old Testament. Columbia, South Carolina: University of South Carolina Press, 1995.

_____. *The Book of Jubilees*, Corpus Scriptorum Christianorum Orientalium, vol. 511, Scriptores Aethiopici, tomus 88. Lovanii: In Aedibus E. Peeters, 1989.

Vaughan, Curtis. *Twenty-Six Translations of the Bible*. 3 vols. Atlanta: American Home Libraries, Inc., 1967.

Vermes, Geza. *The Complete Dead Sea Scrolls in English*. New York: Allen Lane, The Penguin Press, 1997.

Watts, John D. W. *Word Biblical Commentary, Volume 24: Isaiah 1–33*. Waco, Texas: Word Books, Publisher, 1985.

Wenham, Gordon J. *Word Biblical Commentary, Volume 1: Genesis 1–15*. Waco, Texas: Word Books, Publisher, 1987.

Westermann, Claus. *Genesis 1–11: A Commentary*. Minneapolis: Augsburg Publishing House, 1984.

_____. *Isaiah 40–66: A Commentary*. The Old Testament Library. Philadelphia: The Westminster Press, 1969.

Whitney, Orson F. *Life of Heber C. Kimball*. 5th ed. Salt Lake City: Bookcraft, 1974.

Wigoder, Geoffrey, ed. *The Encyclopedia of Judaism*. New York: Macmillan Publishing Company, 1989.

Wildberger, Hans. *Isaiah 1–12: A Commentary*. Minneapolis: Fortress Press, 1991.

Woodruff, Wilford. *Leaves from My Journal*. Faith Promoting Series, no. 3, 4th ed. Salt Lake City, Utah: The Deseret News, 1909.

Young, Edward J. *The Book of Isaiah*. 3 vols. The New International Commentary on the Old Testament. Grand Rapids, Michigan: William B. Eerdmans Publishing Company, 1965–1972.

# About the Author

E. Douglas Clark is an attorney who has consulted at numerous United Nations conferences in New York and around the world on family policy issues. His published works include: *Echoes of Eden: Life Lessons from Our First Parents; The Blessings of Abraham: Becoming a Zion People; The Grand Design: America from Columbus to Zion;* "Abraham" in *Encyclopedia of Mormonism;* "A Prologue to Genesis: Moses 1 in Light of Jewish Traditions" in *BYU Studies* (2006); Foreword for Hugh Nibley's *Abraham in Egypt;* and "Cedars and Stars: Enduring Symbols of Cosmic Kingship in Abraham's Encounter with Pharaoh" in *Astronomy, Papyrus, and Covenant.* He and his wife, Mila, are the parents of three children.